The World in His Hands

The World in His Hands

A Christian Account of Scientific Law
and its Antithetical Competitors

CHRISTOPHER LEE BOLT

WIPF & STOCK · Eugene, Oregon

THE WORLD IN HIS HANDS
A Christian Account of Scientific Law and its Antithetical Competitors

Copyright © 2019 Christopher Lee Bolt. All rights reserved. Except for brief quotations in critical publications or reviews, no part of this book may be reproduced in any manner without prior written permission from the publisher. Write: Permissions, Wipf and Stock Publishers, 199 W. 8th Ave., Suite 3, Eugene, OR 97401.

Wipf & Stock
An Imprint of Wipf and Stock Publishers
199 W. 8th Ave., Suite 3
Eugene, OR 97401

www.wipfandstock.com

PAPERBACK ISBN: 978-1-5326-3661-5
HARDCOVER ISBN: 978-1-5326-3663-9
EBOOK ISBN: 978-1-5326-3662-2

Manufactured in the U.S.A.   MARCH 29, 2019

Scripture quotations are from the ESV® Bible (The Holy Bible, English Standard Version®), copyright © 2001 by Crossway, a publishing ministry of Good News Publishers. Used by permission. All rights reserved.

To my faithful wife Kerri

who is proof God loves me

and in memory of Dr. Lesley Friedman

who introduced me to epistemology.

Contents

Preface | ix

Acknowledgments | xiii

Introduction | xv

Chapter 1   Divine Providence | 1
   Non-Concurrent Theistic Preservation and Government | 7
   Non-Concurrent Cosmological Preservation and Government | 13
   Concurrent Theistic-Cosmological Preservation and Government | 15

Chapter 2   Scientific Implications of Providence | 37
   Scientific Implications of Providence in Theology | 38
   Scientific Implications of Providence in Apologetics | 46
   Scientific Implications of Providence in Science | 80

Chapter 3   Laws of Nature | 96
   Laws of Nature as Regularities | 105
   Laws of Nature as Logical Necessities | 124
   Laws of Nature as Natural Necessities | 130

Chapter 4   Problem of Induction | 138
   Problem of Induction as a Skeptical Concern | 143
   Problem of Induction and Secular Responses | 155
   Problem of Induction and Christian Solutions | 174

Chapter 5   Further Issues | 180
   Further Issue of Miracles | 181
   Further Issue of Islam | 187
   Further Issue of Apologetics | 216

Chapter 6   Conclusion | 220

Bibliography | 223

Preface

My parents are Christians. They taught me that the Bible is God's Word, and based their parenting techniques on it. My parents were faithful in taking me with them to church gatherings. When I was a young boy, virtually everyone I knew was a Christian. Early on, my understanding of the world was shaped by Christian teaching, prayer, and song. One of the songs I remember singing as a boy is called "He's Got the Whole World in His Hands." One version of the song describes God's control of the natural elements in particular, along with the rest of the world, as follows:

> He's got the wind and the rain in His hands
> He's got the wind and the rain in His hands
> He's got the wind and the rain in His hands
> He's got the whole world in His hands.[1]

From the earliest age, I was taught to believe that God is in control of everything. In particular, God is in control of the natural elements. However, I distinctly remember having difficulty articulating a question I had about physical laws. How does God relate to physical laws? My parents and church were telling me that God is in control of the world. My teachers and textbooks were telling me that laws of nature are in control of the world. Which view was correct? Could both views be correct? These were the thoughts with which I began to struggle in elementary school, though I did not get very far. Many years later, I still believe that God is in control of everything, and this book, based on my doctoral dissertation, defends his control of the natural elements in particular.

---

1. Traditional Negro Spirituals, "He's Got the Whole World in His Hands," http://www.negrospirituals.com/songs/he_s_got_the_wole_world_in_his_hands.htm.

My early interest in the topic of this book was reignited as I began to study Christian apologetics. At around the same time, I encountered the Scottish skeptic David Hume's infamous "problem of induction" during my first course in philosophy. Christian apologists consider Hume an enemy of the faith. I thought Hume was wrong about induction, but I was not sure why he was wrong. As I thought more about an answer to Hume, I became even more interested in philosophy and apologetics, and learned that not all apologists are quick to dismiss Hume's skepticism. Presuppositional apologists attempt to undercut the entirety of opposition to the Christian faith with arguments that call attention to the very foundations of thought itself. They seek to turn skeptical worries on the non-Christian, arguing that the religious skeptic is not skeptical enough. The idea of using unbelieving arguments against unbelievers began to haunt and thrill me.

My later courses in philosophy, including epistemology, philosophy of science, medieval philosophy, modern philosophy, pragmatism, and logic kept bringing my attention back to the problem of induction. In epistemology, the problem plagued a strict empiricism. In philosophy of science, the problem served as a major catalyst of change from one scientific methodology to another. In modern philosophy and in logic, my professor mentioned older philosophers having held that the laws of nature were actually an expression of the providence of God. The medieval philosophers attempted to solve the problem through the knowledge of God or Allah, and the pragmatists sought to dismiss it. I became convinced that the most popular secular attempts to solve the problem of induction fail. I also became convinced of the significance of solving the problem of induction for the sake of science.

My desire to immerse myself more fully in the literature surrounding the problem of induction, natural laws, and the providence of God led me to a vast body of literature. I found the argument I was interested in researching and developing was not at all original to the presuppositionalists. A seminary student introduced me to *The Divine Lawmaker: Lectures on Induction, Laws of Nature, and the Existence of God* by John Foster. In this work, Foster addresses each of the topics mentioned in his title. He posits the existence of laws of nature to solve the problem of induction, and points out the new problem of explaining these laws, arguing that "given the problem, we can only achieve a satisfactory account of the situation if we accept that there is a God of the relevant (broadly

Judaeo-Christian) type, and that it is he who is the creator of the natural world and the source of its laws."[2]

In *There is a God: How the World's Most Notorious Atheist Changed His Mind* by Antony Flew and Roy Abraham Varghese, the same argument appears again. Flew writes, "Although I was once sharply critical of the argument to design, I have since come to see that, when correctly formulated, this argument constitutes a persuasive case for the existence of God."[3] Flew cites developments in the area of design that led him to his conclusion, the first of which "is the question of the origin of the laws of nature and the related insights of eminent modern scientists."[4]

Philosopher Alvin Plantinga also picks up on the same argument alluded to above in his book *Where the Conflict Really Lies: Science, Religion, & Naturalism*. Plantinga attempts to connect the problem of induction with the necessity of laws of nature and theism. He contends, "God not only sets laws for the universe, but sets laws we can (at least approximately) grasp."[5] As a *Christian* philosopher and theologian, I think it's beneficial to develop the aforementioned argument in an effort to strengthen and make the argument more explicitly *Christian* theistic. Plantinga does care enough about the threat of Islam to a specifically Christian theistic argument from the laws of nature to briefly address it in a footnote. He explains, "on the whole it seems that the dominant Muslim conception of God is of a more intrusive, unpredictable, incomprehensible divinity."[6] Plantinga's comment serves as a starting point for the explication of other relevant differences between Christianity and Islam. In this book I explore how those differences pertain to laws of nature and the problem of induction.

2. Foster, *Divine Lawmaker*, 2.
3. Flew and Varghese, *There Is a God*, 95.
4. Flew and Varghese, *There Is a God*, 95.
5. Plantinga, *Where Conflict Really Lies*, 277.
6. Plantinga's full comment reads, "There is also an important contrast here between the usual Christian and the usual Islamic way of thinking about God. This is not the place to go into detail into Islamic conceptions of God (even if I knew enough to do so), and of course there are several different Islamic conceptions of God, or Allah, just as there is more than one Christian conception of God. But on the whole it seems that the dominant Muslim conception of God is of a more intrusive, unpredictable, incomprehensible divinity. Rodney Stark points out that a common 'orthodox' claim was that all attempts to formulate natural laws are blasphemous, because they would limit Allah's freedom. See his *Discovering God* (New York: Harper, 2007), p. 367." Plantinga, *Where Conflict Really Lies*, 274n11.

Acknowledgements

THIS BOOK WOULD NOT have been possible were it not for a lengthy list of people who invested time, energy, and money to see me through this project. In addition to the fine folks at Wipf and Stock, without whom this book would not exist, I am grateful for the professors and faculty at The Southern Baptist Theological Seminary, who encourage rigorous intellectual activity at the academic level while remaining true to the faith that was once for all delivered to the saints. In particular, I would like to thank my chairperson, Mark Coppenger, as well as professors Ted Cabal and Steve Wellum for serving on my dissertation committee. James Anderson of Reformed Theological Seminary graciously agreed to serve as external reader.

Other professors and teachers who stand out as having greatly influenced me in my academic career include the philosophy and religion departments at Lynchburg College, which at the time consisted of professors Tom Brickhouse, Lesley Friedman, Ron Martin, Laura Kicklighter, Jeffrey Burke, and James Price, and professors at Central Virginia Community College, especially Tom Sparhawk, Charles Poff, and Kevin Kozerow. Fred Smith mentored me in apologetic engagement and worldview thinking, and long before college, my sixth and ninth grade English teachers gave me a passion for reading and writing.

Forest Baptist Church in Forest, Virginia; Clifton Baptist Church in Louisville, Kentucky; First Baptist Church Ardmore in Ardmore, Alabama; and Elkton Baptist Church in Elkton, Tennessee provided me with loving church families during my time as a member of each and after. My former pastors, Tyler Scarlett, Tom Schreiner, John Kimbell, and Alan Hughes are models of sound Christian thinking and humility. I am also thankful for the guys at Louisville Overstock Warehouse for working with my schedule during my studies, and the many lifelong friends

I made while in seminary, including Ben Askins, Mike Berhow, Mark Warnock, Lucas Almaeda, Lucas Bradburn, Dane Beam, and Randy Syring. A close-knit group of likeminded friends who helped me maintain my sanity throughout my entire academic career includes Brian Knapp, Joshua Whipps, Justin McCurry, Ben Woodring, Nic Heath, Matthias McMahon and Sean Burkes.

My family provided countless blessings to my wife and me during my time in seminary and doctoral studies. I probably could not have completed my studies without the support of my grandmother, Grace Forbes; my parents, Lee and Carol Bolt; my brother-in-law and sister, Boyd and Jennifer Ervin; as well as my in-laws, Larry and Linda Roberts. Most of all I am thankful for the constant support of my beautiful wife, Kerri, and our three wonderful children, Karis, Zoe, and Christian.

Finally, as the apostle Paul similarly writes in Ephesians 1:3–4, blessed be the God and Father of my Lord Jesus Christ, who has blessed me in Christ with every spiritual blessing in the heavenly places, even as he chose me in him before the foundation of the world, that I should be holy and blameless before him.

CHRIS BOLT
Nashville, Tennessee
December 2018

Introduction

PEOPLE OFTEN VIEW SCIENCE and religion as incompatible disciplines.[1] The apparent clash between science and religion is related to the supposed disparity between reason and faith. The proper understanding of the relationship between reason and faith has been a major topic of discussion for philosophers throughout history. The supposedly competing practices of science and religion are thought of as different approaches to knowledge.[2] As two different approaches to knowledge, science and religion are at war, and science is the likely victor.[3] Of course, not everyone agrees with the aforementioned view.

Science dominates the collective Western mind as somewhat of an idol.[4] Yet the benefits of science cannot be ignored. Virtually no area of life is exempt from the benefits of the scientific endeavor and its implications for technology. Not only technology, but medicine and agriculture progress with scientific advancement as well. The prevalent effects of science are felt in the most tangible of ways in common experience.

---

1. Plantinga, *Where Conflict Really Lies*, 5–7. Philosopher Alvin Plantinga comments at length on this popular view. He dates alleged conflict between the disciplines back to "Andrew Dixon White and his rancorous *History of the Warfare of Science and Theology*." Plantinga, *Where Conflict Really Lies*, 5–7. See also Okasha, *Philosophy of Science*, 3.

2. Buddhist author R. G. de S. Wettimuny expresses agreement with this view. Wettimuny, *Buddhism*, 2.

3. Wettimuny exclaims, "The long drawn-out warfare between theology and Science stands eminent. Theology has been forced into a ceasefire now, and the warfare is almost over—a warfare in which the victor, Science, was not to be profited whilst the loser, theology, was all to gain and learn!" Wettimuny, *Buddhism*, 10.

4. Plantinga writes, "Some treat science as if it were a sort of infallible oracle, like a divine revelation—or if not infallible (since it seems so regularly to change its mind), at any rate such that when it comes to fixing belief, science is the court of last appeal." Plantinga, *Where Conflict Really Lies*, xi–xii.

From the moment a person wakes until the time he goes to sleep, he is bombarded by the benefits of science in the practical elements of everyday life. Electricity, lights, hot showers, breakfast cereals, clothing, cars, cell phones, roads, security systems, computers, communications, traffic lights, climate control, and entertainment are just a sampling of the many benefits of science. Educational, political, and marketing strategists often invoke science to substantiate their claims. Even those opposed to various applications of science may rely on apparently scientific claims to refute those with whom they disagree. For example, those with various objections to the supposed science behind vaccines, genetically modified organisms, or prescription drugs often strive to offer a different scientific outlook, whether successful or not.

Society tends to regard science with the utmost respect. At the same time, society remains generally religious. However, as already mentioned, science and religion are frequently thought of as being at odds with one another. The so-called "New Atheism" has only exacerbated the charge that science and religion are incompatible.[5] In his book *Where the Conflict Really Lies: Science, Religion & Naturalism*, philosopher Alvin Plantinga describes the new atheists before explaining that "these new atheists unite with the old atheists in declaring that there is deep and irreconcilable conflict between theistic religion – Christian belief, for example – and science."[6] Plantinga continues, "If there were serious conflicts between religion and current science, that would be very significant; initially, at least, it would cast doubt on those religious beliefs inconsistent with current science."[7] Plantinga goes on to argue that there is no more than a superficial conflict between religion and science.[8]

Demonstrating that no conflict exists between religion and science is a noble task. However, imagine what would happen if one took the aforementioned task a step further. What if it could be shown, not only that science and religion are not in conflict with one another, but that science actually *depends* upon religion?[9] How ironic would it be if science

---

5. For more on the "New Atheism," see Mohler, *Atheism Remix*. Roy Abraham Varghese dismisses the new atheism as "nothing less than a regression to the logical positivist philosophy that was renounced by even its most ardent proponents." Flew and Varghese, *There Is a God*, xv–xxiv.

6. Plantinga, *Where Conflict Really Lies*, xi.

7. Plantinga, *Where Conflict Really Lies*, xii.

8. Plantinga, *Where Conflict Really Lies*, xii–xiii.

9. For example, Plantinga attempts to demonstrate concord between Christian

is in some sense indebted to religion? Moreover, what if the religion that provides the *best* basis for science is *Christian* theism in particular? Such a find would no doubt bolster the apologetic community in the midst of its battles with the new atheists who are now an extremely vocal opposition to the Christian faith. One may conceive of a number of ways to try and demonstrate the dependency of science upon Christian theism. This book provides a philosophical account of the Christian doctrine of providence and its implications for the laws of nature and problem of induction before arguing that Christian theism is thus better equipped to provide a basis for science than are secular and Islamic worldviews.

The Christian doctrine of divine providence is derived from the teaching of Scripture that God is at work in the world as a superior source of provision for creation.[10] The doctrine can be coherently stated in such a way as to remain wholly consistent with science and able to account for the laws of nature and inductive reasoning necessary to scientific inquiry. Commentary from Christian theologians, apologists, and scientists frequently features the widely held belief that the doctrine of divine providence allows for regularity and predictability in the world. Some theologians explicitly recognize this regularity and predictability as providing a basis for science.[11] Apologists develop arguments surrounding the same theme.[12] Many Christian and even some non-Christian scientists recognize the need for particular tenets of the Christian worldview as a basis for their scientific methodology.[13] In a Christian theistic worldview, regularity and predictability are most easily described through the concept of laws imposed upon creation by God.[14] What is the *nature* of

---

belief and science before arguing that science is incompatible with naturalism. Plantinga, *Where Conflict Really Lies*, 191–350.

10. Grudem, *Systematic Theology*, 315.

11. For example, Radford, *Epistle to Colossians*, 177–78; Dunn, *Colossians & Philemon*, 93–94; Barclay, *All-Sufficient Christ*, 63–64; Grudem, *Systematic Theology*, 316–17; Erickson, *Christian Theology*, 394.

12. Modern examples are somewhat obscure. Greg L. Bahnsen used an argument of this type against atheist Edward Tabash. Bahnsen, *Does God Exist?*. Bahnsen repeats the argument a few times in his more famous debate with Gordon Stein. Bahnsen, *Great Debate*. A better argument that attempts to justify the inductive principle is found in Anderson, "If Knowledge Then God," 49–75. Alvin Plantinga hinted long ago in his lecture notes that there might be an argument for the existence of God along such lines. Plantinga, *Two Dozen*.

13. Pearcey and Thaxton, *Soul of Science*, 21.

14. Plantinga, *Where Conflict Really Lies*, 274–75. Plantinga sounds like the

these laws? This book lists three distinct understandings of the laws of nature. The three distinct ways of understanding the laws of nature are as regularities, logical necessities, or natural necessities. Understanding laws of nature as a type of natural necessity is inherent to the doctrine of divine providence and helps answer the problem of induction.[15] This *nomic necessity* is entailed by the fact that God preserves and governs his creation in accord with his perfect nature and will.[16]

The aforementioned view of laws of nature pertains to the problem of induction, a skeptical worry in philosophy. People typically expect the future to resemble the past in relevant ways, and this expectation drives the belief that people are capable of learning from experience.[17] Learning from experience is a significant part of the scientific endeavor. But why should anyone assume that the future will resemble the past? It will not help to claim that since *in the past* the future has resembled the past, it will do so *in the future*, for this response relies upon the very principle which has been called into question, and it is certainly *logically* possible

---

commentators mentioned earlier when he writes, "This constancy and predictability, this regularity, was often thought of in terms of *law*: God sets, prescribes laws for his creation, or creates in such a way that what he creates is subject to, conforms to, laws he institutes." Plantinga, *Where Conflict Really Lies*, 274–75.

15. Plantinga, *Where Conflict Really Lies*, 278. Plantinga writes, "There is still another important way in which theism is hospitable to science: theism makes it much easier to understand what these laws are like. The main point here has to do with the alleged *necessity* of natural law." Plantinga, *Where Conflict Really Lies*, 278.

16. Plantinga explains, "From a theistic perspective, the reason is that God has established and upholds this law for our cosmos, and no creature (actual or possible) has the power to act contrary to what God establishes and upholds. God is omnipotent; there are no non-logical limits on his power; we might say that his power is infinite. The sense in which the laws of nature are necessary, therefore, is that they are propositions God has established or decreed, and no creature—no finite power, we might say—has the power to act against these propositions, that is, to bring it about that they are false. It is as if God says: 'Let c, the speed of light, be such that no material object accelerates from a velocity less than c to a velocity greater than c'; no creaturely power is then able to cause a material object to accelerate from a velocity less than c to one greater than c. The laws of nature, therefore, resemble necessary truths in that there is nothing we or other creatures can do to render them false. We could say that they are *finitely inviolable*." Plantinga, *Where Conflict Really Lies*, 280–81.

17. Plantinga, *Where Conflict Really Lies*, 292. Plantinga writes, "Saying precisely how we expect the future to resemble the past is no mean task; we expect the future to resemble the past in relevant respects; but specifying the relevant respects is far from easy. Nevertheless, we do expect the future to resemble the past, and this expectation is crucial to our being able to learn from experience." Plantinga, *Where Conflict Really Lies*, 292.

that the future will *not* resemble the past in the relevant respects.[18] The theist has an answer here insofar as God is that rational will which stands providentially behind every event and object of the universe concurrently preserving and governing his creation. *Nomic necessity* provides the necessary connection between cause and effect that philosophers have sought after in their attempts to account for scientific success. God imposes laws of nature on his creation and thereby enables the scientist to proceed with his tasks. The theist who adheres to a robust doctrine of divine providence is thus justified in his or her acceptance of inductive reasoning and science. However, one might inquire as to the place of miracles in this understanding of science, as well as competing monotheistic models of science, such as in Islam.

Miracles are rare, revelatory acts of God. Miracles remain a part of God's providential activity while revealing something special about God and his redemptive purposes through nature behaving in a way that it does not usually behave or the laws of nature even seemingly being defied.[19] God need not be thought of as bound by the universe in such a way that he is incapable of superseding its natural operations through his divine power.[20] In Islam, everything in nature follows the command of God.[21] While the obedience of nature to Allah is "voluntary," it is also the default behavior of the world, or "automatic."[22] To be Muslim means to submit to Allah. Thus the entirety of Allah's creation is truly *Muslim*, with the obvious exception of some men and women, who refuse Allah through free will.[23] General theistic principles initially appear to do for the Muslim what they did for the Christian with respect to establishing the laws of nature and justifying the inductive principle, but this assumption is questionable due to relevant differences between the two.

18. The Scottish skeptic David Hume pointed out this problematic observation regarding predictive inference, but Plantinga clarifies it in explaining, "There are plenty of possible worlds that match the actual world up to the present time, but then diverge wildly, so that inductive inferences would mostly fail in those other worlds. There are as many of those counter-inductive worlds as there are worlds in which induction will continue to be reliable. It is by no means inevitable that inductive reasoning should be successful; its success is one more example of the fit between our cognitive faculties and the world." Plantinga, *Where Conflict Really Lies*, 295.
19. McCann, "Creation and Conservation," 311.
20. McCann, "Creation and Conservation," 311.
21. Rahman, *Major Themes*, 65.
22. Rahman, *Major Themes*, 65.
23. Rahman, *Major Themes*, 65.

In summary, after presenting a broad theological and philosophical summary of the doctrine of providence, this book addresses scientific implications of the doctrine. This portion of the book is an attempt at constructive theology based upon historical theological observations. Statements from theologians, apologists, and scientists from various strands of thought are compiled in an effort to compel the reader to believe that the argument of this book is not novel in any negative sense or unpersuasive. However, the original argument will also be improved through philosophical analysis of the character of the laws of nature and the problem of induction. In a later chapter, Christian theism is contrasted with Islam in an effort to show that Islam lacks relevant conceptual tools available in Christian theism. Possible apologetic applications of the argument are then discussed.

Thus, this book is best viewed as a work of constructive philosophical theology with possible apologetic applications. It is mainly philosophical in nature and addresses a number of topics pertaining to subcategories of the discipline of philosophy. These categories include philosophical theology, philosophy of religion, metaphysics, epistemology, and philosophy of science. However, the subject matter of this book also spans several other disciplines. These disciplines include biblical exegesis, systematic theology, and comparative religions. Some evidences from the sciences and history are also provided.

Some readers may notice a heavy emphasis placed upon Christian Scripture. There are at least three reasons for this emphasis. First, I should state at the outset of this work that I am unashamedly Christian. I believe in the death, burial, and resurrection of Jesus Christ for my sins. As I write, I am in agreement with the *Baptist Faith and Message 2000* and the *Chicago Statement on Biblical Inerrancy*. Second, I recognize the necessity of presuppositions when it comes to any work of philosophy. Since I am a Christian, I approach this work from a Christian perspective, with Christian presuppositions. Third, Christian Scripture is simply a part of the subject matter of this book. A positive presentation of providence and its scientific implications relative to a Christian theistic position will of necessity include references to the authoritative canons of Christian theism.

Though I am bound by particular presuppositions, I strive to remain unbiased in my research and writing. Further, my frank acceptance of Christian theism at the outset of my work will not result in reliance upon dogmatic assertions in lieu of nuanced philosophical argumentation. The use of Scripture should not be viewed as a hindrance to a philosophically articulate presentation of the concept of providence and its implications for the philosophy of science. Finally, even the most skeptical reader can approach the present work as a hypothetical view that he or she will, of course, evaluate from within the confines of his or her own philosophical position(s).

Chapter 1

DIVINE PROVIDENCE

THIS CHAPTER PROVIDES A philosophical account of the doctrine of providence with scriptural and historical witness. The term "providence" is not derived strictly from the language of Scripture nor translated from the Hebrew or Greek of the Bible.[1] The term comes from the Latin *providentia*, meaning "foresight" or "forethought."[2] The term "providence"

---

1. The consensus is, "The term 'providence' as it is commonly used in theology normally identifies a cluster of biblical themes, rather than translating a particular word." Rosner et al., *New Dictionary*, 710–11. Theologian Robert Reymond agrees with the aforementioned Bible scholars: "While the word 'providence' (Lat. *providentia*, 'foresight, forethought') is not a biblical word *per se*, the idea that it conveys is everywhere present in the *ad hoc* statements of Scripture to this effect (see Ps. 136:25)." Reymond, *Systematic Theology*, 399. Compare Rosner et al., *New Dictionary*, 711, for the claim that "a precise linguistic basis can certainly be found. For example, W. Eichrodt refers to Job 10:12, which tells of the 'divine superintendence or care by which creatures are preserved' (*Theology of the Old Testament*, vol. 2, p.168); K. Barth derives a concept of providence from the story of the sacrifice of Isaac in Genesis 22:8, 14 (*Church Dogmatics*, vol. 3.3, p. 3)." See also Flint, "Providence and Predestination," 569.

2. Reymond, *Systematic Theology*, 399. Further discussion of the origin of this term is found in Turretin, *Institutes of Elenctic Theology*, 489: "The word 'providence' was called by the Greeks *pronoia* because *proteron noei* (as Favorinus says, *Dictionarium Varini Phavorini* [1538], pp. 1569–70) embraces three things especially: *prognōsin*, *prothesin* and *dioikēsin*—the knowledge of the mind, the decree of the will and the efficacious administration of the things decreed; directing knowledge, commanding will and fulfilling power, as Hugo St. Victor expresses it. The first foresees, the second provides, the third procures. Hence providence can be viewed either in the antecedent decree or in the subsequent execution. The former is the eternal destination of all things to their ends; the latter is the temporal government of all things according to that decree. The former is an immanent act in God; the latter is a transitive action out

simply describes the workings of God in the world with an emphasis upon God as *superior to* and *providing for* his creation. Even though the term itself is not found at all in Scripture, the *concept* is.[3]

A systematic approach must be taken to explaining the aforementioned concept because the whole Bible presents relevant data on the topic. Isolated passages cannot do justice to the doctrine. Even isolated texts which attribute *universal* providential activity to God do not take into account the richness of *particular* applications of their teaching expressed elsewhere in Scripture. For example, while Hebrews 1:3 describes God the Son as sustaining *everything*, the text does not go into detail about what this would mean for God's providential activity with respect to the grass growing.[4] One might even be tempted to overlook that God's sustenance of everything includes his activity of making the grass grow. Further, texts pertaining to the universal providential activity of God do not always address apparent objections to the doctrine from other teachings of Scripture.[5] On the other hand, texts which indicate that God is providentially involved in *particular* aspects of creation do not necessarily justify a conclusion about providence in a *universal* sense. For example, Psalm 147:8 indicates that God makes the grass grow on

---

of God." A more modern explanation may be found in Berkhof, *Systematic Theology*, 165: "While the term 'providence' is not found in Scripture, the doctrine of providence is nevertheless eminently Scriptural. The word is derived from the Latin *providentia*, which corresponds to the Greek *pronoia*. These words mean primarily prescience or foresight, but gradually acquired other meanings. Foresight is associated, on the one hand, with plans for the future, and on the other hand, with the actual realization of these plans. Thus the word 'providence' has come to signify the provision which God makes for the ends of His government, and the preservation and government of all His creatures. This is the sense in which it is now generally used in theology, but it is not the only sense in which theologians have employed it. Turretin defines the term in its widest sense as denoting (1) foreknowledge, (2) foreordination, and (3) the efficacious administration of the things decreed. In general usage, however, it is now generally restricted to the last sense."

3. Systematic theologian Wayne Grudem believes the doctrine of providence follows from the doctrine of creation, but also notes that it is an extra-biblical term, writing, "Once we understand that God is the all-powerful Creator . . . it seems reasonable to conclude that he also preserves and governs everything in the universe as well. Though the term *providence* is not found in Scripture, it has been traditionally used to summarize God's ongoing relationship to his creation." Grudem, *Systematic Theology*, 315.

4. The same is true with respect to texts like Col 1:17 and Acts 17:28.

5. Three notable examples include alleged inconsistencies with human responsibility, with evil, and with miracles.

the hills, but does not necessarily imply that God is actively involved with other parts of creation.[6]

As with any other systematic approach to a teaching of Scripture, philosophy will strongly inform conclusions. Most systematic treatments of the doctrine of providence in Scripture immediately introduce extra-textual, philosophical categories to describe the various aspects of divine providence. Understanding the doctrine of providence at a deeper level begins with a grasp of these categories and how they are related. The doctrine of providence is often divided into the three categories of *preservation, concurrence,* and *government*.[7] For example, systematic theologian Louis Berkhof writes, "Providence may be defined as *that continued exercise of the divine energy whereby the Creator preserves all His creatures, is operative in all that comes to pass in the world, and directs all things to their appointed end*."[8] He explains, "This definition indicates that there are three elements in providence, namely, preservation (*conservatio, sustentatio*), concurrence or cooperation (*concursus, co-operatio*), and government (*gubernatio*)."[9] Likewise, systematic theologian Wayne Grudem follows Berkhof in defining God's providence in terms of *preservation, concurrence,* and *government*.[10] According to Grudem, the doctrine of providence states, "*God is continually involved with all created things in such a way that he (1) keeps them existing and maintaining the properties with which he created them; (2) cooperates with created things in every action, directing their distinctive properties to cause them to act as they do; and (3) directs them to fulfill his purposes.*"[11] The threefold distinction is popular in the Reformed tradition in particular. Mentioning the great detail in which post-reformation Lutheran churches and Reformed churches developed the doctrine of providence, historical theologian

---

6. A persnickety reader might even point out that Ps 147:8 is concerned with grass *on the hills*, and not grass in general. However, Ps 104:14 appears to refer to grass in general and notes its purpose of feeding cattle.

7. For a threefold understanding of providence as well as its history in relation to a twofold distinction, see Berkhof, *Systematic Theology*, 166–67.

8. Berkhof, *Systematic Theology*, 166.

9. Berkhof, *Systematic Theology*, 166.

10. Grudem, *Systematic Theology*, 315.

11. Grudem, *Systematic Theology*, 315. Grudem considers each of these categories separately prior to answering views of providence that are not Reformed, noting that "this is a doctrine on which there has been substantial disagreement among Christians since the early history of the church, particularly with respect to God's relationship to the willing choices of moral creatures." Grudem, *Systematic Theology*, 315.

Gregg Allison writes, "Both groups discussed providence under three headings: *preservation, concurrence,* and *government.*"[12] Though these three aspects of providence are often discussed separately, they are nevertheless closely tied together.

While the three-fold distinction described above is common, preservation and concurrence are sometimes taken as synonyms.[13] Analytic theologian and philosopher Oliver Crisp notes the intimate connection between the doctrines of creation and providence as well as the commonality in post-reformation treatments of the latter doctrine of "the distinction between divine preservation of the creation (*conservatio*), his concurrent activity in upholding and sustaining the creation (*concursus*) and his government of it (*gubernatio*)."[14] However, Crisp adds, "Sometimes the first two of these are conflated, depending on the theory of divine preservation under consideration."[15] He concludes, "Thus, if God preserves the cosmos via concurrently causing all things to occur alongside mundane causes, then God's concurrent activity is a function of his preservation of the created order."[16]

My definition of providence will conflate the two categories of preservation and concurrence as Crisp has described. However, I prefer Crisp's language of concurrence serving as a function of preservation. If concurrence is a function of preservation, then it is also a function of government. In preservation, entities work with God only insofar as they *exist*, and that not of themselves. In government, objects govern themselves in accordance with their natures, but God governs them as well.[17] Moreover, preservation and government are so intricately connected to one another that relegating concurrence to preservation alone is unwarranted. Providence thus consists of the two acts of preservation and government. Another definition of providence describing God's providence as two acts is found in the scholastic theologian Francis Turretin, who contends, "Conservation is that by which God conserves all creatures in

---

12. Allison, *Historical Theology*, 289.

13. Crisp, *Retrieving Doctrine*, 13.

14. Crisp, *Retrieving Doctrine*, 13.

15. Crisp, *Retrieving Doctrine*, 13. Crisp is referring to preservation and concurrence.

16. Crisp, *Retrieving Doctrine*, 13.

17. Here, I highlight the analogous relationship that concurrence shares with preservation *and* government. Concurrence is frequently spoken of with respect to preservation, but not government.

their own state (which is done by a conservation of essence in the species, of existence in individuals and of virtues to their operations)."[18] He continues, "Government is that by which God governs universals and singulars, and directs and draws them out to ends foreappointed by him."[19]

My definition of divine providence divides providence into the two interrelated categories of *preservation* and *government* while *concurrence* describes how God relates to his creation in these two aspects of providence. I will use the following definition of the doctrine of divine providence:

> Divine Providence = df. That action of the Creator to concurrently preserve the existence, nature, and behavior of his creation and to govern it toward its purpose, goal, and end.

The definition provided above includes the two traditional categories of preservation and government but presents concurrence as the activity of God with respect to his creation. Concurrence is thus a *function* of the two aspects of preservation and government in the definition above.[20]

Not only does God preserve, conserve, or sustain the world in existence, but he also governs, guides, or directs it toward its ends.[21] God does so in virtue of concurrence.[22] Concurrence is a function of the philosophical categories of preservation and government, for God is active in both of the aforementioned categories with respect to the *creation* itself.[23]

18. Turretin, *Institutes of Elenctic Theology*, 501.
19. Turretin, *Institutes of Elenctic Theology*, 501.
20. Crisp, *Retrieving Doctrine*, 13.
21. According to Plantinga, "God *conserves* the world, sustains it in being. Apart from his sustaining hand, our universe—and if there are other universes, the same goes for them—would disappear like a candle flame in a high wind. Descartes and Jonathan Edwards, indeed, thought of this divine substance as a matter of re-creation: at every moment God recreates his world. Maybe so, maybe not. The present point is only that God does indeed sustain his world in being, and, apart from that sustaining, supporting activity, the world would simply fail to exist." Plantinga, *Where Conflict Really Lies*, 66–67.
22. Thus Plantinga writes, "Some, including Thomas Aquinas, go even further: every causal transaction that takes place is such that God performs a special act of *concurring* with it; without that divine concurrence, no causal transaction could take place." Plantinga, *Where Conflict Really Lies*, 67,
23. If God is active in preserving and governing the world, then what follows regarding his relationship to time? John Foster offers some helpful comments concerning how God's relationship to time factors into the discussion. He writes, "Under the Judaeo-Christian conception, there is no temporal limitation on the extent of the being's existence. This can mean different things to different Judaeo-Christian theists.

God preserves a *creation* that already exists, and God governs a *creation* with causal natures. Moreover, the doctrine of divine providence establishes that nothing happens according to chance; everything happens in accord with the will of God which preserves and governs the entirety of creation in a *regular* and hence *predictable* way.[24] This regularity and predictability are often noted by exegetes, systematicians, and apologists, as will be discussed in greater detail in the next chapter.

This chapter attempts to show that *non-concurrent theistic* and *non-concurrent cosmological* interpretations of *preservation and govern-*

The almost universal view among ordinary believers is that God is sempiternal—that he exists in time, and that his existence stretches infinitely in both temporal directions. But, against this, a number of theologians have insisted that to locate God in time is, in itself, an unacceptable limitation on the form of his being—that it is something incompatible with his unsurpassable greatness; and, as they see it, the lack of a temporal limitation is simply a consequence of the fact that God's existence is timeless. Given the nature of our investigative concern, this second view can, it seems to me, be set aside. For I do not think that we can make sense of the notion of a personal being existing outside time; indeed, I do not think that we can make sense of the notion of any concrete entity existing outside time. The only way, I think, in which we could make sense of the timeless view of God would be by conceiving of God as an *abstract* entity, such as goodness or love or being. And since we are only interested in the options available in the framework of the personal-agency approach, such a conception is not relevant to our present discussion. As for the claim that locating God in time in some way undermines the traditional view of his greatness, this too seems to me misconceived, though it is not a matter that I want to discuss here. The only point I would stress, in this connection, is that, in recognizing God's existence as temporal, we do not have to think of time as something which is ontologically more fundamental than God. We can recognize time as the essential form of God's existence, but also as something which does not, and cannot, exist without him. I should also point out that, in taking God's existence to be in time, I am leaving open the option of taking his time dimension to be different from ours, though, for simplicity, this is something I shall ignore in my future discussion." Foster, *Divine Lawmaker*, 133–34. Compare Helm, *Eternal God*; Swinburne, *Christian God*, 137–44; Oliphint, *God with Us*.

24. Plantinga echoes the sentiments of exegetes and systematicians: "God so governs the world that whatever happens is to be thought of as 'coming from his fatherly hand'; he either causes or permits whatever does in fact happen; none of it is to be thought of as a result of mere chance. And this governing—'ruling,' as the Catechism has it—comes in at least two parts. First of all, God governs the world in such a way that it displays regularity and predictability. Day follows night and night follows day; when there is rain and sun, plants grow; bread is good to eat but mud is not; if you drop a rock from a cliff top, it will fall down, not up. It is only because of this regularity that we can build a house, design and manufacture automobiles and aircraft, cure strep throat, raise crops, or pursue scientific projects. Indeed, it is only because of this regularity that we can act in any way at all." Plantinga, *Where Conflict Really Lies*, 67. See chap. 5 of this book for a discussion of the place of miracles.

ment should be rejected in favor of *concurrent theistic-cosmological preservation and government*. It is my contention that the *concurrent theistic-cosmological preservation and government* understanding of the doctrine of divine providence is both coherent and consistent with the laws of nature and inductive reasoning necessary for scientific inquiry to be addressed later.

NON-CONCURRENT THEISTIC PRESERVATION AND GOVERNMENT

Non-concurrent theistic preservation and government is a view of providence that denies concurrence between God and creation in preservation and government. This view limits agency or involvement in the acts of preservation and government to God alone. Pantheistic positions tend toward non-concurrent theistic views of providence, and thus serve as an example of the view under consideration. But perhaps the best way to approach the topic of non-concurrent theistic preservation and government is through comparing and contrasting creation and conservation.

One important point of clarification to be made in an explanation of the doctrine of providence concerns the relationship between the act of *creation* and the act of *conservation*. More pointedly, the question is whether these two acts are really distinct from one another. Regarding creation, Crisp writes, "For most Christian theists, God is distinct from his creation, exists *a se*, and, as a consequence, is free to refrain from creating this world or any other metaphysically possible world."[25] He asks, "But is the act of creating the world he does bring about distinct from his act of sustaining that world thereafter?"[26] According to Crisp, one significant thinker who believed that the two acts in question are *not* distinct from one another was the famous American theologian Jonathan Edwards.[27] Edwards held that since the world cannot exist independently of the sustaining power of God, there is a continuous creation of the

---

25. Crisp, *Retrieving Doctrine*, 11.
26. Crisp, *Retrieving Doctrine*, 11.
27. Crisp, *Retrieving Doctrine*, 12. Hugh J. McCann writes, "If the conservation of the world is of a piece with its creation, we may be headed for a 'continuous creation' theory of the sort held by Jonathan Edwards, wherein the world is held to pass away and be recreated at each moment of its existence." McCann, "Creation and Conservation," 306–7.

world by God.[28] This doctrine is much stronger than other accounts of divine preservation.[29] The doctrine posits that the conservation and creation of the world are the same such that the world passes away and is recreated each moment it exists.[30] Another way to state this position is that all efficiency belongs to God and all effects are owing to his agency.[31] Secondary causes do not exist anymore than they did when God created the world *ex nihilo*, for on this view, he creates the whole world *de novo* at every instant.[32]

According to Edwards, "God not only created all things, and gave them being at first, but continually preserves them, and upholds them in being."[33] Edwards appears to distinguish creation from conservation. But then he writes, "God's *preserving* created things in being is perfectly equivalent to a *continued creation*, or to his creating those things out of nothing at *each moment* of their existence."[34] The language of continuous creation will be addressed below. However, when Edwards writes of continuous creation, it is clear from the sentence above that he means creation from nothing each moment. He explains further, "If the continued existence of created things be wholly dependent on God's preservation, then those things would drop into nothing, upon the ceasing of the present moment, without a new exertion of the divine power to cause them to exist in the following moment."[35] Edwards continues, "It will follow from what has been observed, that God's upholding created substance, or causing its existence in each successive moment, is altogether equivalent to an *immediate production out of nothing*, at each moment, because its existence at this moment is not merely in part from God, but wholly

---

28. McCann, "Creation and Conservation," 306–7. Jonathan L. Kvanvig and Hugh J. McCann speak of the "view that was held by Jonathan Edwards: that each of the things God creates somehow begins to exist *anew* at each moment of its duration." Kvanvig and McCann, "Divine Conservation," 15.

29. Crisp, *Retrieving Doctrine*, 12–13. Philosophers Gottfried Wilhelm von Leibniz and George Berkeley hold similarly strong views of divine providence which largely, if not altogether, deny secondary causation.

30. McCann, "Creation and Conservation," 306–7.

31. Hodge, *Systematic Theology*, 578.

32. Hodge, *Systematic Theology*, 578.

33. Edwards, *Original Sin*, 400.

34. Edwards, *Original Sin*, 401.

35. Edwards, *Original Sin*, 401–2.

from him; and not in any part, or degree, from its antecedent existence."[36] Thus, "consequently God produces the effect as much from *nothing*, as if there had been nothing *before*."[37]

There are a number of objections to identifying the act of creation with the act of conservation as Edwards does here. Some will note the theory is intuitively troubling, but more importantly, it is conceptually problematic.[38] Edwards is adamant that apart from God, creation falls out of existence into nothing. But for whatever reason, Edwards seems to miss that God is every bit as present in the traditional view of conservation as he is in the Edwardsian model. The problem with the view set forth by Edwards is not so much with his understanding of God's involvement in preservation as it is with his apparent misunderstanding of the role of creation in preservation. One should agree with Edwards when he states that without God, "things would drop into nothing."[39] However, the hypothetical opponents of Edwards in this passage are not arguing against the presence of God. God is present sustaining created things such that they *do not* "drop into nothing."[40] Surely Edwards would agree. But if God is present so that things *do not* go out of existence, how can God be said to *create from nothing* each moment? Edwards appears to be arguing that God both *fails* to sustain things in existence and *does not* fail to sustain things in existence. He appears to argue that things both *cease* to exist, and *do not* cease to exist. Hence Edwards is mistaken to conclude that God's activity of upholding created things involves "an *immediate production out of nothing*," since there is not *nothing*, but *something*, upon God's initial creation of all things.[41] Edwards' account comes across as rather confusing where the traditional view does not.[42]

36. Edwards, *Original Sin*, 402.
37. Edwards, *Original Sin*, 402.
38. McCann, "Creation and Conservation," 306–7.
39. Edwards, *Original Sin*, 401–2.
40. Edwards, *Original Sin*, 401–2.
41. Edwards, *Original Sin*, 402.

42. These observations are not to suggest that a more nuanced defense of Edwards cannot be offered. For example, consideration of the mechanism by which God sustains the universe in existence, and consideration of the meaning of the term "continuous" are possible routes of defense for those who side with Edwards. Also worth mentioning is the fact that Edwards and others who take a strong view of God's providential activity should not be thought of as outside of Christian orthodoxy, though their view is not the most popular in Christian theology. Here, I attempt to treat the most popular view of divine providence within traditional Reformed theology.

In the traditional view, the creation of the world is creation *ex nihilo*, or creation from nothing, while the sustaining of the world presupposes what has been created *ex nihilo*.[43] In the first, God alone is creating from nothing or from himself, whereas in the second, God is sustaining what has already been created.[44] It is helpful to state this conceptual distinction within the traditional view before moving on to a more substantial objection to the Edwardsian view. The main difficulty with the Edwardsian view is that since the world has no power in and of itself to exist apart from God *it will cease to do so each moment*. Not only does it not follow that the world will cease to exist each moment (see above), but this idea is in violation of the doctrine of divine preservation.[45] On such a view, no entity is ever preserved, but rather each and every entity in the world comes into existence only to go out a moment later, with God recreating a numerically distinct though similar entity in an ongoing process of the world coming into and going out of existence.[46]

A closer look at what the doctrine of creation entails reveals that the coming to be involved in creation is a coming to be from nothing rather than any sort of gradual process of change like that which constitutes every form of creation initiated by humans.[47] The mere fact of instantiated *being* constitutes the "process" of creation *ex nihilo* such that there cannot be any more creation like it.[48] The world cannot come to be in the same sense that it did in creation, and it cannot cease to exist as it once did not exist either.[49] Should the world not exist, it will not exist at all, and even the language of "the world" becomes problematic.[50] The only way that the world could be continually recreated as in the Edwardsian theory of preservation is if it continually ceased to exist, which seems absurd.[51] On this view, each moment of existence would be different from the prior moment, and the thing which exists would be different in each case.[52] Not only is the object of knowledge in this context radically differ-

43. Crisp, *Retrieving Doctrine*, 11.
44. Crisp, *Retrieving Doctrine*, 11.
45. Crisp, *Retrieving Doctrine*, 12.
46. Crisp, *Retrieving Doctrine*, 12–13.
47. McCann, "Creation and Conservation," 307.
48. McCann, "Creation and Conservation," 307.
49. McCann, "Creation and Conservation," 307.
50. McCann, "Creation and Conservation," 307.
51. McCann, "Creation and Conservation," 307.
52. Hodge, *Systematic Theology*, 579.

ent from what seems to be the case intuitively and empirically speaking, but the subject of knowledge is likewise continuously recreated such that identity is forfeit and sensory experience illusory.[53] This theory also leads to occasionalism through the denial of secondary causes.[54] Philosopher Steven Nadler explains, "In its most extreme version, occasionalism is the doctrine that all finite created entities are devoid of causal efficacy, and that God is the only true causal agent. Bodies do not cause effects in other bodies nor in minds; and minds do not cause effects in bodies nor even within themselves. God is directly, immediately, and solely responsible for bringing about all phenomena."[55]

Recall that on Edwards' view no created thing has even the potential to exist on its own.[56] All entities constantly go out of existence to be recreated by God, but this makes God a first cause in every instance with no secondary cause in any instance.[57] Since God literally produces *everything*, nothing can be produced by those things which God creates.[58] There is no efficacy of secondary causes, because secondary causes do not actually exist.[59] No causation exists outside of God, and there is no cooperation on any level between God and that which he creates.[60] This applies not only to a vague conception of the world as a whole, but to every individual entity which comprises it including human thoughts.[61] Note that whatever is the case is such purely because of God and not anything outside of God, so that God is the sole source and cause of evil and moral

---

53. Hodge, *Systematic Theology*, 579. However, Mark Coppenger points out to me that a film projector flashes separate frames upon a screen to create various characters, settings, and other entities bearing definite continuous identities.

54. Hodge, *Systematic Theology*, 579–80. See also McCann, "Creation and Conservation," 306–7. However, note the arguments in defense of occasionalism in Quinn, "Divine Conservation, Secondary Causes, and Occasionalism," 50–73, and Freddoso, "Medieval Aristotelianism and the Case against Secondary Causation in Nature," 74–118.

55. Nadler, "Occasionalism," 626.

56. Crisp, *Retrieving Doctrine*, 12.

57. McCann, "Creation and Conservation," 306–7.

58. McCann, "Creation and Conservation," 306–7.

59. Contrast with Leibniz who does allow for some sense of secondary causation, as well as a theodicy to address the problem of evil which is raised below. McDonough, "Leibniz," 31–60.

60. Hodge, *Systematic Theology*, 579. Although in Leibniz's monadological view there does appear to be a type of cooperation between God and creation.

61. Hodge, *Systematic Theology*, 579.

purity.⁶² This theory looks less like theism, and more like panentheism or pantheism, where the world exists entirely in God, or else everything is God.⁶³ Again, the external world as known by humans, the reality of secondary causation, responsibility, and identity are all called into question on this view.⁶⁴

However, with respect to divine action, there is a sense in which the creation of the world is the same as its conservation. While major aspects of the Edwardsian theory addressed above can be rejected, it is important to acknowledge that God is not any more involved in the creation of the world than he is in its conservation.⁶⁵ Recall that when the universe comes into existence, it does not do so in terms of a *process*, which is significant because the continued existence of the universe is not a process either.⁶⁶ Granting a first moment when the world exists and God is its creator, a process has not taken place, but the mere granting of being by God, and then the world exists.⁶⁷ The creation and sustenance of the world thus occur in one act, for the initial moment of the existence of the world does not differ from any subsequent moment of existence, since each moment is related to God in the same way.⁶⁸ In this sense, but not in the other sense already discussed, one can validly affirm "continuous creation."⁶⁹

---

62. Hodge, *Systematic Theology*, 580.

63. Hodge, *Systematic Theology*, 580. William Rowe claims that "*Pantheism* is the view that God is wholly within the universe and the universe is wholly within God, so that God and the universe are coextensive, but not identical. A related, but distinct view known as *Panentheism*, agrees with pantheism that the universe is within God, but denies that God is limited to the universe. For according to panentheism, the universe is finite and within God, but God is truly infinite and so cannot be totally within or otherwise limited to the finite universe." Rowe, "Does Panentheism?," 65.

64. Hodge, *Systematic Theology*, 580.

65. McCann, "Creation and Conservation," 307. God is every bit as present and active in the sustenance of the world as he is in its initial creation.

66. McCann, "Creation and Conservation," 307.

67. McCann, "Creation and Conservation," 307–8.

68. McCann, "Creation and Conservation," 308.

69. McCann, "Creation and Conservation," 307. McCann thus attempts to clarify that "'continuous creation' should not, then, be interpreted to mean that the world is continually passing away and coming to be. Rather, it is simply a way of making the point that as creator, God is directly responsible for the entire existence of the universe. And on this score, the continuous creation view turns out to be very much on the right track." McCann, "Creation and Conservation," 307. Hodge identifies the aforementioned understanding of continuous creation as the traditional Reformed view: "Others who represent preservation as a continued creation, only mean that the

NON-CONCURRENT COSMOLOGICAL PRESERVATION AND GOVERNMENT

Non-concurrent cosmological preservation and government is a view of providence that denies concurrence between God and creation in preservation and government and limits agency or involvement in the acts of preservation and government to creation alone. One example of a non-concurrent cosmological view of providence is deism. Regarding deism, "By the late eighteenth century, the term came to mean belief in an

---

divine efficiency is as really active in the one case as in the other. They wish to deny that anything out of God has the cause of the continuance of its existence in itself; and that its properties or powers are in any such sense inherent as that they preserve their efficiency without the continued agency of God. This is the sense in which most of the Reformed theologians are to be understood when they speak of preservation as a continuous creation." Hodge, *Systematic Theology*, 577. However, Hodge immediately expresses his discomfort with the language of "continuous creation" because it is not the "idea meant to be expressed." Hodge, *Systematic Theology*, 577. He writes, "It is true that the preservation of the world is as much due to the immediate power of God as its creation, but this does not prove that preservation is creation. Creation is the production of something out of nothing. Preservation is the upholding in existence what already is. This form of the doctrine is therefore a false use of terms. A more serious objection, however, is that this mode of expression tends to error. The natural sense of the words is what those who use them admit to be false, and not only false but dangerous." Hodge, *Systematic Theology*, 577. Using an illustration from J. K. Rowling's *Harry Potter* series, Crisp more helpfully chooses to label this the "radical dependence view" instead of the admittedly confusing "continuous creation." Crisp, *Retrieving Doctrine*, 12. Crisp writes, "Consider the act of thinking of the Mona Lisa. The first instant at which one calls the thought to mind, it begins to exist. Every moment one thinks of the painting thereafter, provided one continues to think of this without interruption, and without being distracted by some other thought, one is conserving that initial thought in the mind's eye. But if one were to stop thinking of the Mona Lisa, the thought of the painting would cease to exist. So, we might say, the initial thought of the painting perdures provided I continue to think it. But if, like Professor Albus Dumbledore, one were able to take a thought from one's mind, and deposit it in a magical thought-repository, or Pensieve, then the thought would continue to exist without my continuing to think it. In which case, the relation between my thought and me is much less radical, since the thought can persist without my consciously sustaining it in being, once it is placed in the Pensieve." Crisp, *Retrieving Doctrine*, 12.

Crisp adds, "This thought experiment should not be pressed too hard. It is only intended to show something of the difference between the dependence of the creation upon the Creator where God preserves an existing creation in being, though, in some sense, the creation perdures—that is, continues to exist under its own steam—and the idea of a radical dependence of the creation upon its Creator. The relation of radical dependence (call it, the *radical dependence view*) should be distinguished from what is sometimes called continuous creation, although not all dogmaticians make this clear." Crisp, *Retrieving Doctrine*, 12.

'absentee God' who creates the world, ordains its laws, and then leaves it to its own devices."[70] This view proffers arguments for the conclusion that the world as a whole sustains itself in existence or that its constituent parts possess the capability to remain in existence.[71] For example, humans have always experienced the world as enduring while they have not, in the same way, experienced God as being responsible for the persistence of existence exemplified by the universe.[72] Thus empirical evidence suggests that the world persists, but the evidence does not appear to indicate that God has anything to do with this persistence of the world. Scientific laws also speak to the conservation of particular aspects of the universe such as its mass and energy.[73] It seems unnecessary to posit a divine source of the sustenance of the universe because scientific laws that are consistent with philosophical or methodological naturalism are already able to account for it.[74] However, these evidences are insufficient.

The endurance of empirical entities does not justify the inference that they persist on their own. Scientific laws do not provide an explanation for the continued existence of the universe either, because they do not *prescribe* anything with respect to the persistence of the universe, but rather *describe* the already existent nature of the universe.[75] Scientific laws pertain to what has already taken place or is taking place at present. Philosopher Hugh J. McCann points out that scientific laws do not describe any process by which objects in the universe move from the past or present into future existence.[76]

Could the behavior of entities account for their continued existence? Supposing an internal mechanism initiates a process of self-existence in an entity, this mechanism would have to be sustained either by the entity itself or by another external mechanism or entity.[77] McCann argues that the mechanism whereby an entity is preserved cannot be sustained by that same entity, and positing another entity whereby the mechanism is sustained leads to an infinite regress, unless God is the external provi-

---

70. Audi, *Cambridge Dictionary*, 216.
71. McCann, "Creation and Conservation," 308.
72. McCann, "Creation and Conservation," 308.
73. McCann, "Creation and Conservation," 308.
74. McCann, "Creation and Conservation," 308.
75. McCann, "Creation and Conservation," 308.
76. McCann, "Creation and Conservation," 308.
77. McCann, "Creation and Conservation," 308–9.

dential sustainer.[78] Suggesting that the world has a disposition not only to behave the way that it does, but to continue to exist ignores the fact that dispositions are reducible to the behaviors of structural elements within entities, which is the same attempted explanation offered above.[79] In the end, the world can have no intrinsic explanation for its persistence in existence, but must be preserved through the same divine creative activity which brought it into existence in the first place.[80]

Scientific laws do not prescribe or even describe the self-conservation of entities, but apply to physical interactions which already presuppose the existence of the world and are irrelevant to concerns about its continued existence.[81] Implicit in these metaphysical observations is the realization that there is no inconsistency between the doctrine of divine preservation and the laws of conservation in science.[82] It may even be the case that the laws of conservation in science, as all other so-called laws of nature or scientific laws, are dependent upon God for their existence and consistency through time and space every bit as much as the universe is dependent upon him for its existence and preservation.

CONCURRENT THEISTIC-COSMOLOGICAL PRESERVATION AND GOVERNMENT

The refutation of the two non-concurrent views of divine providence above leaves a properly qualified continuous creation which allows for secondary causes and a universe which is wholly dependent upon God for its existence, nature, and behavior. The doctrine of divine providence is clearly consistent with the application of natural theology in the previous section, and the doctrine is thoroughly developed in systematic

---

78. McCann, "Creation and Conservation," 308-9. Following McCann, positing further internal mechanisms leads to an infinite regress. Trying to imagine what such a mechanism might look like is a difficult, if not impossible, task from the start. Such a mechanism would operate in the context of the continuum of time, but this would entail that for any time that the process inherent to the mechanism in question is initialized, it must have an effect at some future time that both accounts for the endurance of the respective entity through time and does not account for any endurance at all, since the future time must be immediately subsequent to the initial time with no gap in between the two points. McCann, "Creation and Conservation," 308-9

79. McCann, "Creation and Conservation," 309.
80. McCann, "Creation and Conservation," 310.
81. McCann, "Creation and Conservation," 310.
82. McCann, "Creation and Conservation," 310.

theologies throughout history. Moreover, the doctrine of providence is consistent with Scripture.

One passage which explicitly speaks to the issues raised in the present discussion is Colossians 1:16–17, which states, "For by him all things were created, in heaven and on earth, visible and invisible, whether thrones or dominions or rulers or authorities—all things were created through him and for him. And he is before all things, and in him all things hold together." Paul begins his letter to the believers at Colossae with a typical Pauline greeting and expression of thanks to God for the faith and love exhibited by those who heard and understood the gospel. Paul describes the content of the prayers he makes on behalf of the recipients of his letter before transitioning into transfer language and a proclamation of redemption in the Son which leads to a great christological hymn. In this christological hymn Paul claims that the Son is the image of the invisible God, firstborn of all creation, creator, sustainer, head of the church, beginning, firstborn from the dead, preeminent, indwelt by the fullness of God, and reconciler. The description of the Son as sustainer in Colossians 1:17 affirms that "in him all things hold together."

Note that *creation* is mentioned first in this passage, followed by the explanation that everything was created for Christ, which is an allusion to *government*, and finally the strong claim that "in him all things hold together," which is taken in the literature to allude not only to *preservation* and *government*, but especially to describe *concurrence*.[83] The word trans-

---

83. The Greek text of Colossians 1:17b is τὰ πάντα ἐν αὐτῷ συνέστηκεν. All things in him hold together. The αὐτῷ clearly refers to the "Son" of Colossians 1:13. The subject of the verse is Jesus Christ the Son. Colossians 1:17 follows Colossians 1:16d in taking τὰ πάντα to refer to the universe, or all that is created. Harris, *Colossians & Philemon*, 43. In Colossians 1:15–20 there is a thematic emphasis on the phrase τὰ πάντα, but the main theme of the passage is Christ, and they are not the same. Christ holds a position of ultimacy over his creation. See Dunn, *Colossians & Philemon*, 93.

What theologians refer to as the "Creator-creature-distinction" is thus assumed by the text. However, the substance of the passage really concerns what one might term the "Creator-creature-*relation*." Thus Dunn writes, "The thematic emphasis on τὰ πάντα and on Christ's ultimacy in relation to τὰ πάντα is continued. Once again the theme reflects Jewish reflection on Wisdom. According to Sir. 1:4 'wisdom was created before all things' (προτέρα πάντων ἔκτισται σοφία), and the second-century-BCE Jewish philosopher Aristobulus notes Solomon's observation (Prov. 8:22–31) that 'wisdom existed before heaven and earth' (Eusebius, *Praeparatio Evangelica* 13.12.11)." Dunn, *Colossians & Philemon*, 93.

Following Harris, the ἐν αὐτῷ in Colossians 1:16a serves as a guide to taking ἐν αὐτῷ in Colossians 1:17b as the locative "in him." Harris, *Colossians & Philemon*, 43. Again, the αὐτῷ clearly refers to the "Son" of Col 1:13. Harris, *Colossians & Philemon*,

lated "hold together" is the Greek συνέστηκεν which is a philosophical term used outside the New Testament in contexts addressing the order of the cosmos.[84] Many other passages of Scripture describe the various

---

43. The subject of the verse is still Jesus Christ the Son. Dunn mentions that the use of the aforementioned preposition ἐν was a common one in contexts of God and the universe, writing, "Such use of the prepositions 'from,' 'by,' 'through,' 'in,' and 'to' or 'for' was widespread in talking about God and the cosmos. So particularly pseudo-Aristotle, De mundo 6: ὅτι ἐχ θεοῦ πάντα χαί διά θεοῦ συνέστηχε; Seneca, Epistulae 65.8: 'Quinque ergo causae sunt, ut Plato dicit: id ex quo, id a quo, id in quo, id ad quod, id propter quod'; Marcus Aurelius, Meditations 4.23: ἐχ σοῦ πάντα, ἐν σοῖ πάντα, εἰς σὲ πάντα; so also Philo, De cherubim 125-26: τὸ ὑφ' οὗ, τὸ ἐξ οὗ, τὸ δι' οὗ, τὸ δι' ὅ; and already in Paul (Rom. 11:36 and 1 Cor. 8:6, as partially also in Heb. 2:10)." Dunn, Colossians & Philemon, 91. It is worth noting that one of the words used by pseudo-Aristotle above is συνέστηχε, a word that appears again in Col 1:17b.

84. The συνέστηκεν in Col 1.17b is the third person singular perfect active indicative of συνίστημι. Harris points out that the subject of συνέστηκεν is neuter and plural. Harris, Colossians & Philemon, 43. The term means "to come to be in a condition of coherence, continue, endure, exist, hold together." Danker, A Greek-English Lexicon, 973. According to Harris, the term is an intransitive perfect having a present meaning that "in him all things hold together," and he adds, "What Christ has created he maintains in permanent order, stability, and productivity. He is the source of the unity (συν-, together) and cohesiveness or solidarity (συν-ίστημι, cohere) of the whole universe. But it is not impossible that συνίστημι denotes subsistence rather than coherence: 'all things have their existence in him' (W. Kasch, TDNT 7:897). Commentators who regard v. 17 as transitional ... and therefore as dealing with both creation and redemption argue that this vb. indicates that both the physical universe and the Church owe their coherence to Christ, and that πρὸ πάντων (v. 17a) denotes his priority over the new creation as well as the old." Harris, Colossians & Philemon, 43.

The text teaches that everything holds together in Christ. As alluded to in the previous note, there is also a theme outside of Scripture wherein the universe is ordered according to the mind and will of some given deity. For example, Plato and Pseudo-Aristotle attribute the coherence of the universe to their deities and even use the same word the apostle Paul later uses to indicate an imposition of order upon the contingent realm. Jewish thought likewise ascribed the sustenance of the universe to the wisdom of God, while Philo posits the logos as the rational explanation behind all of the parts of the universe. Radford, Epistle to Colossians, 177. So also Dunn, "Likewise, although the thought of the universe as held together by divine agency is characteristic of wider Greek philosophic thought (see, e.g., pseudo-Aristotle, cited above in 1:16; W. Kasch, TDNT 7.897), in Jewish thought this is attributed particularly to the divine Logos: thus Sir. 43:26 maintains that 'by his word all things hold together' (ἐν λόγῳ αὐτοῦ σύγκειται τὰ πάντα) and similarly in Philo (Quis rerum divinarum heres 23, 188; De fuga 112; De vita Mosis 2.133; Quaestiones in Exodum 2.118) and in Wis. 1:6-7 Wisdom, God, and Spirit are merged into each other with the description τό συνέχον τὰ πάντα ('that which holds all things together')." Dunn, Colossians & Philemon, 93. Paul is working with this background in mind but going much further to say that Jesus Christ is that, "living bond of the world's order, the source and secret of 'that unity and solidarity which makes it a cosmos instead of a chaos.'" Dunn, Colossians & Philemon, 93. Following

aspects of divine providence, but this particular text is one of the most explicit and exhaustive, and is well suited for observations to be made later regarding the scientific implications of the doctrine of providence.[85]

J. B. Lightfoot, Radford adds, "Cp. Heb. i. 3, 'upholding all things by the word of his power', i.e. not merely sustaining the universe but carrying it forward to its goal." Radford, *Epistle to Colossians*, 177.

With regard to this pervasive rationality and bond of the universe Dunn explains, "In identifying this function with Christ ('in him') the intention presumably was not to reduce the person of Christ to a personification, but to shed the further light of Christ on that personification: paradoxical as it may seem, the wisdom which holds the universe together is most clearly to be recognized in its distinctive character by reference to Christ." Dunn, *Colossians & Philemon*, 94. Dunn continues, "This will mean, among other things, that the fundamental rationale of the world is 'caught' more in the generous outpouring of sacrificial, redemptive love (1:14) than in the greed and grasping more characteristic of 'the authority of darkness' (1:12)." Dunn, *Colossians & Philemon*, 94. The Son created the cosmos, but it is not the case that the Son *merely* created the cosmos. Paul proclaims the great truth that Christ is also the one in whom all things continuously hold together. William Barclay summarizes the truth of this text well: "As Paul sees it, Jesus Christ is not only the agent of creation, he is also the one in whom 'all things hold together' (Col. 1:17). It would be perfectly possible to think of a creator who made the world and then left the world to itself, of one who, as it were, set the world going and then left the world to its own devices. A watchmaker, for instance, may make a watch, but once he has made it and sold it, it is out of his hands. But to Paul, Jesus Christ was more than the creating power and personality; he is, as J. B. Lightfoot puts it, 'the principle of cohesion in the universe.' He makes the universe 'a cosmos instead of a chaos,' an ordered and orderly and reliable whole instead of an erratic and unpredictable muddle. This is a very great thought." Barclay, *All-Sufficient Christ*, 62–63.

85. Rosner et al., *New Dictionary*, 711. Scripture is full of examples of God's providentially sustaining and caring for his creation. Popular examples of books that speak of God's providence include Job and Pss. Matt 6:25–30 and Rom 8:28 are often cited to alleviate worry and bring comfort to God's people. "The idea goes beyond that of a general power which preserves cosmic life and order; the power is exercised specifically (Matt. 10:29)." Rosner et al., *New Dictionary*, 711. Christians readily affirm this view of God's workings in the natural order. It is a serious misunderstanding of providence to think that the results of scientific inquiry can refute the doctrine. As mentioned and explained in Rosner, "The development of the natural sciences over the centuries has increased human understanding of the causes operative within nature, but this leaves the biblical idea of providence unaffected. The Bible is concerned not with the mechanics of divine sustaining and the causal ordering of nature but with the knowledge, power, will and manifest activity of God. God's being and action is the basic reality which undergirds cosmos and history, and the biblical witness is interested in this fundamental fact rather than in its precise form and inner nature." Rosner et al., *New Dictionary*, 711.

However, providence extends beyond the natural order. According to texts like Acts 17:28 and Heb 1:3, God keeps all created things existing and maintaining their properties. Grudem, *Systematic Theology*, 315. See also Allison, *Historical Theology*, 289. God

Another text often raised in connection to providence is the portion of Hebrews 1:3 which states that "he upholds the universe by the word of his power."[86] The author of Hebrews begins his work by explaining that God spoke to ancient Israel through the prophets. He then contrasts this means of God's speaking to his people with the speech of God in the last days through the Son of God, who has been appointed to the position of the heir of God, and who is identified as the creator of the world. Continuing his description of the Son, the author states that the

---

also directs all created things in those actions which correspond to their respective properties such that both God and his creatures effect changes within the cosmos; however God's efficacy is universal and primary, meaning that God brings about every event in the universe, whereas creaturely causes are secondary and particular. Grudem, *Systematic Theology*, 315. Allison explains the relationship between first and second causes in Reformed thought in the context of concurrence: "The second aspect of providence, concurrence, brings the working of God together with the working of his creation: 'God not only gives and preserves to secondary causes the power to act, but immediately influences the action and effect of the creature, so that the same effect is produced not by God alone, nor by the creature alone, nor partly by God and partly by the creature, but at the same time by God and the creature, as one and the same total efficiency—that is, by God as the universal and first cause, and by the creature as the particular and secondary cause.' Specifically, 'the *first cause* is that which is entirely independent; but upon it all other things, if there are any, depend; this is God. A *second cause* is that which recognizes another cause prior to itself, upon which it depends; such are the efficient created causes . . . depend on the first cause as for their existence so also for their operation.' Examples of secondary causes include the law of gravity, the bonding of chemicals to produce amino acids, the orbit of the planets and stars, and the human will exercising its prerogative to either obey God or sin against him. With their doctrine of concurrence, the post-Reformers did not allow for the idea that these secondary causes act independently of God, nor that the secondary causes become primary causes (with God, now the secondary cause, helpless to direct them or dependent on them), nor that God's activity and the activities of secondary causes are completely different. Yet these theologians affirmed the real activity of such secondary causes. In his work of concurrence, God acts together with all that he has created in a way that is consistent with each thing's nature." Allison, *Historical Theology*, 289–90.

Finally, God directs every created thing so that it fulfills his purposes. Grudem, *Systematic Theology*, 315. Allison is helpful here again, explaining, "The third aspect of providence is government, which is 'an act of divine providence by which God symmetrically arranges each and every creature, in its particular strength, actions, and suffering, to the glory of the Creator and the good of this universe, especially to the salvation of the godly.' This government applies to both inanimate (or nonrational) things and living (or rational) beings. Indeed, there is one system of government for inanimate things, another system for living creatures. Furthermore, 'The end [purpose] of providence is the glory of God and the salvation of the elect.'" Allison, *Historical Theology*, 290.

86. The Greek text reads "φέρων τε τὰ πάντα τῷ ῥήματι τῆς δυνάμεως αὐτοῦ."

Son is the "radiance of the glory of God and the exact imprint of his nature," meaning that the glory of God has now come to rest in the heir of all things, the Son, who is of the same nature as God the Father. The next part of verse three is most relevant to the current discussion of divine providence, for it is claimed that the Son, in addition to everything else said about him in the preceding verses, "upholds the universe by the word of his power." However, some commentators question whether the passage is so clearly referring to the Son, rather than the Father.

New Testament commentator Gareth Lee Cockerill focuses on the close identification of the Father and Son in the passage.[87] He finds ambiguity surrounding whether it is the word of the Father or the word of the Son that bears all things.[88] Cockerill understands this ambiguity to call attention to the contiguous identities of Father and Son.[89] John Calvin explains, "The demonstrative pronoun 'His' can be construed equally well as referring either to the Father or to the Son: it can be rendered as 'the Father's' or as 'His own.'"[90] Taking the context into account and following the most popular reading, Calvin concludes "His" refers to the Son, which is the best understanding of the text.[91] The Son is said to uphold the universe by his word of power. The content of verse three complements the content of verse two, placing the power of the Son on display through his acts of creation and providence.[92] New Testament scholar Simon J. Kistemaker points out the flow of the verse from a description of the *person* of Christ to a description of the *work* of Christ.[93] He notes,

---

87. Cockerill, *Epistle to Hebrews*, 95. Even in distinguishing the Father from the Son, Cockerill writes, "The universal heir and agent of creation is also the one who sustains the universe." Cockerill, *Epistle to Hebrews*, 95.

88. Cockerill, *Epistle to Hebrews*, 95.

89. Cockerill, *Epistle to Hebrews*, 95.

90. Calvin, *Epistle of Paul*, 9.

91. Calvin, *Epistle of Paul*, 9. Calvin defends his view: "I am inclined to accept the latter rendering because it is more widely received and best suits the context. Literally it reads 'by the Word of His power', but the genitive has the force of an adjective in accordance with Hebrew idiom. There is no point in the torturous explanation of some of the effect that Christ upholds all things by the Word of the Father, that is by Himself, because He is the Word. There is no need of such a forced exposition, for Christ is not called ῥῆμα but λόγος. Word, here, simply means will, and the gist is that Christ who upholds the whole world by His will alone, nevertheless did not refuse the task of accomplishing our purification." Calvin, *Epistle of Paul*, 9.

92. Kistemaker, *Exposition*, 30.

93. Kistemaker, *Exposition*, 30.

"From a discussion about the being of the Son, the writer proceeds to an explanation of the Son's activity, which involves caring for all things."[94] The sustaining work of Christ is thus viewed by Kistemaker as a *caring* work, an insight to be repeated later. In the text of Hebrews, the Son is presented as the one through whom God created the world, and those in the early church "were filled with the thought that the One who had created the world would also be the One who redeemed it."[95] More than that, the Son was thought of as the one who sustains the world, rather than creating it and leaving it alone.[96]

Not all commentators agree that the verse pertains to the metaphysical preservation of the universe. For example, New Testament professor George Wesley Buchanan rejects the majority view of Hebrews 1:3 as describing metaphysical sustenance and opts instead for an interpretation regarding the authority of the Son.[97] According to Buchanan, "The Son has authority over everything since he is given legal authority and is supported in everything he does 'by the word of [God's] power.'"[98] Calvin also views the passage as affirming the authority of the Son. He writes, "Christ, to whom is given supreme authority, is to be listened to before all others."[99] However, unlike Buchanan, Calvin takes the passage to affirm the *verbal* authority of the Son upon the basis of the *metaphysical*

---

94. Kistemaker, *Exposition*, 30.
95. Barclay, *Letter to Hebrews*, 15.
96. Barclay, *Letter to Hebrews*, 15. Barclay writes, "The sustaining power belongs to Jesus. These early Christians had a tremendous grip of the doctrine of *providence*. They did not think of God as creating the world and then leaving it to itself. Somehow and somewhere they saw a power that was carrying the world and each life on to a destined end. They believed,
  'That nothing walks with aimless feet;
  That not one life shall be destroy'd,
  Or cast as rubbish to the void,
  When God hath made the pile complete.'" Barclay, *Letter to Hebrews*, 15.
97. Buchanan, *To Hebrews*, 7–8. Buchanan writes, "'Bearing everything by the word of his power' does not picture the Son playing the part of Atlas carrying the world on his shoulder, nor in the sense that God is the 'sustainer of the world' or 'age' (*sōbēl 'ōlām*) (Exod R. 64c, §36:4). Rather, as ambassador or apostle, the Son has authority over everything since he is given legal authority and is supported in everything he does 'by the word of [God's] power.' He speaks for the One who sent him." Buchanan, *To Hebrews*, 7–8.
98. Buchanan, *To Hebrews*, 7–8.
99. Calvin, *Epistle of Paul*, 9.

authority of the Son.[100] The description of the Son, including his work of providence, proves that supreme authority is given to him, and thus he must be listened to.[101] Commentator James T. Draper takes this argument a step further, not just arguing that the Son's providential maintenance of all things merits listening to his word, but arguing that the providential power of the Son is indicative of his *superiority* to the prophets.[102] This explanation fits the context nicely.

The same word through which all things were created also sustains all things.[103] Frederick F. Bruce draws a connection between the creating and sustaining word when he notes, "The creative utterance which called the universe into being requires as its complement that sustaining utterance by which it is maintained in being."[104] New Testament professor Donald Hagner, too, draws the parallel between the power of the Son in creating the universe and his power in continuing to uphold it.[105]

Calvin defines the use of "uphold" in the passage as "to care for and to keep all creation in its proper state."[106] Recall Kistemaker also notes

---

100. Calvin, *Epistle of Paul*, 9.

101. Calvin, *Epistle of Paul*, 9. Calvin writes, "Christ, to whom is given supreme authority, is to be listened to before all others." Calvin, *Epistle of Paul*, 9. The supreme authority refers to the description of the person and work of Christ in the passage, and the fact that people must listen to him upon that basis refers to the derivative authority of his word.

102. Draper, *Hebrews*, 18. Draper writes, "He is maintaining all things by the word of his power. Because of that, he is superior to the prophets." Calvin, *Epistle of Paul*, 9.

103. Calvin, *Epistle of Paul*, 17–18.

104. Bruce, *Epistle to Hebrews*, 49.

105. Hagner, *Hebrews*, 4. Hagner reasons, "As the Son was instrumental in the creation of the universe (v. 2), so the continuing significance of the Son is seen, in the fifth clause, in his sustaining the universe with his powerful word. Philosophers of every age are prone to ask what it is that underlies reality—that is, what dynamic sustains and makes coherent all that exists. Our author, further revealing his Christocentric perspective, finds the answer in the mighty word of the Son. This view also finds parallels in Paul and John. When John uses 'Word' (*logos*) to describe Jesus, he uses a term that has both Jewish and Greek associations. For the Greek philosophers *logos* was the underlying principle of rationality that made the world orderly, coherent, and intelligible. Without using the technical term *logos*, Paul argues in similar fashion: 'He is before all things, and in him all things hold together' (Col. 1:17, RSV). Although the author of Hebrews does not use the specific term *logos* in this passage, the idea that Christ sustains the universe, is behind it all, and keeps it all going (as the present participle sustaining indicates), is parallel." Hagner, *Hebrews*, 4–5.

106. Calvin, *Epistle of Paul*, 9.

this work of the Son "involves caring for all things."[107] Moreover, Calvin connects Christ's care to his goodness.[108] Calvin writes, "He sees that everything will quickly disintegrate if it is not upheld by His goodness."[109] In Draper's words, "God takes individuals, nations, nature, and history and maintains them by the word of his power."[110]

Draper describes the work of the Son as carrying.[111] He writes, "By the very word of his power, Jesus Christ is carrying all things toward their appointed end."[112] A common theme of commentaries on this passage is contrasting the activity of the Son with the activity of Atlas. Commentators are quick to note that this act of carrying should not imply that the Son is anything like Atlas. For example, Robert H. Smith writes, "The Son is hardly being pictured like Atlas bent beneath the weight of the world upon his shoulders."[113] Bruce shares Smith's sentiment, echoing

---

107. Kistemaker, *Exposition of Epistle*, 30.

108. Calvin, *Epistle of Paul*, 9.

109. Calvin, *Epistle of Paul*, 9. One might object to the ideas of Christ's care and goodness in upholding the universe by raising the problem of natural evil. Natural evil includes potentially harmful aspects of the created order such as hurricanes, tornadoes, earthquakes, and tsunamis. Animals experience pain, suffering, and death. So do humans. How can a Christian account for these evils if God's providence is good? According to Gen 3, a consequence of human sin is a curse on creation itself. This curse is seen in the aforementioned experiences of pain, suffering, and death, whether they come about as the direct result of natural disasters or not. The biblical view of evil is one of hope that God will bring forth good from out of the evil. See, for example, Gen 50:20 and Rom 8:28. The death of Christ is the surest of all proofs that God brings good from evil. Thus even turmoil in the natural order is part of God's good plan. On a more practical level, if God were to suspend regular operations of the natural order to prevent every consequence of the curse, innumerable difficulties for regularity in the natural order would follow. A chaotic creation is the realm of a chaotic God, rather than a God who cares.

110. Draper, *Hebrews*, 18.

111. Draper, *Hebrews*, 17.

112. Draper adds, "In another place, the writer of Hebrews asserts that 'through faith we understand that the worlds were framed by the word of God' (11:3). The word that proceeded out of the mouth of God was the word of his power. When God wills something, it is accomplished completely and finally. When God created this universe, he did not turn away to go off and leave it. He has been carrying it on toward its completion." Draper, *Hebrews*, 17–18.

113. Smith, *Hebrews*, 32–33. Smith makes a number of interesting comments on the passage by drawing on his knowledge of Jewish tradition: "A Jewish tradition teaches that the world rests upon three things: Torah, worship of God, and deeds of loving service (M. Pirqe Aboth 1:2). As the tranquility of the world and life itself are threatened by crime and evil (M. Pirqe Aboth 5:1), harmony and life are enhanced by

also Draper's implication that the providential activity of government is described in this text.[114] Bruce writes, "He upholds the universe not like Atlas supporting a dead weight on his shoulders, but as one who carries all things forward on their appointed course."[115] Kistemaker likewise posits the presence of government in this passage, as he writes, "That word in itself signifies a forward motion, although not in the sense of an Atlas whose movement is torturously slow because the weight of the globe nearly crushes him."[116] He continues as follows:

> The Son carries "all things" to bring them to their destined end. And he does this by a mere utterance ("by his powerful word"). Christ, the ruler of the universe, utters a word, and all things listen in obedience to his voice. No other motions are necessary, for the spoken word is sufficient.[117]

Again, it is clear that more than a mere emphasis on preservation is present in the text. Government is present as well. Hughes also argues that the work of the Son "involves not only support but movement, the carrying forward and onward of all things to the predestined consummation which is also implicit in their beginning."[118] Thus Hughes sees not only

---

these three, and indeed without them the world would relapse into chaos. The author of Hebrews is echoing the Christian conviction that the powers and energies resident in the Son are what keep the world from collapsing (cf. Heb. 11:3; Col. 1:17). That which sustains, upholds, and bears the world is not the law proclaimed on Sinai, not some esoteric knowledge granted to a spiritual elite, not wisdom available in the tradition of sages, and surely not political or financial clout, but only his word of power, the message declared at first by the Lord (2:3). People must attend to that if they are really to live." Smith, *Hebrews*, 32–33.

114. Bruce, *Epistle to Hebrews*, 48–49.
115. Bruce, *Epistle to Hebrews*, 49.
116. Kistemaker, *Exposition*, 30.
117. Kistemaker, *Exposition*, 30.
118. Hughes, *A Commentary*, 45. Hughes continues, "God creates the world in accordance with his will and purpose, and what he has created he sustains and directs toward the fulfillment of that purpose. Nor does the fall of man into sin, with its dire effects on the created order (Gen. 3), frustrate the will of the Creator; for the new creation, or the renewal of creation, in Christ is precisely the undoing of the fall and the bringing to fruition of all God's purposes in the original creation. Moreover, throughout the period that separates the beginning from the fulfillment the world is dependent on God for the continuance of its existence: were it not for the sustaining providence and government of God, all would relapse into non-existence. This emphasis is common in the patristic and medieval commentators." Hughes, *A Commentary*, 45. The summary provided by Hughes points toward the Trinitarian nature of the work of Christ as well. He writes, "Not only, then, did the universe come into existence

preservation in Hebrews 1:3, but government as well. And after commenting on the Lord Jesus Christ carrying the weight of all of creation in his hand, and disposing of it through wisdom and power, the Puritan John Owen writes, "Such is the nature and condition of the universe, that it could not subsist a moment, nor could anything in it act regularly unto its appointed end, without the continued supportment, guidance, influence, disposal, of the Son of God."[119] Owen, too, sees the two aspects of providence discussed above on this particular passage, namely, preservation and government. Barclay writes of the early Christians, "Somehow and somewhere they saw a power that was carrying the world and each life on to a destined end."[120]

Finally, much is made of Acts 17:22–28 in relation to divine providence and a pantheistic view in particular.[121] Having introduced a self-existent, self-sustaining God and all of creation's radical dependence upon him, the apostle Paul grounds his claims by explaining, "for 'In him we live and move and have our being'; as even some of your own poets have said, 'For we are indeed his offspring'" (Acts 17:28). The first part of this final verse of the passage in question is extremely valuable to the current discussion of divine providence.

---

through the Son (v. 2), but the whole created order is sustained in being and carried on to its appointed destiny by *his word of power*. The Son, so to speak, is the nucleus of creation: 'in him all things hold together' (Col. 1:17); and the purposeful coherence of the whole is achieved by his word. This word, which is the expression of his will, is essentially a *dynamic* word; that is to say, it is always and inevitably a word which effects its intended purpose. The word of the Son is not other or less than the word of the Father, for he who himself is the Word is the perfect and harmonious expression of the mind and will of God. The word of the Word is infallibly effective precisely because it is one with the word of the Father." Hughes, *A Commentary*, 46.

119. Owen, *Hebrews*, 6.

120. Barclay, *Letter to Hebrews*, 15.

121. In this passage, the apostle Paul stands in the middle of the Areopagus and challenges the men of Athens regarding their religiosity (Acts 17:22). He notes an altar they have to an unknown god, and uses it as an opportunity to proclaim his God to them (Acts 17:23). Paul identifies this God as the creator of the world and everything that exists in the world, Lord of all, and the God who does not live in temples made by human beings (Acts 17:24). The God Paul proclaims to the Athenians is not served by humans because he does not need anything, but rather humans derive everything from this God (Acts 17:25). Humans even derive their nationalities, histories, and geographies from God (Acts 17:26). The hope is that people might seek and find God, who is not far from them (Acts 17:27). John Stott asserts, "If it were not for sin which separates us from him, he would be readily accessible to us." Stott, *Message of Acts*, 286.

Theologian John R. W. Stott believes this line to be "a quotation from the 6th century poet Epimenides of Cnossos in Crete."[122] However, much debate exists regarding the source of the first poetic line the apostle Paul quotes.[123] Paul is quoting from a pagan philosopher, presumably because Scripture would have been quite foreign to Paul's Athenian audience, and presumably because Paul desires to build a bridge of appeal for the sake of clarity and persuasion.[124] However, New Testament scholar John Polhill is skeptical that there are two quotes in Acts 17:28, arguing instead that the apostle Paul is attempting to utilize familiar terminology with the Greeks.[125] Polhill writes, "The phrase 'in him we live and move and have our being' seems to have been a more or less traditional Greek triadic formula."[126]

A general concern about the relationship of Paul's statements to a pantheistic or panentheistic understanding of the universe is common in commentaries on this passage. Calvin starts his discussion of this text, "I grant that the apostles, according to the Hebrew idiom, often use the preposition *in* instead of *per*, 'by'; but because the expression 'we live in God' is more emphatic and more expressive, I did not see fit to change it."[127] The difficulty here is one surrounding not only the fact that Paul

---

122. Stott, *Message of Acts*, 286.

123. Peterson, *Acts of Apostles*, 499. Peterson writes, "Some have argued that Paul is citing words originally addressed to Zeus in a poem attributed to Epimenides of Crete, who flourished in the sixth century BC. However, we do not have the original poem, and there are similar assertions by other Greek writers (e.g., Dio Chrysostom, *Or.* 12.43). Whatever the source, Paul will have been using these words to convey the biblical truth that God, not merely the creation, is the environment in which we exist (cf. 14:17). As a personal being he can be known, understood, and trusted. In the syntax of the sentence, the words '*as some of your own poets have said*' most naturally relate to what follows. Paul goes on to quote Aratus of Cilicia (*Phaenomena 5*), a philosopher-poet from the third century BC, who said of Zeus, "'we are his offspring'" (*tou gar kai genos esmen*). The poet will have understood these words in a pantheistic sense, but Paul appears to have viewed them in the light of the image of God theology in Genesis 1:26-27 (see further below). He recognized that a search for God had been taking place in the Greco-Roman world, but condemned the result—the idolatry which was everywhere present and the ignorance of the true God which it betrayed (vv. 22-25). In short, he indicated that the search had been ineffective because of human blindness and stubbornness (cf. Rom. 1:18-32)." Peterson, *Acts of Apostles*, 499-500.

124. Polhill, *Acts*, 375.

125. Polhill, *Acts*, 375.

126. Polhill, *Acts*, 375.

127. Calvin, *Acts of Apostles, 14-28*, 119. Calvin explains, "For I have no doubt that Paul means that we are in some way contained in God, because He dwells in us by His

quotes from a pagan source, but the way English speakers read the preposition in question. Calvin chooses to leave the stronger connotation of "in" in lieu of "by," and does so in such a way that he entails a different reading than the mere use of "by" would merit.[128] Polhill is emphatic, "Paul surely did not understand this in the Greek sense, which would emphasize the pantheistic view of the divinity residing in human nature."[129] Rather, "His view was that of v. 25: God is the giver of life and breath and all that is."[130]

Even though Calvin's rendition of the text more readily lends itself to a pantheistic reading as described above, he is careful to distinguish Paul's description of the work of the Spirit in the world from pantheism. He writes, "For the power of the Spirit is diffused through all parts of the world, to keep them in their place; and to supply the energy to heaven and earth which we see, and also movement to living creatures."[131] He continues, "This does not mean the way that crazy men talk nonsense about all things being full of gods, and even the very stones being gods, but that by the wonderful activity and instigation of His Spirit God preserves all that He has created out of nothing."[132] Calvin thus takes this text to describe, as do Colossians 1:17 and Hebrews 1:3, the preservation and government of the world by God, particularly here through the Spirit.[133] So then, "This verse also teaches that the world was not created by God once, in such a way that afterwards He abandoned His work, but that it endures by His power, and that the same One who was once its Creator is its perpetual ruler."[134]

Bede quotes Augustine to the effect that people do not exist *in* God in the sense of a substance within another substance, but rather in the sense that "*he brings it* [our existence] *about; and this is his work, whereby he contains all things.*"[135] God orders the world in virtue of his wisdom,

---

power. And therefore God Himself distinguishes Himself from all creatures so that we may realize that strictly speaking He alone is, and that we truly subsist in Him, seeing that He quickens and sustains us by His Spirit." Calvin, *Acts of Apostles, 14–28*, 119–20.

128. Calvin, *Acts of Apostles, 14–28*, 119.
129. Polhill, *Acts*, 375–76.
130. Calvin, *Acts of Apostles, 14–28*, 376.
131. Calvin, *Acts of Apostles, 14–28*, 120.
132. Calvin, *Acts of Apostles, 14–28*, 120.
133. Calvin, *Acts of Apostles, 14–28*, 120.
134. Calvin, *Acts of Apostles, 14–28*, 120.
135. Bede, *Venerable Bede Commentary*, 143–44.

and "*It is through this 'ordering' that 'in him we live and move and are.'*"[136] Augustine concludes "*that if he withdrew this work of his from things, we would neither live nor move nor be.*"[137] Bede adds, "And a little further on he [Augustine] says: *Heaven and earth and all things which are in them, namely all spiritual and bodily creatures, do not remain in being in themselves, but in him, surely, of whom it is said, 'in him we live and move and are,' because although every part can exist in the whole of which it is a part, nevertheless the whole itself does not exist, except in him by whom it was made.*"[138]

Another commentator on the passage, theologian Ajith Fernando, presents a simple explanation of this verse. He writes, "Since God is the immanent sustainer of creation, everyone's life depends on him (v. 28)."[139] Calvin states the same, using this realization from the text to make an argument from the greater to the lesser.[140] Thus Colossians 1:17, Hebrews 1:3, and Acts 17:28 are three texts of Scripture which appear to teach the doctrine of providence with its three aspects of concursus, preservation, and government. Other more systematic considerations bear upon a proper scriptural understanding of the doctrine of providence as well.

According to Calvin, believers differ from unbelievers in that they see the *continuing* work of God, although unbelievers have the capacity to see "the wisdom, power, and goodness of the author in accomplishing such handiwork."[141] Calvin believes the character of God as revealed in creation is self-evident even to those who do not want to see it and that unaided reason can also contemplate, "some general preserving and

---

136. Bede, *Venerable Bede Commentary*, 144.
137. Bede, *Venerable Bede Commentary*, 144.
138. Bede, *Venerable Bede Commentary*, 144.
139. Fernando, *Acts*, 475.
140. Calvin, *Acts of Apostles, 14–28*, 120. Calvin explains, "Paul has put the most important thing in the highest place, so as to pass down, step by step, to *being*; in this sense, 'Not only is there no *life* for us except in God, but there is not even *movement*, no, and what is more, there is no *being*, which is an inferior thing to both of them.' I say that life is superior in men, because not only do they have sensation and movement in common with the brute beasts, but they are endowed with reason and intelligence. Accordingly Scripture justifiably honours that unique gift, with which God has distinguished us, with a separate description of its own." Calvin, *Acts of Apostles, 14–28*, 120.
141. Calvin, *Calvin*, 197. Calvin writes, "For even though the minds of the impious too are compelled by merely looking upon earth and heaven to rise up to the Creator, yet faith has its own peculiar way of assigning the whole credit for Creation to God." Calvin, *Calvin*, 197.

governing activity, from which the force of motion derives."[142] He concludes, "In short, carnal sense thinks there is an energy divinely bestowed from the beginning, sufficient to sustain all things."[143] Natural theology can take us so far, "But faith ought to penetrate more deeply, namely, having found him Creator of all, forthwith to conclude he is also everlasting Governor and Preserver—not only in that he drives the celestial frame as well as its several parts by a universal motion, but also in that he sustains, nourishes, and cares for, everything he has made, even to the least sparrow [cf. Matt 10:29]."[144] Here, as before, Calvin insists upon the good and caring nature of God's providence. Though fortune and chance have dominated mortal reckoning of seemingly random happenings, the doctrine of God's providence precludes such an explanation of events.[145]

In Calvin's view, while every object possesses its own properties, objects do not exercise any power unless directed by God; therefore, Calvin views entities "nothing but instruments to which God continually imparts as much effectiveness as he wills, and according to his own purpose bends and turns them to either one action or another."[146] The doctrine of providence follows from the doctrine of creation and the doctrine of the omnipotence of God so that, for Calvin, omnipotence is "not the empty, idle, and almost unconscious sort that the Sophists imagine, but a watchful, effective, active sort, engaged in ceaseless activity."[147] Further, God's omnipotence is "one that is directed toward individual and particular motions."[148] One of the ways in which humans discern that God is omnipotent is in virtue of his governing providence. Calvin explains, "For he is deemed omnipotent, not because he can indeed act, yet sometimes ceases and sits in idleness, or continues by a general impulse that order of nature which he previously appointed; but because, governing heaven

---

142. Calvin, *Calvin*, 197.

143. Calvin, *Calvin*, 197.

144. Calvin, *Calvin*, 197–98.

145. Calvin, *Calvin*, 198. Calvin claims that "anyone who has been taught by Christ's lips that all the hairs of his head are numbered [Matt. 10:30] will look farther afield for a cause, and will consider that all events are governed by God's secret plan." Calvin, *Calvin*, 198.

146. Calvin, *Calvin*, 198.

147. Calvin, *Calvin*, 198. Calvin similarly argues that if God is called "Ruler" in more than name only then it follows he rules wisely and dispositionally rather than blindly and ambiguously. Calvin, *Calvin*, 202–3.

148. Calvin, *Calvin*, 202–3.

and earth by his providence, he so regulates all things that nothing takes place without his deliberation."[149] God's government extends to all of his works, and "those as much defraud God of his glory as themselves of a most profitable doctrine who confine God's providence to such narrow limits as though he allowed all things by a free course to be borne along according to a universal law of nature."[150] Universal providence not only includes God's watching over the order he has put into nature, but his exercising special care of each of the things he has created.[151] Especially important to note in the work of Calvin is the strong emphasis upon the good and caring nature of God revealed through providence. The significance of this point will be seen more clearly in later chapters.

Returning to Scripture, Calvin infers the doctrine of providence from John 5:17, Acts 17:28, and Hebrews 1:3 and writes, "Therefore we must prove God so attends to the regulation of individual events, and they all so proceed from his set plan, that nothing takes place by chance."[152] Along this same line of thought, Calvin offers a rather strong argument that God is in immediate control of the weather and seasons.[153] He proposes the following hypothetical to illustrate the naturalistic view:

---

149. Calvin, *Calvin*, 202–3. Does evil take place without his deliberation? Greg Allison comments, "Of course, one of the major issues raised by this position is the problem of evil: If God is all-powerful and exercises control over everything in his creation, what can explain the presence of evil and suffering in the world? Even those who do not hold such a view have still had to wrestle with this issue." Allison, *Historical Theology*, 277. The problem of evil is a difficulty to be worked through by all Christians, not just those adhering to a Reformed perspective. Calvin's view allows evil to be ascribed to the creaturely cause of an event in terms of fault, while absolving the God who faultlessly brings good out of evil.

150. Allison, *Historical Theology*, 197–98. If God does not have control over the elements, but leaves them up to the laws of nature, it follows that humans, too, are left to the mercies or mercilessness of impersonal, uncaring, and morally neutral laws of nature. Allison, *Historical Theology*, 197–98.

151. Allison, *Historical Theology*, 203. The fact that God exercises special care over each of his creatures does not entail that nothing bad ever happens to them. Here, as elsewhere with the problem of evil, God has a sufficient reason for the evil he permits. If physical laws were rescinded every time they threatened physical harm to a particular creature, more creative creatures would no doubt take immediate advantage of the situation, threatening harm for the sake of advantage over physical laws. This hypothetical is one of many that might explain what morally sufficient reasons God has for allowing natural evil in the world.

152. Allison, *Historical Theology*, 203.

153. Allison, *Historical Theology*, 203.

> Suppose we grant that the beginning of motion is with God, but that all things, either of themselves or by chance, are borne whither inclination of nature impels. Then the alternation of days and nights, of winter and summer, will be God's work, inasmuch as he, assigning to each one his part, has set before them a certain law; that is, if with even tenor they uninterruptedly maintain the same way, days following after nights, months after months, and years after years. But that sometimes immoderate heat joined with dryness burns whatever crops there are, that at other times unseasonable rains damage the grain, that sudden calamity strikes from hail and storms—this will not be God's work, unless, perhaps because clouds or fair weather, cold or heat, take their origin from the conjunction of the stars and other natural causes.[154]

Calvin complains that if the hypothetical above were the case, then no room is left for the fatherly care of God, whether by favor or judgment.[155] The process is impersonal and fatalistic, rather than showing God's actual caring involvement with the world.[156] Calvin cites Scriptures where God is said to show his favor through watering the earth including Leviticus 26:3–4 and Deuteronomy 11:13–14 and 28:12, and shows his judgment when it does not rain, or when it hails and storms in Leviticus 26:19, Deuteronomy 28:22, Isaiah 28:2, and Haggai 2:18.[157] Again, the emphasis is upon the immanence of God in caring for everything that happens in his creation. Rather than making God out to be a distant, fatalistic, and cold force that blindly determines the course of events on earth, God is presented as a good, nurturing, and caring God who watches over and intentionally directs his creation.

Calvin also makes a persuasive argument for the universality of God's providential care by appealing to Matthew 10:29.[158] In this text, "Christ says, without exception, that not even a tiny and insignificant sparrow falls to the ground without the Father's will."[159] The point of the text is not that God watches over only sparrows, but that *even* the

---

154. Allison, *Historical Theology*, 203–4.
155. Allison, *Historical Theology*, 204.
156. Allison, *Historical Theology*, 204.
157. Allison, *Historical Theology*, 204.
158. Allison, *Historical Theology*, 204.
159. Allison, *Historical Theology*, 204.

most seemingly insignificant things come about by God's direction.[160] Interestingly, Calvin points out that the universe was made for humanity, and hence we can look for purpose in the government of God in his creation.[161] According to Scripture, even seemingly chance events are due to the providential working of God.[162] Thus Calvin writes, "From this we gather that his general providence not only flourishes among creatures so as to continue the order of nature, but is by his wonderful plan adapted to a definite and proper end."[163]

> We do not, with the stoics, contrive a necessity out of the perpetual connection and intimately related series of causes, which is contained in nature; but we make God the ruler and governor of all things, who in accordance with his wisdom has from the farthest limit of eternity decreed what he was going to do, and now by his might carries out what he has decreed. From this we declare that not only heaven and earth and the inanimate creatures, but also the plans and intentions of men, are so governed by his providence that they are borne by it straight to their appointed end.[164]

Theologian Millard Erickson also divides providence into two closely related aspects.[165]

> One aspect is God's work of preserving his creation in existence, maintaining and sustaining it; this is generally called preservation or sustenance. The other is God's activity in guiding and directing the course of events to fulfill his purposes. This is termed government or providence proper. Preservation and government should not be thought of as sharply separate acts of God, but as distinguishable aspects of his unitary work.[166]

---

160. Allison, *Historical Theology*, 204.

161. Allison, *Historical Theology*, 204. This truth becomes even more readily apparent in the creation itself as scientists reveal more about the fine tuning of the universe.

162. Allison, *Historical Theology*, 205–6. Scripture testifies that God controls whatever happens in nature, such as the movement of winds and seas. Moreover, the provision of bread, which includes an innumerable number of factors in nature, is due to the favor of God. Allison, *Historical Theology*, 205–6.

163. Allison, *Historical Theology*, 205–6.

164. Allison, *Historical Theology*, 207.

165. Erickson, *Christian Theology*, 414.

166. Erickson, *Christian Theology*, 414.

In preservation, God maintains the existence of creation and protects it from harm or destruction, as well as provides for any need had by the entities of creation, as noted in numerous passages of Scripture.[167] Creation is not self-sufficient, nothing remains in existence by its own power, and Erickson points out, "Both the origination and the continuation of all things are a matter of divine will and activity."[168] The second aspect of providence is government, where God acts in the universe in order that all events fulfill the plan of God for his universe.[169] Government is "the purposive directing of the whole of reality and the course of history to God's ends. It is the actual execution, within time, of his plans devised in eternity."[170]

Theologian John Frame adds to this picture of providence. Because the natural world is the creation of God, as emphasized in Scripture, it is also extremely personalistic.[171] While angels and humans are involved in the work of the world, natural events proceed from God.[172] The Bible does not affirm anything like an impersonal set of natural laws that govern the universe, although this observation does not completely preclude the concept of natural law, nor does the Bible give any place to the idea that natural events occur at random.[173] Behind the secondary causes of nature, whether they appear to be law-like or random, stands the personal force who is the God of the Bible.[174] Frame explains, "Quantum mechanics may demonstrate a randomness in the finite world, that is, events without finite causes. But it can never demonstrate negatively that those events have no causation at all, that is, that they are independent even of God's determination."[175] God is at work with his creation in concursus to sustain and direct it toward its ends.

---

167. Erickson, *Christian Theology*, 414.

168. Erickson, *Christian Theology*, 414.

169. Erickson, *Christian Theology*, 420.

170. Erickson, *Christian Theology*, 420. Erickson continues, "This governing activity of God extends over a large variety of areas. God is described as controlling nature, so much so that its elements are personified as obeying his voice." Erickson, *Christian Theology*, 420.

171. Frame, *Systematic Theology*, 146–47.

172. Frame, *Systematic Theology*, 147.

173. Frame, *Systematic Theology*, 147.

174. Frame, *Systematic Theology*, 147–48.

175. Frame, *Systematic Theology*, 147n11.

Some have objected to the doctrine of concursus on philosophical grounds. Two objections will be examined here in hopes of better explaining how the doctrine of concursus looks in more philosophical categories. Theologian Michael Horton takes up an objection from philosopher Frank Dilley to the doctrine of concursus.[176] He quotes from Dilley as follows:

> In short, the dilemma is this: if there is genuine unity of action, two parties doing exactly the same act at the same time, then there is no duality of causes; and if there is duality of causes, then there is no unity of action. If it is not possible to conceive of two sets of free causes operating conjointly in exactly the same action, then it is not possible to satisfy the conditions by which one would be able to say that both naturalistic (and human) and theological explanations are valid. Hence the seeming plausibility of the joint-case solution breaks down. The alternative to conservatism and liberalism turns out to be a delusion.[177]

Dilley's argument starts with a definition of what he refers to as "unity of action, two parties doing exactly the same act at the same time."[178] Since the two parties involved do exactly the same act, there is no distinction between what the two parties actually do, from which it follows that there is no distinction between them as particular types of causes.[179] On the other hand, if the two parties involved act in different causal senses, then there is no "unity of action."[180] Therefore, there is no way to satisfy requirements whereby one might be able to affirm both a theistic (God) and cosmological (nature and human) explanation for an event, at least according to Dilley.[181]

Horton responds to the argument from Dilley by precluding his notion of unity in action from the discussion at the start, noting that "it is one thing to decree the safe passage of a ship in time to be carried out through secondary agents and quite another to guide the ship to its destination as its captain."[182] A duality of causes *does* exist in this scenario, as it does in all others, but if two genuinely different causes exist in every

---

176. Horton, *Covenant and Eschatology*, 90.
177. Horton, *Covenant and Eschatology*, 90.
178. Horton, *Covenant and Eschatology*, 90.
179. Horton, *Covenant and Eschatology*, 90.
180. Horton, *Covenant and Eschatology*, 90.
181. Horton, *Covenant and Eschatology*, 90.
182. Horton, *Covenant and Eschatology*, 90.

scenario, then it does follow, as Dilley points out, that there cannot be any unity of action.[183] Horton concedes the point and replies that the objection is simply not a problem since "Dilley demands too much of *concursus* by insisting that it must preserve a unity of action (despite dual causality) that, as we have already seen, is not only unnecessary but impossible, given the distinction between creator and creature."[184] He continues, "The effect of a concursive event (note 'event,' not 'action,' since the argument here is that there are many 'actions' involved, on the part of two or more agents) is referred to the secondary agent precisely because it is that agent's actions that are most directly recognized as producing it."[185]

The second objection Horton faces comes from philosopher of religion David Griffin. According to Horton, "Griffin holds that 'the primary-secondary cause version of double agency assumes the sufficiency of each cause and that the idea of two sufficient causes for one event is self-contradictory.'"[186] For example, if God, the primary cause acts in such a way to cause it to rain, and a cloud, the secondary cause acts in such a way to cause it to rain, then both the agency of God and the agency of the cloud are involved in the rain event. Griffin's aforementioned objection understands each of the two aforementioned agents a sufficient cause for the rain. Either God sufficiently causes the rain such that no place is left for the cloud, or else the cloud sufficiently causes the rain such that no place is left for God. But to posit both God and the cloud as sufficient causes for the rain is to propose a self-contradictory state of affairs. Horton responds, "But the doctrine of *concursus* does not assume the sufficiency of each cause."[187] Horton clarifies as follows:

> In any case, the response to Griffin is essentially the same as that made to Dilley: primary and secondary causality each entail subsidiary actions that are proper to each agent. One must not confuse the totality of a produced event (whose diversity is itself discernible upon reflection) with a unity of action or sufficiency of each cause.[188]

---

183. Horton, *Covenant and Eschatology*, 90.
184. Horton, *Covenant and Eschatology*, 90–91.
185. Horton, *Covenant and Eschatology*, 91.
186. Horton, *Covenant and Eschatology*, 91.
187. Horton, *Covenant and Eschatology*, 91.
188. Horton, *Covenant and Eschatology*, 91.

In divine concursus there are two agents, or actions, or causes, and one event.

Both God and creation are present in preservation, and both God and creation are at work in government. Providence is thus, as defined and described above, God's work of concurrently preserving and governing his creation in a concurrent theistic cosmological model.

Chapter 2

Scientific Implications of Providence

THE PREVIOUS CHAPTER PROVIDED a philosophical account of the Christian doctrine of divine providence. This chapter discusses some implications of the doctrine of divine providence for the laws of nature and problem of induction. In chapter 3, a more detailed analysis of the concept of the laws of nature is presented, and chapter 4 turns to address the problem of induction. Since the laws of nature and problem of induction are philosophically relevant to the scientific endeavor, the content of this chapter is presented as pertaining to the scientific implications of providence. The scientific implications of the doctrine of divine providence are evident to theologians who have commented on texts of Scripture which speak of divine providence, Christian apologists who have sought to integrate theology and science for the sake of positive theistic argumentation, and both Christian and secular scientists who have sought proper presuppositions underlying their work in the natural realm.

A sampling of the evidence from the aforementioned categories of theologians, apologists, and scientists is offered below to establish the link between divine providence and science. Providing such evidence not only serves to establish the aforementioned link, but corroborates the argument of this book, that Christian theism is better equipped to provide a basis for science than are secular and Islamic worldviews. The argument presented in this book is not novel, but the hope is that the argument is more explicitly developed within the context of a Christian worldview.

SCIENTIFIC IMPLICATIONS OF PROVIDENCE IN THEOLOGY

One of the recurring themes of commentary written on Colossians 1:16–17 is the observation that science can proceed upon the premise of Christ's providential care of his creation.[1] For example, one commentator speaks of the control and guidance of Christ entailing the order and unity of the universe and references the *Epistle to Diognetus*, where "God is described as sending to men not an angel or any other minister in His service, 'but the very Artificer and Creator of the universe Himself . . . whose mysteries all the elements faithfully observe.'"[2] He suggests that these mysteries are the laws of nature which are, "not impersonal tendencies but the secret counsels of the living Word."[3] Similarly, Dunn wants to link the language of Colossians 1:17b back to what he calls "Platonic-Stoic cosmology."[4] He takes this cosmology to be "the belief that there is a rationality (Logos) which pervades the universe and bonds it together (cf. Heb. 1:3) and which explains both the order and regularity of natural processes and the human power of reasoning resonates with this rationality."[5] While Dunn may be overstating his case linguistically or historically, he is right to see a metaphysical truth in Colossians 1:17b with significant consequences for epistemology. Not only is the universe coherent and regular, but human minds are created in such a way that they fit this natural order.[6] Note also Dunn's reference to Hebrews 1:3, another text mentioned in the previous chapter regarding the Christian doctrine of providence. Dunn sees Colossians 1:17 and Hebrews 1:3 as teaching metaphysical and epistemological truths relevant to the laws of nature and the scientific endeavor.[7] He even claims, "In the modern era

---

1. Radford, *Epistle to Colossians*, 177–78; Dunn, *Colossians & Philemon*; Barclay, *All-Sufficient Christ*, 63–64.

2. Radford, *Epistle to Colossians*, 177.

3. Radford, *Epistle to Colossians*, 177–78.

4. Dunn, *Colossians & Philemon*, 93–94.

5. Dunn, *Colossians & Philemon*, 93–94.

6. This observation is similar to a philosophical concept to be discussed later known as *adequatio intellectus ad rem*. Plantinga, *Where Conflict Really Lies*, 295–96. Versions of it may be found in Thomas Reid and Immanuel Kant as well.

7. Stated implications of the doctrine of providence for the laws of nature are virtually non-existent in the commentaries on Heb 1:3 and Acts 17:28. A number of commentaries on Acts do not even address Acts 17:28, but skip it and go on to 17:29. However, commentaries on Col 1:17 sometimes include references to Heb 1:3 and

Newtonian physics and the scientific investigation of 'the laws of nature' were premised on a similar axiom."[8] Barclay states the matter especially well in mentioning that early Christian thinkers saw Jesus Christ as the "principle of cohesion in the *physical universe*" in terms of their Logos doctrine.[9]

> He who created the universe put his own laws into the universe. As Lightfoot put it, "The law of gravity is an *expression* of his mind." There is something very great here. The laws of nature are the laws of God. It is because the mind of God, the Logos, the Divine Reason, the Son, Jesus Christ—they all mean the same—is in and through the universe that the universe has the marvelous order and the dependable, reliable, predictable order that it has. The scientist, the mathematician, the astronomer, the nuclear physicist, if they only knew and realized it, are discovering the laws of God all the time, and it is his reason that guides them. The universe is as it is, because the Spirit of Christ is in it to order and to control.[10]

However, New Testament commentators are not the only theologians who have noticed the scientific implications of texts pertaining to the providence of God.

Systematic theologians who discuss the doctrine of providence have not missed the metaphysical and epistemological implications of the truths expressed above either. Grudem mentions that God causes all things that he preserves to keep their created properties such that particular entities like water, grass, paper, and rock all continue to act in accordance to their natures.[11]

> God's providence provides a basis for science: God has made and continues to sustain a universe that acts in predictable ways. If a scientific experiment gives a certain result today, then we can have confidence that (if all the factors are the same) it will give the same result tomorrow and a hundred years from tomorrow. The doctrine of providence also provides a foundation for technology: I can be confident that gasoline will make my car run today just as it did yesterday, not simply because "it has

---

Acts 17:28, as do systematic theologies that address divine providence.
8. Dunn, *Colossians & Philemon*, 94.
9. See Barclay, *All-Sufficient Christ*, 63.
10. See Barclay, *All-Sufficient Christ*, 63–64.
11. Grudem, *Systematic Theology*, 316.

always worked that way," but because God's providence sustains a universe in which created things maintain the properties with which he created them. The *result* may be similar in the life of an unbeliever and the life of a Christian: we both put gasoline in our cars and drive away. But he will do so without knowing the ultimate reason why it works that way, and I will do so with knowledge of the actual final reason (God's providence) and with thanks to my Creator for the wonderful creation that he has made and preserves.[12]

Millard Erickson is more focused in his comments on the implications of God's providence. Erickson begins by noting the metaphysical basis for the regularity and constancy of the world: "God's work of preservation also means that we can have confidence in the regularity of the created world. It is possible to plan and to carry out our lives because there is constancy to our environment."[13] He continues with the epistemological implications of the metaphysical truth stated above:

> We take this fact for granted, yet it is essential to any sort of rational functioning in the world. We are able to sit down in a chair because we know it will not vaporize or disappear. Barring a practical joke by someone while our back is turned, it will be there.[14]

Then he discusses even the negative implications of rejecting the doctrine of providence.

> Yet from a purely empirical standpoint, there is no real basis for such an expectation. In the past, we have found that our expectations of the future proved true when that future became present. Thus, we assume that our present expectations of the future, because they resemble previous expectations of now past futures, will be fulfilled. But this argument assumes the very thing that it purports to establish, namely, that future futures will resemble past futures. That is equivalent to assuming that the future will resemble the past. There really is no empirical basis for knowing the future until we have had a chance to actually experience that future. While there may be a psychological tendency to expect a certain thing to occur, there are no logical

---

12. Grudem, *Systematic Theology*, 316–17.
13. Erickson, *Christian Theology*, 394.
14. Erickson, *Christian Theology*, 394.

grounds for it, unless there is a belief that reality is of such a nature that it will persist in existence.[15]

Erickson's observations are deeply philosophical. Although he does not call it by name, what Erickson is describing above is what has become known as the problem of induction. This philosophical problem will be discussed in chapter 4. Erickson attempts to solve the problem by considering the Christian view of providence, "The assumption that matter persists, or that the laws of nature will continue to function, brings us into the realm of metaphysics. The Christian's belief at this point is not in a material or impersonal ground of reality, but in an intelligent, good, and purposeful being who continues to will the existence of his creation, so that ordinarily no unexpected events occur."[16] Though Erickson is a theologian, his argument is deeply philosophical, and carries with it a slightly polemical tone. He, like other theologians, believes a Christian metaphysic is found behind the ability to rationally function in the world.

Philosopher Lydia Jaeger has focused in on the narrower place of laws of nature in the biblical witness. In the context of science, and more specifically, the laws of nature, Jaeger writes, "Even a cursory reading of the Old Testament reveals the duality of its thinking about nature."[17] She continues, "On the one hand, natural phenomena are tied to rules, to a stable order; on the other, the Lord causes them through immediate action. Halfway between these two types of assertions there are some texts that speak of the effects of the divine Word in nature."[18] In the biblical account of nature, the established order of creation is harmonized with God's direct action, and the biblical authors sometimes affirm the presence of both even in the same passage without fear of contradiction.[19] Jaeger mentions that "regularities of nature, both animate and inanimate, serve as examples to attest to the truth of God's threats and promises (Matt. 16:2–3; 24:32)."[20] Again, Jaeger has laws of nature in mind, without which the biblical witness to spiritual consequences would not even make sense. Here, Jaeger sounds similar to Calvin in the previous chapter. Important to note also is the fact that the Old Testament contains the bulk of

15. Erickson, *Christian Theology*, 394.
16. Erickson, *Christian Theology*, 394.
17. Jaeger, *Einstein*, 139.
18. Jaeger, *Einstein*, 139.
19. Jaeger, *Einstein*, 139–40.
20. Jaeger, *Einstein*, 140–41.

passages pertaining to laws of nature, but New Testament passages factor into the general biblical picture of laws of nature as well. For example, "The Sermon on the Mount uses the Old Testament language describing the divine actions that govern meteorological and biological phenomena and establishes a direct link between divine action in nature and God's providential caring for man (Matt. 5:45; 6:26–30)."[21] More importantly, Jaeger points to some of the passages on providence discussed earlier. She writes, "There is one area where the New Testament expresses the Old Testament vision of nature in greater depth: a number of New Testament authors stress Christ's role in the Creation and maintenance of the world (John 1.3; 1 Cor. 8:6; Col. 1:16–17; Heb. 1:2–3; Rev. 3:14)."[22]

> Here we see an indirect link to the idea of law of nature, insofar as Christ recapitulates, in his person, the role of wisdom in Creation. In the same line of thought, John applies to Jesus the title of *Logos*, which corresponds both to the *ḥokmâ* of the Old Testament, with its continuation in the Jewish tradition, and to the unifying principle of the world in Stoic philosophy. These facts allow us to establish a (cautious) link between the natural order and intra-Trinitarian life. In this regard, we must of course recall the fundamental dependence of Creation with respect to God's Trinitarian nature: God can create beings that are radically different from him and yet dependent on him, for he unites in his essence both the One and the Many.[23]

Jaeger's view of the laws of nature is thus Christocentric, while it also alludes to the Trinitarian nature of the Christian God. The previous study of texts on divine providence emphasized the role of Christ the creator in sustaining his creation. Christological acts can be seen as Trinitarian as well, but Jaeger seems to have something further in mind concerning the Trinitarian nature of God and his relation to creation.[24] She references the ultimate relationship of the one and many in Trinity. Jaeger sees implications for the laws of nature not merely in particular texts of the Old and New Testament, but in the Bible as a whole and, in this instance, in such orthodox systematic beliefs as the doctrine of the Trinity. This Trinitarian aspect of theology and its possible relevance to laws of nature is discussed in chapter 5.

21. Jaeger, *Einstein*, 141.
22. Jaeger, *Einstein*, 141.
23. Jaeger, *Einstein*, 141. The Hebrew term *ḥokmâ* is "wisdom."
24. See, for example, John 5:19.

Returning to Jaeger's discussion of textual implications for laws of nature, the book of Job is mentioned as containing "texts that are very rich in teachings on nature, the best known undoubtedly being the speech of the Lord (chaps. 38–41)."[25]

> The book emphasizes both the efficacy of God's action in natural phenomena and the regularity of these phenomena, for nothing can escape the divine government, whose hallmark is wisdom. Several texts help us to understand how these two truths are articulated, and how the idea of law of nature fits into the more general framework of biblical revelation.[26]

The Lord's speech in Job is important, not just for its subject matter, but because the Lord's voice in the book is certainly the correct one, included as it is with the failed attempts of Job's friends to comfort him in his many afflictions. Job's friends, nevertheless, appear to agree with the Lord's speech regarding his providential care of nature.[27]

So, for example, Eliphaz recognizes God as the source of rain in Job 5:9–10 while Bildad strongly affirms the efficacy of secondary causes in Job 8:11 with respect to plant life and ascribes the order and peace of the heavens to the government of God in Job 25:2–3.[28] Elihu recognizes God as just judge and governor in Job 34:10–17, a legislator who is constrained by his own righteous character, and who reveals his goodness in sustaining the lives of his creatures.[29] Yet, Elihu also knows that as judge, God also works through nature (creation) to bring about just punishments. In expressing this knowledge, Elihu makes reference to natural phenomena.

---

25. Jaeger, *Einstein*, 142. Jaeger ties the book's treatment of nature to its answer to the problem of suffering: "Observation of nature is in fact part of the overall plan of the book: faced with incomprehensible suffering, the believer can take comfort in the control that the Lord maintains over the world. The description of nature—and in particular in its more frightening aspects—serves to illustrate the smallness of man and the sovereign power of God." Jaeger, *Einstein*, 142.

26. Jaeger, *Einstein*, 142.

27. Jaeger, *Einstein*, 142–43. Jaeger explains the significance of this point: "We have not noted any appreciable difference in the approach to nature among the different characters that intervene in the course of the dialogue. On the one hand, they base their arguments on divine sovereignty, which naturally leads them to highlight God's immediate action. On the other, they appeal to God's justice and wisdom, thus introducing the notions of regularity and of law." Jaeger, *Einstein*, 142–43.

28. Jaeger, *Einstein*, 143.

29. Jaeger, *Einstein*, 143.

> Elihu ends his speech with a long tirade on the divine action in nature (36:26–37:24). He evokes meteorological phenomena, for the most part violent: rain, lightning, thunder, wind, ice. His words reflect the anthropocentric concept of nature, typical of other Old Testament texts that establish a link between God's action in Creation and the blessings or punishments intended for men. Thus, Elihu can say, of these meteorological phenomena, that "through them, he judges the nations" (36:31).[30]

Elihu is careful to distinguish between the creator and creature in his doctrine of providence, emphasizing the word of God in bringing about these natural phenomena.

> Elihu puts particular emphasis on God's word: "He says to the snow: Fall on the ground! He says it to the rains, even to the strongest rains" (37:6; see also vv. 2–5). The verb ṣàwâ ("command," "order") serves to describe God's action on the clouds (37:12). The same verse contains the word taḥbulôt ("direction," "art of governing"), which is often used in the sphere of politics and government. The fact that Elihu refers to God's word as mediating divine action on nature implies some reservations about a concept of interaction that might too naively identify the divine with natural phenomena, an identification that, in any case, Israel's transcendent monotheism forbids.[31]

Again, the word of God serves as mediator between God and his creation. This protects the distinction between the creator and his creation. Although God is certainly immanent in his creation, he remains transcendent, and hence distinct from creation. The transcendent immanence of God is foreign to many other world religions. Jaeger contrasts the concept of God's transcendence with animism.

> Moreover, the transcendence of the divine invites us to see God as revealing himself in ephemeral phenomena, in opposition to the animist attitude that assigns springs, mountains, or trees as places of residence of the divine. And even ephemeral

---

30. Jaeger, *Einstein*, 143–44.

31. Jaeger, *Einstein*, 144. Jaeger again links observations about nature to the overall point of the Book of Job, "Terrifying meteorological phenomena, which man can neither predict nor control, further highlight the control that God exercises in any situation. This emphasis is particularly well suited to the purpose served by observation of nature in many passages of the Book of Job (and in particular in the Lord's speeches): to reassure the believer who faces adversity and suffering that God is sovereign." Jaeger, *Einstein*, 144.

> phenomena that serve to reveal the divine presence are never identified with it: in fact, even in the lengthiest descriptions of theophany, God is never identified with natural phenomena. These phenomena can be his clothing, his voice, his angry breath, or even the smoke from his nostrils and fire from his mouth, but never God himself, his Being... Consequently, careful descriptions of God avoid the strongest expressions; rather; they speak of the winds as his messengers or of the lightning bolts as his servants, who do his bidding.[32]

God shakes the mountains, Earth, and sun, which is significant because they symbolize the stability of nature.[33] Chaos in nature is represented by the sea, which God controls, and the gods correspond to the stars, which are merely the creation of God.[34] The providence of God is a polemic against pagan conceptions of nature. Providence is revealed through "normal" and "abnormal" natural activity.[35] Jaeger sees this description of providence as a shift toward the concept of natural order, even though nothing is stated at this point in the text of Job regarding laws of nature.[36] She sees that the author is able to affirm God's ordering the surface of water in one line, followed by God's shaking heaven in the next, so that "the author shows no discomfort in expressing, in a single breath, the establishment of limits, of order, and disruption of that order."[37] This shows that the God who sets up the order in nature maintains control over that order.[38]

> The establishment of the created order and its perfect control by God are closely connected to biblical monotheism. The assurance expressed in this text is only possible because of the character of the God of Israel, who is both all-powerful and entirely wise—in contrast to the concepts of the divine among neighboring peoples:
>
> Usually in ancient Near Eastern mythologies the god of wisdom is distinguished from the god of power. Because these two qualities do not exist in a single god of the pantheon, there

---

32. Jaeger, *Einstein*, 144–45.
33. Jaeger, *Einstein*, 145–46.
34. Jaeger, *Einstein*, 146.
35. Jaeger, *Einstein*, 146.
36. Jaeger, *Einstein*, 146.
37. Jaeger, *Einstein*, 147.
38. Jaeger, *Einstein*, 147.

is no god that is able to accomplish his full intentions. In contrast, the God of Scripture possesses both qualities supremely. There is no other cosmic being that is his equal in any way.[39]

Laws of nature are hence rather difficult to establish in the context of other world religions. This topic will be explained in more detail in the following section. For now, it will do to call attention to the fact that the laws of nature fit well with and are implied by a Christian view of divine providence, even though this is not necessarily the case with non-Christian views. The laws of nature fit so closely with a biblical understanding of divine providence that Jaeger actually argues something akin to the term is found in the biblical text.[40] The words *ḥòq* and *ḥuqqà* are argued for as being "among the most important terms to express the idea of law in the natural domain, although they are not the only ones."[41] Thus Christian Scripture has something to say about laws of nature.

SCIENTIFIC IMPLICATIONS OF PROVIDENCE IN APOLOGETICS

Not surprisingly then, apologists for the Christian faith have attempted to construct arguments based upon scientific implications of the doctrine of providence and other related doctrines. Most of these arguments seem to begin by denying the existence of God for the sake of argument, and examining the relevant epistemological consequences which follow from a non-Christian, or at any rate, non-theistic, metaphysic.

For example, the Dutch theologian and presuppositional apologist Cornelius Van Til argued, "Non-Christians are never able to, and therefore never do, employ their own methods consistently."[42] What, in example, might he be referring to? In the context of this quote, the principle of induction is the first item he attacks. To this end Van Til quotes A. E. Taylor regarding the uniformity of nature:

> The fundamental thought of modern science, at any rate until yesterday, was that there is a "universal reign of law" throughout nature. Nature is rational in the sense that it has everywhere a coherent pattern which we can progressively detect by the steady

39. Jaeger, *Einstein*, 146–47.
40. She makes this argument on pp. 147–48 of *Einstein*.
41. Jaeger, *Einstein*, 148.
42. Van Til, *Defense of Faith*, 125.

application of our own intelligence to the scrutiny of natural processes. Science has been built up all along on the basis of this principle of the "uniformity of nature," and the principle is one which science itself has no means of demonstrating. No one could possibly prove its truth to an opponent who seriously disputed it. For all attempts to produce "evidence" for the "uniformity of nature" themselves presuppose the very principle they are intended to prove.[43]

Here, Van Til has the laws of nature in view, per the quote from Taylor. Van Til adamantly believes these laws presuppose the existence of the Christian God, and will go on to argue that any position denying the existence of that Christian God is a position fraught with difficulties accounting for these laws of nature.[44] He states his argument as follows:

> Our argument as over against this would be that the existence of the God of Christian theism and the conception of his counsel as controlling all things in the universe is the only presupposition which can account for the uniformity of nature which the scientist needs. But the best and only possible proof for the existence of such a God is that his existence is required for the uniformity of nature and for the coherence of all things in the world.[45]

Van Til thus assumes that the providence of God is the basis for belief in the uniformity in nature presupposed by science. Van Til's move here is interesting, for he does not then argue *for* the existence of God based upon his observation, but rather states that, unless one *presupposes* the existence and activity of God in the world, then one has no basis upon which to pursue the scientific endeavor.[46] Interestingly, Van Til claims that it is specifically *Christian* theism that is the *only* principial basis for scientific knowledge. He does not appear to give any reason as to why this might be the case.

---

43. Van Til, *Defense of Faith*, 125.

44. Van Til, *Defense of Faith*, 125–26. Perhaps one would give Van Til's thought more credit had he not asserted that it is the Christian God in particular who accounts for the uniformity of nature. Even if Van Til's argument is for general theism, his assertions barely scratch the surface of what such an argument must offer to be found persuasive. More will be said about this matter below.

45. Van Til, *Defense of Faith*, 125–26.

46. For those curious as to how unbelievers "presuppose" the existence of God, see Rom 1:18–25. Van Til does not, to my knowledge, offer a philosophically robust treatment of what he means by "presupposition." At any rate, he does not do so here.

One other example of a Christian apologist with an argument from providence and laws of nature is Greg L. Bahnsen, who used such an argument against atheist Edward Tabash.[47] Unfortunately, Tabash did not seem to follow Bahnsen's presentation and resorted to emotional appeals regarding the doctrine of hell.[48] Presumably Bahnsen would have used a similar approach against atheist philosopher Michael Martin (the debate was cancelled by Martin) as evidenced from Bahnsen's lecture given in lieu of the debate.[49] Bahnsen also mentions the argument several times in his most famous debate with atheist Gordon Stein.[50] However, the Stein debate has been severely criticized in numerous ways.[51] Bahnsen was not always clear regarding what his actual argument *was*.

Perhaps the closest Bahnsen came to a clear statement of the argument used in the aforementioned debates is found in his massive work on apologist Cornelius Van Til.[52] Even here, Bahnsen's argument must be pieced together by following his footnotes and references to other chapters of his book. In the midst of a discussion on the place of traditional theistic proofs in the apologetic method championed by Van Til and Bahnsen, Bahnsen offers a new formulation of the cosmological argument for the existence of God.[53] He does so by critiquing a premise of the cosmological argument.

---

47. Bahnsen, *Great Debate*.
48. Bahnsen, *Great Debate*.
49. Bahnsen, *Debate That Never Was*.
50. Bahnsen, *Great Debate*.
51. See, for example, Clark, "A Reformed Epistemologist's Response," 256, who comments negatively on the debate (ellipses mine), "I have listened to the tapes . . . of the debate between Gregory Bahnsen, presuppositional apologist, and Gordon Stein, defender of atheism. Quite frankly, I found Bahnsen's arguments precious thin and his approach wearisome—he simply repeated over and over that unbelievers have no grounds for reason and then offered the briefest defense of his view that only Christian theism provides grounds for reason. Van Til, I'm afraid, had a similar awkward tendency to prefer assertion over argument. Perhaps the presuppositionalists are right when they claim that only Christian theism can provide any grounds for reason, meaning, and the natural sciences. But making the case that this is so requires an enormous amount of research, thought, and argument. A paragraph or two scarcely suffice." See also Choi, "Transcendental Argument," 232–33. Choi deals a gigantic blow to Bahnsen's argument as it appears in the Stein debate by arguing that "Bahnsen's actual argument in that debate—insofar as it can be reconstructed so as to be deductively valid—fails to establish Bahnsen's purported claim for his TAG—i.e., that *Christian* theism is the necessary precondition for proving anything at all." Choi, "Transcendental Argument," 232–33.
52. Bahnsen, *Van Til's Apologetic*, 617–19.
53. Bahnsen, *Van Til's Apologetic*, 617–19.

If the premise that "Everything has a cause" is interpreted in a more familiar way, as having an empirical impetus based on observation, then it refers to our ordinary and natural experiences. In that case, the cosmological argument proceeds upon an insecure foundation, for nobody knows from empirical experience that every single object and event in this world has a cause; nobody has observed everything. Moreover, if the causal principle is empirically interpreted, then "everything" means more precisely "each and every particular thing within the universe of experience," and "has a cause" means more specifically "has a natural cause."[54]

How might this crucial premise of the cosmological argument be established? Bahnsen draws heavily upon the Scottish skeptic David Hume to show that the premise is in serious question granting certain assumptions.

> For Hume, there is no empirical (and thus no rational) basis for attributing necessity to the regular sequences of events we have experienced. We expect a heavy object to drop to the ground when we let go of it, not because of sound scientific reasoning, but simply because of the psychological habit of associating one event with another. We have become accustomed to things happening in that way, even though there is no intellectual basis for predicting that they will do so in the (unperceived) future.[55]

Bahnsen does not deny, even per Hume, that people *expect* some sort of necessity between events. He does not deny that people reason inductively. Rather, Bahnsen is sifting for the basis of inductive reasoning within an unbelieving view of the world. Elsewhere he writes the following:

> Unbelievers who have been both brilliant and honest about this matter have openly conceded that they have no rational basis for believing that the future will resemble the past. We may have observed that event B followed event A many times in the past, but to know that B *necessarily* follows A (i.e., that the relation is causal), calls for reference to a metaphysical principle (namely, that the future will be like the past) for which the unbeliever has no warrant or right. As Bertrand Russell was driven to conclude: "The general principles of science, such as the belief in the reign of law, and the belief that every event must have a cause, are as completely dependent upon the inductive principle as are the beliefs of daily life. All such general principles are

54. Bahnsen, *Van Til's Apologetic*, 618.
55. Bahnsen, *Van Til's Apologetic*, 337n161.

believed because mankind have found innumerable instances of their truth and no instances of their falsehood. But this affords no evidence for their truth in the future, unless the inductive principle *is assumed*." Assumed? But that is what was supposed to be proved! Russell was aware of his defeat: "Hence we can never use experience to prove the inductive principle without begging the question. Thus we must . . . forgo all justification of our expectations about the future."[56]

Bahnsen asks the following:

> What rational basis is there for the assumption of natural uniformity, which is taken for granted in all inductive reasoning? Regardless of what specific answers are offered in response, they are certainly not based on empirical observation and inductive generalizations! Such answers are philosophical in nature.[57]

Bahnsen is thus closed to any merely empirical justifications of the inductive principle he views as in some sense behind the traditional cosmological argument. The premise is based not in observation alone, but deeper metaphysical commitments. For Bahnsen, the existence of the Christian God is one of these deeper metaphysical commitments.

> God knows Himself, of course, perfectly and comprehensively. He knows His holy character. He knows all propositional truths and possibilities, as well as their conceptual or logical relations. He knows His plan for every detail of creation and history, as well as the relations between all events and objects. His understanding is infinite and without flaw. Moreover, it is in terms of His creative and providential activity that all things and events are what they are. God's thinking is what gives unity, meaning, coherence, and intelligibility to nature, history, reasoning, and morality. In terms of this picture of the knowing process, man can search for causal relationships and laws (thinking God's thoughts after Him about the patterns, classifications, or kinds of things He creates and providentially controls).[58]

Bahnsen has set forth what he considers an unbelieving metaphysical view of the world and its resultant epistemological failures, as well as a Christian metaphysical view of the world and its epistemological fruits.

---

56. Bahnsen, *Van Til's Apologetic*, 618–19.
57. Bahnsen, *Van Til's Apologetic*, 642–43.
58. Bahnsen, *Van Til's Apologetic*, 223.

SCIENTIFIC IMPLICATIONS OF PROVIDENCE

With this metaphysical backdrop in mind, he is ready to state his rather unique approach to what he calls the cosmological argument.

> A presuppositional version of the cosmological argument amounts to the general presuppositional argument (i.e., the transcendental argument that God is the precondition of rational intelligibility), applied to the particular notion of causation. As Christians, we maintain that we can rationally prove God's existence from causation. We can show the unbeliever that causal reasoning or the "inductive principle" (compare the belief in the uniformity of nature) is not only taken for granted by all men, but is rationally necessary for our scientific inferences, our use of language, and our practical experience. However, when the worldview of the Bible is set next to the worldview of unbelief (in whatever form it takes) for mutual analysis, the causal principle is seen to be intelligible only within the Christian framework of thought.[59]

Bahnsen believes he has refuted all non-Christian attempts to justify the inductive principle through his reliance upon the thoroughgoing skepticism of unbelieving philosophers David Hume and Bertrand Russell.[60] He believes the traditional cosmological argument fails to prove anything because its premise pertaining to causation cannot be supported on a merely empirical basis. This apparently inevitable failure is not the case when it comes to the Christian worldview.

> But the Christian worldview does not have this intellectual dilemma of justifying the causal principle (inductive or scientific reasoning). It is transcendentally justified by the inner coherence of our presupposed worldview, or within its wider context, being entailed by both the nature and promises of God (cf. chap. 4.5 above). The unbeliever may be unwilling to resort to a "theological rationale" to justify the foundational belief (the causal principle) that is necessary to the rationality of science, but it is the only rational alternative to "forgo[ing] all justification of our expectations about the future." The presuppositional cosmological argument points out that unbelief must destroy rationality in order to save it. The unbelieving worldview cannot provide a

---

59. Bahnsen, *Van Til's Apologetic*, 618.
60. Whether he actually has accomplished so much is, of course, no small matter of debate.

cogent reason for what we necessarily assume in all our reasoning. Thus, it is entirely unreasonable not to believe in God.[61]

Bahnsen's attempt at arguing his case raises many questions. For now, it is worth noting that Bahnsen's voice is included along with a number of others who have attempted to make *something* of the skeptical musings of philosophers concerning the inductive principle which, as will be demonstrated, depends upon some concept of the laws of nature. Bahnsen does not believe the inductive principle should be dispensed with, but that the principle is necessarily assumed in all human reasoning. Bahnsen is not arguing as a skeptic, in other words, or even in virtue of a *reductio ad absurdum*, but as someone who grants the inductive principle (uniformity of nature, regularity, or causation) and then attempts to draw out the metaphysical preconditions for the truth of that premise.

A much clearer and much more modest proposal of the argument mentioned above pertaining specifically to the doctrine of providence and its scientific implications is found in an article from philosopher James N. Anderson.[62] While Anderson does not follow Bahnsen in his approach to this apologetic argument, like Bahnsen, he relies heavily on Van Til and Hume. Anderson begins by calling Hume's so-called problem of induction to mind.

> The infamous "problem of induction," brought forcefully to our attention by Hume, refers to the deceptively difficult task of accounting for the rationality (construed in terms of truth-directedness) of inductive inferences. Why should it be thought eminently reasonable to make generalizations about future events on the basis of past events or to posit "causal laws" on the basis of finite observations of coincidental occurrences? Such inferences are grounded on the assumption of uniformity and order in nature, but the task of *justifying* that assumption without reasoning in a vicious circle has proven all but intractable. This is hardly an abstruse, irrelevant concern detached from the realities of everyday life; on the contrary, it brings into question the rationality of all scientific investigation and such mundane practices as looking both ways before crossing the road.[63]

Anderson attempts to state Van Til's argument formally as follows:

---

61. Bahnsen, *Van Til's Apologetic*, 619.
62. Anderson, "If Knowledge Then God," 49–75.
63. Anderson, "If Knowledge Then God," 65–66.

24. If theism is not the case, then one cannot account for the uniformity of nature presupposed by inductive reasoning.
25. If one cannot account for the uniformity of nature presupposed by inductive reasoning, then beliefs based on inductive reasoning are not warranted.
26. Beliefs based on inductive reasoning are warranted.
27. Therefore, theism is the case.[64]

Anderson is much more modest in his approach to this argument than either Van Til or Bahnsen. Anderson does not make an exclusivist claim regarding Christianity, but argues for general theism as the basis of inductive reasoning.[65] He does so by hypothesizing regarding the denial of theism in (24). Even though Anderson's argument is much more modest than Bahnsen's, one still notes the possible difficulty of establishing the first premise of this argument. Here too, the uniformity of nature is taken as the basis of warranted beliefs resulting from inductive reasoning. Anderson, like Bahnsen, is not truly a skeptic regarding the inductive premise. He does not claim that inductive reasoning is unjustified or unwarranted. In fact, in (26) he assumes the opposite: working from the premise that inductive reasoning *is* warranted. The syllogism is deductively valid. If its premises up to this point are true, then the conclusion follows, and Anderson has successfully offered an argument for the existence of God from the inductive principle. Again, Anderson, as so many other theologians and apologists, appears to believe, at least insofar as he follows Van Til on this matter, that the doctrine of divine providence has particular apologetic import in terms of its implications for the laws of nature and, in this case, warrant for the inductive principle.

It is worth noting here, as Anderson does, that "premises (24) and (25) are understood to refer to an inability *in principle* rather than one indexed to a particular reasoner."[66] Thus, the "charge of epistemic level confusion can be avoided."[67] Anderson explains, "If Susan cannot account for the uniformity of nature, it does not follow that her inductively inferred

---

64. Anderson, "If Knowledge Then God," 66.

65. The fact that Anderson does not argue for the *Christian* God in particular here does not entail that he does not attempt to do so elsewhere, just as any other Christian apologist does, moving from some general concept of God to the Christian God in particular.

66. Anderson, "If Knowledge Then God," 6n50.

67. Anderson, "If Knowledge Then God," 6n50.

conclusions are unwarranted; but if the uniformity of nature cannot be accounted for *in principle*, by *any* human reasoner, then the warrant of *all* inductively inferred conclusions is cast into doubt."[68]

Finally, philosopher Alvin Plantinga hinted long ago in his lecture notes that there might be an argument for the existence of God along the lines of skepticism about inductive reasoning.

> Hume pointed out that human beings are inclined to accept inductive forms of reasoning and thus to take it for granted, in a way, that the future will relevantly resemble the past. (This may have been known even before Hume.) As Hume also pointed out, however, it is hard to think of a good (noncircular) reason for believing that indeed the future will be relevantly like the past. Theism, however, provides a reason: God has created us and our noetic capacities and has created the world; he has also created the former in such a way as to be adapted to the latter. It is likely, then, that he has created the world in such a way that in fact the future will indeed resemble the past in the relevant way. (And thus perhaps we do indeed have *a priori* knowledge of contingent truth: perhaps we know *a priori* that the future will resemble the past.) (Note here the piece by Aron Edidin: "Language Learning and A Priori Knowledge"), *APQ* October 1986 (Vol. 23/ 4); Aron argues that in any case of language learning a priori knowledge is involved. This argument and the last argument could be thought of as exploiting the fact that according to theism God has created us in such a way as to be at home in the world. (Wolterstorff.)[69]

Plantinga believes humans are at home in the world. Not only did God create such that human faculties meet up to the way the world works, but the non-human creation itself operates in accordance with the providential will of God through what theologians, apologists, and scientists have described as laws of nature.

Establishing the necessity of Christian theism for the laws of nature, induction, or science is a rather ambitious, if not impossible, enterprise. Some apologists have attempted to strengthen the persuasiveness of their

---

68. Anderson, "If Knowledge Then God," 6n50. Anderson notes, "For a discussion of epistemic level confusion, see William P. Alston, 'Level Confusions in Epistemology,' *Midwest Studies in Philosophy* 5 (1980): 135–50." Anderson, "If Knowledge Then God," 6n50.

69. Plantinga, "Two Dozen." Plantinga has developed his argument further, as will be seen later on.

arguments by aiming to establish general theism rather than Christian theism in particular, even though these apologists would still identify themselves as Christians. Another means of attempting to establish Christian theism as a more viable basis for the scientific endeavor than other theistic world religions is the use of a cultural apologetic. The cultural apologetic is a simple, often overlooked, yet persuasive method of apologetic engagement. The method is introduced here, and an attempt made to explain how it might apply to corroborating the scientific implications of the doctrine of divine providence. Consider first an analogous case for Christianity from the cultural apologetics of morality.

Philosopher and apologist Mark Coppenger explains the concept of cultural apologetics beginning with the charges often brought against Christians and Christianity regarding its supposed moral inferiority.[70] His apologetic "is designed to push back against such criticism, arguing that Christianity is morally superior as well as true."[71] Coppenger notes that his work is "not meant as a knockdown proof of Christianity."[72] This recognition in and of itself might be seen as an improvement over those apologists noted above who argue a much stronger claim with respect to Christian theism. Regardless, Coppenger "will seek to demonstrate that the moral and cultural center of mass of genuine Christianity is clearly superior to that of its competitors."[73] Note that although Coppenger focuses mainly upon ethics, he mentions the cultural impact of Christianity as well. One will appeal to this cultural impact of Christianity when making a case for the superiority of Christianity over other world religions in terms of the scientific enterprise.

Coppenger sets forth a number of principles for his apologetic method that are worth mentioning here.

1. If Christians claim that God is infinite in power and knowledge and that his commands are wise and good, then obedience should result in wonderful things, which should reflect well on tenets of the faith.

2. Evidence of negative social impact, if and where it occurs, is problematic for Christianity; it makes the case for a sovereign,

---

70. Coppenger, *Moral Apologetics*, 1.
71. Coppenger, *Moral Apologetics*, 1.
72. Coppenger, *Moral Apologetics*, 1.
73. Coppenger, *Moral Apologetics*, 1.

self-revealing, benevolent God more difficult, and it demands explanation.

3. True ideas do not, in the end, have negative social impact; they bring light and life to society.[74]

Although Coppenger is making the case primarily for a superior Christian ethic, one could easily adapt each of these premises to fit a cultural apologetic for the beneficial scientific implications of Christian theism. For example, the character of the Christian God not only supplies a sound metaphysical basis for science, but living out a consistent Christian worldview should lead to acknowledgement of the value of science for knowing God's world and his ways of governing it, at the very least. Those places and times that Christianity has negatively affected or hindered any true scientific progress hurts the witness, attractiveness, and believability of Christianity as a worldview and calls for some sort of apologetic defense. Finally, if Christianity is true, it should be expected to help, rather than harm society even in the realm of science, which is neither an objectionable nor unreasonable discipline from the standpoint of Christian theism. Coppenger himself, arguing that cultural apologetics serve both negative and positive purposes in apologetics, quotes apologist Francis Schaeffer to the effect that science was helped in a positive manner by Christianity, writing, "As Francis Schaeffer demonstrated, the Reformation did much to foster the arts, science, and technology."[75] In quoting philosopher and apologist William Lane Craig in an effort to push back against Craig's apparent disdain for cultural apologetics, Coppenger writes, "Craig remarks, 'In Europe, we have seen the bitter fruit of secularization, which now threatens North America.'"[76] Coppenger continues, "I hope to show or remind the reader that the 'bitter fruit' of rejecting Christianity extends well beyond the intellectual climate to the well-being of society in general."[77] Thus Coppenger is concerned for the general well-being, or health, of society. In my view, a healthy society is, among other things, a scientific society.[78]

---

74. Coppenger, *Moral Apologetics*, 4.
75. Coppenger, *Moral Apologetics*, 5.
76. Coppenger, *Moral Apologetics*, 5.
77. Coppenger, *Moral Apologetics*, 5.
78. I am not giving way to *scientism* here. A healthy society is *at least* a scientific one. This truth does not preclude other marks of a healthy society, such as a civil government, education, ethics, and the like. Coppenger would likely agree. For example,

In moving forward to present a cultural apologetic for the positive impact of the doctrine of divine providence upon society, and in virtue of its providing a philosophical assumption that is so crucial to science, I want to note three points. First, if it is the case that the Christian account of things is true, then Scripture is also true. Scripture would lead one to believe not only that God is providentially at work in the world, but that this Christian aspect of metaphysics is the only way the world actually *is*. Although other world religions might offer something quite *similar* to Christianity in terms of this metaphysic, in the end they offer relevantly *different* metaphysics, and thus it makes sense that the Christian metaphysic involving God's providence has positive implications for laws of nature, for induction, and for science, whereas non-Christian metaphysics do not. If a Christian worldview is assumed as *true* from the outset (and to make this assumption is what it means to be a Christian), then it follows that science is *actually* dependent upon a Christian metaphysic. Of course, this argument would not be overly convincing to a non-Christian.

How then might the aforementioned observation be used in such a way as to persuade the non-Christian, rather than merely appealing to the faith of the Christian? One way to argue the point is to offer evidence that science simply does not comport well with non-Christian religious worldviews, but that it does in fact comport well with a Christian worldview. There are at least two ways of accomplishing this task of establishing Christianity as providing a solid context from within which the scientific endeavor might be carried out. The first is to provide evidence of the impact of Christianity upon society in scientific terms, whether in virtue of Christianity as a worldview, particular Christian tenets, or Christian scientists. This evidence may be contrasted with evidence of the impact of non-Christian religions upon society in scientific terms. The second is to simply point out the raw fact that the modern scientific worldview

---

Coppenger writes that we should avoid "deference to such faiths as Hinduism, with its caste system; Islam, with its sharia-driven dhimmitude; Animism, with its indifference to science, its worship of nature and overweening superstition; Buddhism, with its irrationality and self-absorption; Atheism, where humanity [is] arbitrarily definable and morally unaccountable; Shintoism, with its ancestor worship; Cults, with their sexual adventurism; Utopianism, with its love of tyranny; Scientism, which spawned eugenics; Rationalism, which yields radically divergent conclusions depending upon the premises: 'garbage in garbage out.'" Coppenger, "Therapeutic Nihilism."

shared by most people today in civilized societies began in a Christian cultural context, and not anywhere else.[79]

When assembling information of scientific thought regarding the Christian doctrine of providence, and its relation to laws of nature in particular, one must not miss the obvious. Though Christianity is sometimes thought of as opposed to the scientific endeavor, it is in fact an old friend of science. Modern science itself stems from a *Christian* context and not any other: "It was Christianized Europe that became the birthplace of modern science—there and nowhere else."[80] Why might it be the case that modern science would arise in such a context? One reason might be that Christianity as a thoroughgoing view of the world provides certain assumptions relied upon heavily within the scientific realm. One of these assumptions, no doubt, is the assumption of laws of nature. Whether or not this assumption is the driving force behind every cultural advantage of Christianity in the history of science is not ascertainable through a cultural apologetic alone. However, it does not follow from this realization that the doctrine of divine providence is to be excluded from the list of potential candidates for metaphysical assumptions that make science possible, and hence grant it the cultural influence it holds over much of the world. In fact, it is quite reasonable to believe that the doctrine of divine providence is one of the main tenets of the Christian faith with strong enough scientific implications to radically affect the course of history. Evidence for this claim will be provided in terms of a cultural apologetic. Emphasis is placed upon the presence of the belief in laws of nature pertaining to the Christian cultural apologetic from science. Chapter 5 provides further argumentation that Islam fails to encourage or accommodate a scientific worldview because, even though other considerations might be brought to bear upon the discussion, Islam does not comport with modern scientific understandings of laws of nature and induction that are able to be accounted for within the context of a Christian view of the world.

As already noted, modern science arose in a Christian context. Before providing more positive evidence in defense of the role of Christianity in the history of science, it is helpful to turn to the negative task of showing how problematic other religious worldviews are when it comes

---

79. See the comments to this effect from Alfred North Whitehead in the following section of this chapter. See also the comments from Nancy R. Pearcey and Charles B. Thaxton below.

80. Pearcey and Thaxton, *Soul of Science*, 21.

to providing a basis for the scientific endeavor, often in terms of their incapacity to accommodate needed assumptions regarding the laws of nature and induction.

Divine providence leads to belief in an orderly universe. One of the ways an orderly universe has been described is through the concept of the laws of nature.[81] Remove the assumption of divine providence, and one is left with little, if anything, to base the laws of nature upon. For example, "People in pagan cultures who see nature as alive and moved by mysterious forces are not likely to develop the conviction that all natural occurrences are lawful and intelligible."[82] Of course, the ability to comprehend such regularities is also a presupposition of science. Pearcey and Thaxton explain the difficulty with the following example:

> A cross-cultural comparison can help clarify the point. Joseph Needham, a student of Chinese culture, asks in his book *The Grand Titration* why the Chinese never developed modern science. The reason, he said, is that the Chinese had no belief either in an intelligible order in nature nor in the human ability to decode an order should it exist. As Needham writes:
>
> There was no confidence that the code of Nature's laws could be unveiled and read, because there was no assurance that a divine being, even more rational than ourselves, had ever formulated such a code capable of being read.
>
> The Chinese did sense some order in nature, but they conceived of it as an inherent necessity inscrutable to the human mind. "It was not an order ordained by a rational personal being," Needham explains, "and hence there was no guarantee that other rational personal beings would be able to spell out in their own earthly languages the pre-existing divine code of laws which he had previously formulated."[83]

Problems with anti-scientific metaphysics are not limited to animists and the Chinese.

Greeks also struggled with how to contemplate a rational order to the universe. Pearcey and Thaxton point out, "In all other religions, the creation of the world begins with some kind of pre-existing substance

---

81. Pearcey and Thaxton, *Soul of Science*, 26.

82. Pearcey and Thaxton, *Soul of Science*, 26. According to Pearcey and Thaxton, "In every culture, of course, craftsmen have developed rough and ready rules of procedure. But when they encounter an irregularity or anomaly, they simply accept it as part of the inscrutable nature of things." Pearcey and Thaxton, *Soul of Science*, 26.

83. Pearcey and Thaxton, *Soul of Science*, 29.

with its own inherent nature."[84] This metaphysic is important as goes science because, "as a result, the creator is not absolute and does not have the freedom to mold the world exactly as he wills."[85] As an example of the negative consequences of this widely held view, Pearcey and Thaxton offer the Platonic forms of ancient Greece.[86]

> In Plato's creation myth, the creator (demiurge) is an inferior deity who did not create from nothing; he merely injected reason (Ideas) into reason-less matter. And even that he did imperfectly because matter was stubborn stuff, capable of resisting the rational structure imparted by the Ideas. In short, this is a creator whose hands are tied, as Hooykaas writes, in two respects:
> He had to follow not his own design but the model of the eternal Ideas; and second, he had to put the stamp of the Ideas on a chaotic, recalcitrant matter which he had not created himself.[87]

While Platonic ideas or forms are often attacked on other grounds, and are rarely, if ever thought of in the context of science, it is evident from this work in cultural apologetics that the forms create difficulties for a would-be scientific worldview along the lines of the laws of nature. Though the forms could be set forth as problematic in their own right, Pearcey and Thaxton take the observation of Hooykaas a step further and draw out the logical, and hence cultural, implications of the Platonic doctrine. Regarding the negative influence this doctrine had upon science in Greek society, Pearcey and Thaxton write,

> As a result, the Greeks expected a level of imprecision in nature, a certain fuzziness at the edges. If some facts did not fit their theories, well, that was to be expected in an imperfect world. Individual things were, after all, only rough approximations to the rational Ideas or Forms. As historian Dudley Shapere explains, in Greek thought the physical world "contains an essentially irrational element: nothing in it can be described *exactly* by reason, and in particular by mathematical concepts and laws."[88]

---

84. Pearcey and Thaxton, *Soul of Science*, 27.
85. Pearcey and Thaxton, *Soul of Science*, 27.
86. Pearcey and Thaxton, *Soul of Science*, 27.
87. Pearcey and Thaxton, *Soul of Science*, 27–28.
88. Pearcey and Thaxton, *Soul of Science*, 28.

Animists, Chinese, and Greeks appear to have some difficulties with scientific procedure in *practice*, because, in their case, they have difficulties with scientific procedure in *principle*. Their non-Christian metaphysics simply do not provide the sort of confidence in the laws of nature and the human ability to know them that Christianity does. As a result, societies made up of large numbers of animists, Chinese, and Greeks have not offered much in the way of science. Their societies have, historically, not been well-off with respect to this extremely important human endeavor.

Another religious worldview that struggles with science is Buddhism. This non-Christian religious worldview is worth examining in detail, not only because it is becoming so popular in the United States, but because some of the reasons Buddhism struggles with science might be difficulties with Islam as well.[89] The Buddhist view of science is far from monolithic. Various strands of Buddhist thought result in a plethora of opinions amongst Buddhists concerning science. Some Buddhists attempt to avoid science through what is known as the Middle Way of Buddhism. Many view science in an extremely negative light. Other Buddhists believe scientific discoveries corroborate the superiority of Buddhism in an apologetic fashion. None of these three approaches is an acceptable understanding of science.

Some Buddhists posit Buddhism as the Middle Way between religion and science. Buddhism becomes a mediating position between the two error-laden extremes of religion and science. Thus Buddhism is "above" the alleged disagreements between religion and science. It encompasses the good that is found in both disciplines, but ultimately fits into neither category.[90] To interpret Buddhism as religion or science is a mistake. Buddhists consider it tolerant and compassionate to work *outside* of religion and science in order to point out and correct their faults.[91] Neither ecclesiastical authority nor the interpretations of scientists are the subject matter of Buddhism.[92] Rather, Buddhism taps into the source of all wisdom encompassed in eternal natural laws.[93] Such laws speak to the

---

89. These difficulties will be more closely examined in chap. 5 with respect to Islam.

90. Wettimuny, *Buddhism*, 7. Wettimuny, a Buddhist author, states, "Buddhism holds a peculiar relation to both Religion and Science in that it permits itself of being interpreted either as a religion, that is as a faith, or as a science, that is as a workable hypothesis, *if it is not rightly comprehended.*" Wettimuny, *Buddhism*, 7.

91. Wettimuny, *Buddhism*, 8–9.

92. Wettimuny, *Buddhism*, 12–13.

93. Wettimuny, *Buddhism*, 12–13. Buddhist doctrine, according to Wettimuny,

causal orderliness of relationships.[94] This idea is thoroughly grounded in at least one important Buddhist tenet called "dependent origination."[95]

Dependent origination is the name of a central doctrine of Buddhism.[96] According to Kogen Mizuno, "This doctrine teaches that phenomena occur through conditions; all that comes into being is dependent on something else."[97] Another word for "dependent origination" is "causality."[98] Virtually everything in Buddhism is described in terms of dependent origination. Mizuno goes so far as to call it, "both a basic doctrine of Buddhism and the core of Buddhist truth."[99] Further, "The basic formula of dependent origination is 'When this exists, that exists; with the arising of this, that arises. When this does not exist, that does not exist; with the cessation of this, that ceases.'"[100] The doctrine sounds similar to an account of causation as discussed in the philosophy of science. However, the doctrine is prone to misunderstanding, and one might read a non-religious understanding into Buddhist causation in an attempt to make it scientific.[101] Thus, some clarification is needed.

While it is true that dependent origination is much *more* than causation in nature, it certainly is not *less* either. Dependent origination includes twelve parts.[102] These twelve aspects of dependent origination should be thought of as spiritual realities, and not primarily as causal

---

"deals not with the actions of individuals or the dictates of ecclesiastical authority revealed or unrevealed, but with the natural laws that stand true for all time, and therefore with that with which wisdom and truth are concerned." Wettimuny, *Buddhism*, 12–13.

94. Wettimuny, *Buddhism*, 12–13. Wettimuny quotes Buddhist Scripture to explain, "This nature of things just stands, this causal orderliness, the relatedness of this to that." Wettimuny, *Buddhism*, 12–13.

95. Mizuno, *Essentials of Buddhism*, 135.

96. Mizuno, *Essentials of Buddhism*, 135.

97. Mizuno, *Essentials of Buddhism*, 135.

98. Mizuno, *Essentials of Buddhism*, 135.

99. Mizuno, *Essentials of Buddhism*, 135. Mizuno continues, "Primitive sutras point out that 'one who sees dependent origination sees the Law; one who sees the Law sees dependent origination' and that 'one who sees dependent origination sees the Law, and one who sees the Law sees me [the Buddha].'" Mizuno, *Essentials of Buddhism*, 135.

100. Mizuno, *Essentials of Buddhism*, 135–6.

101. For example, note the concerns of Wettimuny, *Buddhism*, 242–57.

102. Mizuno, *Essentials of Buddhism*, 147–48.

interactions in nature.[103] Nevertheless, causality in nature can serve as an *illustration* of what dependent origination is *like*.[104] While it is true that "it is religious causality that is important to Buddhism," religious or spiritual causality is not the *only* type of causality.[105] Rather, "dependent origination encompasses two types of causality: general or physical (or external) and religious or mental (or internal)."[106] It is the general or physical category with which one is concerned when it comes to science.

Even given the apparently scientifically advantageous set of beliefs described above, a negative attitude toward science is common amongst Buddhists.[107] In this view, modern scientific thinking is outside the teachings of the Buddha, who forbade speculation on matters that do not tend toward nirvana.[108] For example, Southern Buddhism is focused upon practical matters and morality, and thus gives little regard to science.[109]

Other Buddhists reject science because of metaphysical commitments. For example, some Japanese and Chinese Buddhists are united in their adherence to "a philosophy of absolute and monistic Idealism" at the core of their beliefs.[110] In this view, there is no distinction between reality and experience.[111] Science pertains to a secondary reality of multiplicity rather than the one absolute truth.[112] However, the negative attitude toward science amongst Buddhists is shared by some who do not

---

103. Wettimuny, *Buddhism*, 242–57.

104. Mizuno, *Essentials of Buddhism*, 137.

105. Mizuno, *Essentials of Buddhism*, 137.

106. Mizuno, *Essentials of Buddhism*, 137.

107. See, for example, Lopez, "Future of Buddhist Past," 883–96, and Harrison, "A Scientific Buddhism?," 861–69.

108. Pratt, "Buddhism and Scientific Thinking," 14. Pratt explains, "The Buddha taught his disciples not to speculate on matters that profit not, that do not tend to absence of passion, to quiescence, supreme wisdom, Nirvana." Pratt, "Buddhism and Scientific Thinking," 14.

109. Pratt, "Buddhism and Scientific Thinking," 14.

110. Pratt, "Buddhism and Scientific Thinking," 14. All is one. The Buddha nature is *in* and *is* everything.

111. Pratt, "Buddhism and Scientific Thinking," 14.

112. Pratt, "Buddhism and Scientific Thinking," 14. Pratt notes, "The Buddhist world-formula has room for every conceivable kind of purely empirical fact." Pratt, "Buddhism and Scientific Thinking," 14–15. Pratt quotes Tai Hsu to the effect that people using science are like blind men feeling different parts of an elephant and never arriving at an understanding of the whole. Pratt, "Buddhism and Scientific Thinking," 14–15.

hold to absolute monism.[113] This "mystical" group of Buddhists includes "the Ch'an sects in China, the Zen sects in Japan, and, in addition, a large portion of those Buddhists . . . called metaphysical."[114]

The Northern Buddhists are the Amida sects in Japan and China like the Shin and Jodo.[115] The Northern Buddhists "are the most advanced and up-to-date members of the Buddhist world" because they have adopted Western methodology in their religious education.[116] This group of Buddhists came into contact with some modern scientific thought of the West, but has no other relationship with science.[117] Recently, a growing number of Buddhists have thought Buddhism to be self-sufficient to the point of rejecting science.[118] Some other Buddhists have even called Buddhism "emphatically non-scientific."[119] A similar sentiment is expressed by those who understand science as essentially materialistic, and hence opposed to spiritual practice.[120] On this view, science is limited to the external, objectively quantifiable world whereas Buddhism works with the internal, subjectively experienced world accessible not through scientific

---

113. Pratt, "Buddhism and Scientific Thinking," 15.

114. Pratt, "Buddhism and Scientific Thinking," 15. The "metaphysical" category is Pratt's. He quotes Tai Hsu as claiming, "The central core of Buddhism science cannot reach, for Buddhism has to do with inward illumination, the direct insight into the reality of the universe, an intuitive experience only acquired by one himself, where all logic, analogy, or scientific method or hypothesis are of no avail." Pratt, "Buddhism and Scientific Thinking," 15.

115. Pratt, "Buddhism and Scientific Thinking," 16–17.

116. Pratt, "Buddhism and Scientific Thinking," 16–17.

117. Pratt, "Buddhism and Scientific Thinking," 16–17.

118. Pratt, "Buddhism and Scientific Thinking," 16–17. Pratt relates the story of "a letter from Professor Suzuki of the Otani Buddhist College in Kyoto (received just before I started for Chicago)" in which he writes, "Formerly Buddhists were glad to welcome a scientific approach to their religion. But nowadays a reaction seems to have taken place among them. Instead of relying on scientific arguments for the rationalization of the Buddhist experience they are at present trying to resort to its own dialectics. There is a growing conviction among the Buddhists that their philosophy does not require the support of Western logic, especially of modern science." Pratt, "Buddhism and Scientific Thinking," 16–17.

119. Pratt, "Buddhism and Scientific Thinking," 16–17.

120. English, "On the 'Emptiness,'" 156. English claims, "It is true that the starting points of western science and Buddhism could not be farther apart, the former restricting its purview to the 'external', objective world mapped out by instrumental measurements, and the latter focusing mostly on the 'internal', experiential world explored through meditation." English, "On the 'Emptiness,'" 156.

inquiry but Buddhist meditation.[121] Finally, while many have understood Buddhism to correspond in general to a Western rational empiricist epistemology, there are questions as to whether or not this interpretation of Buddhist epistemology is simply projected from a modern scientific framework onto the teachings of the Buddha.[122]

Not all Buddhists are opposed to science. Buddhist sects like the Kegon and Shingon are metaphysically committed to the ultimate nature of plurality as opposed to unity, and hence their view is very close to naturalism.[123] Some practitioners of the Kegon and Shingon sects, as well as a few Japanese Zen Buddhists, have attempted to bring Buddhism into a closer relationship with science.[124] Professor Nurakiya teaches at a Zen college in Tokyo, Japan, and has mixed materialist philosophy with his Buddhism in order to accomplish this task.[125] However, Nurakiya, and other modern scientifically minded Buddhists, compose only a very small minority of Buddhists and are not at all representative of the religion, especially its Ch'an (Chinese) and Zen (Japanese) varieties which look to inner vision to apprehend true light.[126] Here, "science can contribute only in a very preliminary and crude fashion; and once the vision has been gained, nothing else is of much importance."[127] Science has also played a role in South and Southeast Asia where "Buddhism has latent capabilities for making common cause with some of the central features

---

121. English, "On the 'Emptiness,'" 156.

122. Evans, "Epistemology," 67. Evans notes, "In two previous papers (Evans 2007, 2008), I called into question what Frank Hoffman (1982) has called the 'Buddhist empiricism hypothesis', the interpretation of Buddhist epistemology as empirical and rational in a modern Western sense. That interpretation, I believe, is a projection of modern orientations that obscures the understanding of knowledge and the means of pursuing it advocated by the Buddha of the *Nikàyas*." Evans, "Epistemology," 67.

123. Pratt, "Buddhism and Scientific Thinking," 15. Pratt writes, "The small Kegon sect, and the large sect of Shingon (which draws most of its philosophy from Kegon), while asserting with other Buddhist thinkers the ultimate identity of the Many and the One, lay their emphasis upon multiplicity rather than unity." Pratt, "Buddhism and Scientific Thinking," 15. He adds, "And a few members of both sects—we might call them the radical left—carry this tendency to the extent of something very like what we know as Naturalism." Pratt, "Buddhism and Scientific Thinking," 15.

124. Pratt, "Buddhism and Scientific Thinking," 16.

125. Pratt, "Buddhism and Scientific Thinking," 16.

126. Pratt, "Buddhism and Scientific Thinking," 16.

127. Pratt, "Buddhism and Scientific Thinking," 16. Although one might argue that environmental ethics, for example, are important. See Chapple, "Thomas Berry," 147–54.

of modernization, particularly with a new self-corrective life style and community of inquiry spreading swiftly throughout the earth."[128]

The main role of science in Buddhism appears to be the Buddhist use of Western science to explicate teachings of Buddhism in an apologetic fashion.[129] Even those who assert that Buddhism is "emphatically non-scientific" call attention to correlations between traditional Buddhist concepts and major ideas in modern Western science.[130] This use of science is merely illustrative and quite unlike its traditional use. However, other Buddhists have embraced systems of logic that closely parallel Western conceptions of logic and scientific reasoning.

Diṇnāga (or Dignāga) was a Buddhist logician who provided the sort of material in his *Compendium of the Means of True Knowledge* (*Pramāṇasamuccaya*) that will come to bear upon any Buddhist attempt at articulating scientific principles.[131] For example, Diṇnāga's theory of inference pertains to *induction*, which is a crucial aspect of science.[132] Diṇnāga's logic was the basis upon which later de-

---

128. Jacobson, "Buddhism, Modernization, and Science," 155. Jacobson notes, "The special sciences may be taken as illustrating this new life-style and community, though in fragmentary and highly specialized form." Jacobson, "Buddhism, Modernization, and Science," 155.

129. Pratt, "Buddhism and Scientific Thinking," 15–16. Aparna Sharma expresses concerns that Buddhists might also be misunderstanding scientific discoveries in their zeal for such an apologetic. Sharma, "Buddhism and Science," 78.

130. Pratt, "Buddhism and Scientific Thinking," 17–18. Pratt writes, "Buddhist thought anticipated the modern Western notions of the spatial world by many centuries. Tai Hsu points out that in ancient times men thought of heaven as above and earth beneath: then came Copernicus, who taught that the sun was the center of our system. Now we have arrived at the idea that there is no one center anywhere in the astral universe. This supports the Buddhist idea of the great unlimited Void, embracing numberless worlds, all interwoven like spiders' webs. In their conception of time, also, ancient Buddhist thinkers—and in fact Indian thinkers of various schools—were far in advance of our Western ancestors. The Sukhavati Vyuha refers to a series of eighty-one hundred thousand niyutas of kotis of past Buddhas who succeeded each other long before the appearance of Gotama, at the rate of one in perhaps five thousand years. A niyuta is one million and a koti ten million, and I leave it to you to determine how many years are here involved; it will, of course, be eighty-one hundred thousand times five thousand times one million times ten million." Pratt, "Buddhism and Scientific Thinking," 17–18.

131. *Encyclopedia Britannica Online*, s.v. "Dignāga," http://www.britannica.com/EBchecked/topic/163392/Dignaga.

132. Matilal and Evans, "Buddhist Logic," 1. According to Matilal, "Diṇnāga's theory of inference may briefly be stated as follows: When we infer some fact or item or characteristic belonging to some object on the basis of our knowledge of some

velopments in Buddhist philosophy would come about, including, most significantly, the work of Dharmakīrti.[133]

Other than his philosophy, not much can be known about the Indian Buddhist philosopher Dharmakīrti, and explaining Dharmakīrti's philosophy in any great detail is beyond the purposes of this chapter, but he appears to have held to what philosophers call a "causal theory of properties."[134] His understanding of these points in the philosophy of science leads one to hold, "a causal theory that makes no separation at all between *what* something is and what it does."[135] Unfortunately, there are substantial objections to Dharmakīrti's theory based upon his various comments and attempts to resolve potential difficulties with his theory.[136]

The Dalai Lama has spurred both Buddhists and Western scientists on toward a continuous dialogue.[137] In 1985, the Mind and Life Institute was formed for the purpose of gathering the Dalai Lama and other Tibetan Buddhists together with Western scientists.[138] The first gathering was in 1987 and it was followed by many more meetings up to the present day.[139] The Dalai Lama has even published a book on the topic of the relationship between science and spirituality.[140] Quite obviously then, the Dalai Lama represents a part of Buddhism that is completely open to science. He no doubt understands the importance of science,

---

other characteristic belonging to the same object the second characteristic (variously called '*liħga*' or '*hetu*', 'inferential sign' or 'indicator-reason') must have the 'triple-character.'" Matilal and Evans, "Buddhist Logic," 1.

133. *Encyclopedia Britannica Online*, s.v. "Dignāga." See also Matilal, "Buddhist Logic and Epistemology," 1.

134. In this view, "Particulars have causal properties, that is, powers (*śakti*) or 'fitness' (*yogyatā*) to produce such and such results, in that they will produce those results when the right 'complete collections' (*sāmagrī*) of circumstances and other properties are united. And what makes any property what it is consists in the contribution it makes to the potential causal behaviour of what has it." *The Stanford Encyclopedia of Philosophy*, s.v. "Dharmakīrti," http://plato.stanford.edu/archives/fall2012/entries/-dharmakiirti.

135. *The Stanford Encyclopedia of Philosophy*, s.v. "Dharmakīrti," http://plato.stanford.edu/archives/fall2012/entries/-dharmakiirti.

136. *The Stanford Encyclopedia of Philosophy*, s.v. "Dharmakīrti," http://plato.stanford.edu/archives/fall2012/entries/-dharmakiirti. See also Gillon, "Dharmakīrti and His Theory," 77.

137. Yong, "Buddhism and Science," 177.

138. Yong, "Mind and Life," 46.

139. Yong, "Mind and Life," 46.

140. The Dalai Lama, *The Universe in a Single Atom*.

and probably its pervasive nature in the world as well. His commitment to science brings a kind of credence to his Buddhist faith in the modern, and especially Western, world. Nevertheless, the history of Buddhism in terms of its outright rejection of and incompatibility with science are impossible to deny.

Buddhist views of the relationship between Buddhism and science are at least as varied as the forms of Buddhism that exist in the world. Some view Buddhism as the superior Middle Way between religion and science and are thus rather dismissive of both. Others seem to feel more threatened by science as a concept, and thus choose to interact with it. However, their assessment of the scientific endeavor is almost wholly negative, for the Western view of the world typically used in science is foreign to the Buddhist metaphysical scheme. Still others approve of science. Of those who favor the scientific discipline, some use what has already been discovered as apologetic ammunition, while others devote themselves to the development of the sciences within Buddhist circles, borrowing from the work that has been done in Christianized societies. The Buddhist view of the relationship of Buddhism to science really depends upon to which Buddhist one is referring. However, for all of their disagreements, Buddhists seem to agree on the premise that science, for all of its value, is not the most significant route to knowledge or the ultimate goal of life. This premise is true for Christians as well, but Christianity has not led to anything like the type of anti-scientific view of the world that exists in Buddhism. While Buddhism appears to affirm something like the laws of nature, they are thought to exist in similar fashion to the Platonic forms mentioned earlier, and are said to be of more spiritual value to the Buddhist system than descriptive of the nature of ultimate reality, which for many Buddhists, is either radically monist or radically atomistic.

Islam is far removed from Buddhism, or so one would think.[141] Islam appears to share many of its core beliefs with Christianity, so much so that some commentators in comparative religions lump the two world religions, along with Judaism, into the same camp. But Islam differs from Christianity. That Islam differs from Christianity is no less true when it comes to the scientific endeavor. Not only does Islam suffer from problems in its basis for science, problems which will be argued more fully in chapter 5, but these problems have become evident to a certain extent in

---

141. Chap. 5 argues that Islam is not as far removed from Buddhism as one might think, at least with regard to its understanding of ultimate reality.

SCIENTIFIC IMPLICATIONS OF PROVIDENCE 69

the scientific impact of Islam on the societies historically saturated with Islamic doctrine.

To be sure, some Muslim commentators are out to paint a rather rosy picture of the relationship between their religion and science, to say the least. Unfortunately, this picture is far from sustainable in light of the facts of what little Islam has contributed to science. To say that Islam has offered little by way of its contributions to science is not the same as stating that it has had nothing at all to offer. Nevertheless, some Muslims attempt to exaggerate the role that Islam plays in the scientific endeavor.

For example, author Muhammad 'Ali al-Hashimi claims that the Qur'an creates "a serious objective and scientific mentality that stayed away from idle pursuits, myths and trivia, and encouraged scientific research, investigation of transmitted reports and the pursuit of scientific truths, far removed from conjecture, whims and desires and blind imitation."[142] How much did the Qur'an really encourage research in science? The answer to this question can be determined, to some extent, by looking at the quality and quantity of science carried out by adherents to the lifestyle prescribed by the Qur'an. Muhammad 'Ali al-Hashimi writes of "the peace, harmony and freedom of research enjoyed by the Muslim scholars."[143] He writes also of "the fact that Islam encouraged the pursuit of knowledge and counted the scholars' efforts to learn and discover as acts of worship."[144] While these claims are at the very least questionable, the following claim appears to be patently false:

> This bond between science and religion in the Muslim society had a great impact in encouraging the scholars and motivating them to seek more knowledge. This is the opposite of what we know of other nations in which there was a conflict between science and religion, or between reason and the texts that had been handed down. Many Muslim scholars were scholars in both shari'ah and medicine, mathematics, chemistry, physics, astronomy, geography and philosophy, such as Ibn Rushd, al-Fakhr ar-Râzi, al-Khawârizmi, Ibn an-Nafees, Ibn Seena, Jâbir ibn Ḥayyân and others.[145]

The so-called conflict between religion and science, as well as supposed contradictions between what is learned through the intellect and what

---

142. Al-Hashimi, *Ideal Muslim Society*, 347.
143. Al-Hashimi, *Ideal Muslim Society*, 347.
144. Al-Hashimi, *Ideal Muslim Society*, 347.
145. Al-Hashimi, *Ideal Muslim Society*, 347.

is learned through the text of Scripture, are figments of this Muslim's imagination. From what has been explained in the previous section, one can see that many Christians believe their sacred texts to support the scientific endeavor, rather than contradicting it or creating anything like a dichotomy between the Christian religion and science.

Muhammad Ali Al-Hashimi asserts that the church and scientists fought each other in medieval Europe, and meanwhile, "the mosque in the history of Islam and the Muslims was a shady oasis, a peaceful and welcoming spot for study circles and scholars throughout the history of the Muslim ummah."[146] Even if one assumes the aforementioned author is correct, the rhetorical flourishes of his statements are exaggerations, as when he writes, "For a lengthy period between the sixth and twelfth centuries C.E., Europe was living in the deepest darkness, at the time when the sun of Islamic civilization was shedding its rays on the east and the west."[147] He continues as follows:

> At that time the Muslim scholars, encouraged by the teachings of Islam, were enthusiastically seeking knowledge from Greek, eastern and other sources. They then began to develop those sciences further and add new sciences in many fields. Thus Islamic civilization pushed the world forward after it had been dominated by ancient Greek science.[148]

One of the difficulties of this claim has already been mentioned. Greek and Eastern knowledge is already lacking in terms of its contributions toward science, and so it does not help the scientific credibility of Islam to explain that Islamic civilization was borrowing from Greek and Eastern sources. Further, it may be true that, "The Muslims were the first to invent decimal fractions, algebra, trigonometry and geometry, and the first to discover zero, which had been unknown in Europe."[149] But even then, citing these supposed inventions of Islamic civilization does very little, if anything, to bolster the credibility of Islam with regard to science, since citing these realms of knowledge as scientific advancement conflates knowledge in general with empirical scientific discovery in particular, a

---

146. Al-Hashimi, *Ideal Muslim Society*, 348.
147. Al-Hashimi, *Ideal Muslim Society*, 348.
148. Al-Hashimi, *Ideal Muslim Society*, 348.
149. Al-Hashimi, *Ideal Muslim Society*, 348. The literature leans toward ascribing even these mathematical principles to Indian origins.

problem that is common in Muslim apologetics for the supposed scientific contributions of Islamic society.[150]

Another flawed approach to defending the legitimacy, and sometimes even the superiority, of Islam with respect to its scientific achievement is to cite the supposed Islamic preservation of ancient texts crucial to the undisputed scientific advancements of the Christianized West. For example,

> The Muslims collected the Greek legacy and translated it into Arabic in a trustworthy and sincere manner. It is well known that the Greek legacy that was transmitted to Europe was translated first into Arabic, then into Latin, and that it was the Arabic translation that saved it from being lost altogether.[151]

Referring to the aforementioned body of knowledge and supposed Muslim corrections and additions to it, Muhammad Ali Al-Hashimi writes, "This is what subsequently encouraged European scholars to advance in various fields of knowledge and to make new inventions and discoveries."[152] He continues, "They would not have made the great achievements that they did if they had not taken the tools of knowledge from Islamic civilization at its peak."[153] Yet, according to Muhammad Ali Al-Hashimi's own words, the knowledge he claims was passed from Islam to Christianized Europe was initially taken from the Greek and Eastern thinkers by the Muslims.[154] Even granting that the author states the account of this transmission of knowledge honestly and faithfully, what is to be learned from it regarding Islam? That Islamic societies should be known for passing on modified knowledge that was not their own, and that came from other societies that could not offer very much, if anything, in the way of scientific progress either? This account, even if one grants that it is completely true, seems far removed from a cultural apologetic for the scientific superiority, or even the fact of the mere scientific contribution, of Islam.

Although scientist Michael Robert Negus comes across as much less polemical in tone, and much more sober and scholarly, he does

---

150. Mathematics is also *deductive* in nature, while science is very much *inductive* in nature. Islamic contributions to mathematics say very little about Islamic contributions to science.

151. Al-Hashimi, *Ideal Muslim Society*, 348–49.

152. Al-Hashimi, *Ideal Muslim Society*, 349.

153. Al-Hashimi, *Ideal Muslim Society*, 349.

154. Al-Hashimi, *Ideal Muslim Society*, 348.

corroborate some of the claims of Muhammad Ali Al-Hashimi above. He writes of the growing Islamic empire and its contributions to science as follows:

> The Empire was held between the ninth and the twelfth centuries as a single vast unifying power. Its significance cannot be overestimated in constituting a foundation for the development of much of modern science. During the seventh to the ninth centuries Islamic scholars, working with the immense collection of Greek, Egyptian and Oriental documents in Alexandria (cf. Nasr, 1976:9), made a vast number of translations and compilations into Arabic. This effectively opened up the whole of the extant knowledge of the ancient worlds and, very importantly, ensured its eventual survival for the West and for us today.[155]

Again, this transmission of knowledge establishes nothing with regard to novel scientific thought produced in the Islamic empire, nor does it even establish the transmission of *scientific* knowledge, as opposed to mathematical knowledge, or just knowledge in general. It seems that if any Muslim contribution was forthcoming from the period of time known as the "Golden Age" of Islam, it was the contribution of some mathematical thinking and terminology. Negus explains as follows:

> A group of *hukamā* (singular *hakīm*), 'natural philosophers', developed medicine, astronomy and mathematics. They refined algebra, improved and popularized arithmetic, founded plane and spherical trigonometry and developed the physics of optics. Their influence on the West was so great that many Arabic words are still used in these disciplines, words such as algebra, algorithm, zenith, azimuth, nadir; other words such as alcohol and alkali came into the English language in the context of the chemical processes involved in alchemy, itself an Arabic word.[156]

---

155. Negus, "Islam and Science," 327. Negus describes the Islamic empire, "The development of science in Islam is inseparably bound up with the expansion of the Islamic Empire. After the death of Muhammad, in 632, the four Caliphs established the *dār al-islām*, the 'Territory of Islam.' Very soon the territory ruled by Islam included Persia, Syria, Egypt and Mesopotamia. By the year 750 the territory had expanded to an empire stretching from Spain to India and including extensive parts of northern Africa." Negus, "Islam and Science," 327.

156. Negus, "Islam and Science," 327–28. Negus further explains the translation, and hence transmission of valuable philosophical works by Muslims to the Europeans, "During the course of the twelfth century scholars working in Sicily and Toledo translated the manuscripts that had been written during the Golden Age from Arabic into Latin. These included translations of philosophical works. Thus Thomas Aquinas (d.

SCIENTIFIC IMPLICATIONS OF PROVIDENCE 73

Most of these developments do not immediately pertain to science, and so they do not undercut the general argument of the cultural apologetic offered here.

To be fair, Muslims could have made some small contributions to the scientific enterprise, such as the physics of optics cited above. But even these contributions do not serve to bolster the Muslim case for scientific acumen by much, and they certainly do not establish scientific superiority, especially when one contrasts the quality and quantity of scientific advancements stemming from Islam with the quality and quantity of scientific advancements coming out of societies that were overwhelmingly Christian, or adhered to a Christian worldview. One example of an apparently legitimate scientist in the Islamic tradition was Ibn al-Haytham, who is also known as Alhazen.[157] Negus describes his work:

> He was outstanding in astronomy and in mathematics. His special success was in optical studies of lenses and mirrors. He compiled tables of the angles of incidence and refraction of light rays (published in his book *kitāb al-manādhir*) and so had the data required to discover Snell's Law. He extended his studies to determine the angle of refraction of the sun's light as it passed through the atmosphere (see Nasr, 1987), and thereby estimate the height of the atmosphere. He applied his studies of refraction to explain the optical properties of the eye.[158]

Alhazen is not the only example of a Muslim scientist. Negus continues:

> Another *hakīm*, named Abū Rayhān al-Bīrunī (973–1051), in his astronomical studies, described the Earth as a sphere after observing the shadow of the Earth in lunar eclipses; by means of observations and trigonometric calculations he was able to calculate with some accuracy the circumference and radius of the Earth. These sophisticated observations were provoked because, for the *hukamā*, science was integral to Islam and equivalent to piety.[159]

1274) was able to read translations of the works of Plato and Aristotle as well as the thoughts of tenth-century Ash'arite theologians. Moreover Aquinas employed a secretary who could translate from Arabic into Latin." Negus, "Islam and Science," 328.

157. Negus, "Islam and Science," 328.

158. Negus, "Islam and Science," 328.

159. Negus, "Islam and Science," 328. Negus notes, "The material presented in this chapter can only hint at the quality of science in Islam during the Golden Age; those wishing to read further are recommended the two excellent volumes by Nasr (1968; 1976) referenced in the Bibliography." Negus, "Islam and Science," 328. Unfortunately

Negus cites technological inventions including scissors, machines to lift water, and machines to weigh metals.[160] Interestingly, Negus quite willingly admits, "Traditional Islamic science at its best in the Golden Age was a blend of deductive and inductive reasoning, although the latter was much rarer than the former."[161] Indeed, most of the "science" cited thus far by apologists for the Muslim contribution to science has not been scientific at all, but rather mathematical or technological in non-inductive ways, ways which rely very little, if at all, upon the idea of a divine providence. The use of inductive reasoning by Muslim scientists will resurface in chapter 5. For now, it will suffice to point out that the case for Islamic science has been very weak, at least with respect to establishing that Muslims have worked off similar principles to what Christians have available to them to make just as many wonderful contributions to the history of science as have the Christians.

Virtually every treatment of the history of Islam and science describes how the Muslims copied from other cultures. The British physicist Peter E. Hodgson describes the world domination enjoyed by Islam between the eighth and fourteenth centuries.[162]

> At the height of its temporal power the Muslim civilization controlled a vast territory from the Pyrenees, through Spain and the coastal regions of North Africa, to Baghdad and beyond as far as the Pamirs. Muslim armies crossed the Pyrenees into France as far as Poitiers and in the East captured Constantinople, invaded the Balkans and reached the gates of Vienna. The literary heritage of ancient Greece first passed to the Byzantine Empire. There the Nestorian Church was established in the fifth century. The Nestorians were persecuted by the Byzantines and emigrated to Mesopotamia, where they founded a centre of intellectual activity at their capital Gondisapur (Jundishapur). There they translated many of the Greek works on philosophy, science and medicine into Syriac. This city became the scientific centre of the new Islamic Empire. From there many scholars came to their capital Damascus in the late seventh and early eighth century; they were mainly Jews and Nestorian Christians (O'Leary, 1949; Sabra, 1987). Through them the Muslim scholars inherited the

---

for Negus, Eratosthenes of Cyrene was actually the first person to calculate the circumference of the earth.

160. Negus, "Islam and Science," 328.
161. Negus, "Islam and Science," 329.
162. Hodgson, *Theology and Modern Physics*, 41.

SCIENTIFIC IMPLICATIONS OF PROVIDENCE 75

works of the ancient Greeks and extended their knowledge, particularly in medicine, mathematics, astronomy and philosophy. Early in the ninth century, the caliphs Harun al-Rashid and al-Memun founded a school for translation and a library in Baghdad, and this soon surpassed Gondisapur as a scholarly centre. Means were provided for Christian scholars to travel to collect Greek manuscripts and bring them back for translation. The Nestorian Christian Ibn Masawagh headed an institute in Baghdad that translated ancient texts. His pupil Hunayn wrote many medical treatises and translated all the known Greek works into Arabic. Indian, Syriac and Persian texts were also translated (Singer, 1959).[163]

In terms of a cultural apologetic, even this detailed account of Islam's past does not bode well for it. Did Islam provide a context wherein scientific reasoning, and in particular, inductive reasoning, could flourish? Did Islamic civilization actually produce or contribute anything original to the human story of scientific achievement? Even when cast in a positive light, and even at the height of Islamic civilization, it appears that Islam did no such thing. If the evidence provided here is some of the best regarding the Muslim contribution to science, then Islam neither provided a suitable context for science nor did it offer anything substantial by way of original scientific discovery. Rather, Muslims appear to have copied from other cultures and transmitted that information to the West.

Of course, there is nothing *wrong* with learning from other societies or even translating or passing that information along. But note that translating and transmitting information, even modified information, is not the same as *producing* such information. Oddly, when it comes to the discussion of the historical relationship between Islam and science, writers on the subject consistently mention the Muslim work to transmit texts and concepts from other societies, which does not actually indicate anything with respect to scientific contributions from within the religion of Islam. Hodgson notes one Muslim scientist who was proud of the aforementioned work, but in so doing also reveals where the supposed great achievements of Islam actually originated.

> This willingness to learn from other civilizations was emphasized by the scientist and philosopher Ibn Ya'qub al-Kindi: 'We ought not to be ashamed of appreciating truth and of acquiring it wherever it comes from, even if it comes from races different

---

163. Hodgson, *Theology and Modern Physics*, 41.

from us." In this way they learned Greek philosophy and science, Persian literature, Indian medicine and mathematics, and some aspects of Egyptian and Babylonian science (Hoodbhoy, 1991, p.96). The diffusion of new knowledge throughout the Islamic Empire was greatly facilitated from the end of the seventh century by the ready availability of paper, made by techniques learned from the Chinese.[164]

If Hodgson's account is correct, then at its height, Islam received its philosophy from the Greeks, science from the Greeks, literature from the Persians, medicine from the Indians, mathematics from the Indians, and a little more science from the Egyptians and Babylonians. These cultural contributions from non-Muslim civilizations were captured on paper that came from copying a Chinese method of paper-making. This account does nothing to bolster a scientifically superior image of Islamic civilization.

Nevertheless, Hodgson believes, "As a result of this scholarly activity, the Islamic Empire in its prime was far more advanced than the Western powers."[165] Even if true, one struggles to see how Hodgson's statement could be true in terms of Islam itself. Islam may have been advanced in terms of its appropriated material, but certainly not in its ability to create similar material, or in its competency to use said material to launch its own cultural (or for the purposes of this book) scientific advances. In fact, Hodgson's next statements are revealing. Hodgson believes the Islamic empire "would seem to be well placed to become the cradle of modern science."[166] Hurting the cultural apologetic for Islam, and helping Christianized Europe, Hodgson continues, "And yet in the following centuries the lead was lost and the West surged ahead, eventually to reach heights far greater than the Muslims ever achieved."[167] He finishes, "Although they had a start of 500 years, Muslim scholars never developed modern science themselves, and eventually had to learn it from the West."[168] The

164. Hodgson, *Theology and Modern Physics*, 41–42.
165. Hodgson, *Theology and Modern Physics*, 42.
166. Hodgson, *Theology and Modern Physics*, 42. Hodgson writes, "Unified by a well-developed language, extending over most of the civilized world, possessing numerous libraries and astronomical observatories, with a tradition of technical excellence and a respect for learning and many thinkers of high intelligence, it would seem to be well placed to become the cradle of modern science." Hodgson, *Theology and Modern Physics*, 42.
167. Hodgson, *Theology and Modern Physics*, 42.
168. Hodgson, *Theology and Modern Physics*, 42.

SCIENTIFIC IMPLICATIONS OF PROVIDENCE 77

case is quite strong that Islam has contributed almost nothing to science. Of course, one only has the evidence provided in the authors treated here. Hodgson does offer another way out for those interested in defending the scientific contributions of Islam when he writes, "It should be mentioned that our present knowledge of Islamic science is very incomplete as there are very many unpublished manuscripts that have not been analyzed."[169] Unfortunately, if one were to attempt to construct an argument upon unpublished and unexamined Muslim manuscripts, one would be making an argument from silence. Moreover, there is no reason to think that obscure manuscripts will yield anything different in terms of quality or quantity of scientific contribution, and if we extrapolate from the data we do possess regarding this topic, it even seems terribly unlikely that new manuscripts will offer anything worthwhile.

This study need not lead one to believe that there were no Muslim scientists at all, and an effective cultural apologetic argument does not require a defense of such a strong claim.[170] Hodgson points out, for example, "Medicine was practiced throughout the Islamic Empire, hospitals were established in many cities, and the care of the sick was given high priority."[171] Muslim philosophers al-Razi and Ali Ibn-Sina are mentioned as contributing to medicine through their writings, but evidence of scientific acumen in Islamic civilization in the realm of medicine is quite sparse.[172] Hodgson even includes a Christian in his list of contributors to Islamic medicine. He writes, "In Damascus the Christian physician Ibn al-Quff taught medicine and wrote one of the first treatises on surgery."[173] But this was an accomplishment for Christianity, not Islam, even given that it took place in a Muslim land. Insofar as the discipline of mathematics is related to science, Muslims appear to have several achievements to offer.[174] Yet here too the Muslims borrowed heavily from non-Muslims,

---

169. Hodgson, *Theology and Modern Physics*, 42.

170. However, the case against the idea that Muslims have contributed to science at all is quite strong.

171. Hodgson, *Theology and Modern Physics*, 42.

172. Hodgson, *Theology and Modern Physics*, 42.

173. Hodgson, *Theology and Modern Physics*, 42.

174. Hodgson, *Theology and Modern Physics*, 43. Hodgson provides a list: "The Persian al-Kwarizmi wrote on algebra in Arabic and showed how mathematical methods can be used to solve inheritance problems. The mathematician Tabit Ibn-Korra translated the works of Euclid, Apollonius, Archimedes and Ptolemy, and developed geometrical methods to solve cubic equations. The poet Omar Khayyam classified algebraic equations and explored the connections between algebra and geometry. Other

since "the Greeks developed geometry, and the Hindus arithmetic and algebra, and this knowledge passed to the Muslims."[175] The Muslims did seem to excel at astronomy, borrowing from Ptolemy, but nevertheless making some improvements upon his work.[176] However, here, too, Hodgson cites non-Muslim scientists living in Muslim lands, providing no help for Islam in terms of the cultural apologetic.[177] To make matters worse, astronomy was strongly opposed by several notable Muslim thinkers:

> In the twelfth century scientific work was discouraged due to the influence of al-Ghazali, who thought that it would lead to the loss of belief in the Creator. He maintained that one only needs to know what is required for the performance of duties obligatory for Muslims. Medicine is encouraged for its utility, whereas physics is useless. Muhsin Fayd Kashani thought that knowledge that is not useful for the hereafter is not needed, so that, for example, it is sufficient to learn only the simplest astronomy. Thereafter most scientific writers were Jews, of whom the most eminent was the philosopher Maimonides.[178]

Again, Maimonides was a Jew, not a Muslim. His contributions to science do not count in Islam's favor. If alchemy is more than mere quackery, namely, the predecessor of chemistry, then Islam may have contributed something to science by way of alchemy.

> The earliest Arabic writer on alchemy was Jabir (Geber), followed by Rhazes, who also wrote extensively on medicine. Jabir classified minerals as spirits, metals and pulverizable substances. Rhazes had a relatively well-equipped laboratory and was the first to suggest the familiar division into animal, vegetable and mineral. He distinguished six types of mineral: spirits, metals, boraxes, salts, stones and vitriols. Alchemy was practiced

---

Arab mathematicians include al-Battani and Abu-al-Wafa, who derived trigonometrical formulae. The Arabs applied mathematics to physical and astronomical problems. Many advances were made in arithmetic, algebra, geometry and trigonometry, as we are reminded by Arabic terms such as algebra and logarithm." Hodgson, *Theology and Modern Physics*, 43.

175. Hodgson, *Theology and Modern Physics*, 43.
176. Hodgson, *Theology and Modern Physics*, 43.
177. Hodgson, *Theology and Modern Physics*, 43–44.
178. Hodgson, *Theology and Modern Physics*, 44.

in Spain, and it was through the Spanish alchemists that their knowledge reached the Latin West.[179]

Hodgson nevertheless calls the experiments of the alchemists "fruitless" and also states, "Many of the leading Arabic scholars denounced alchemy as a worthless enterprise."[180]

Muslim resistance had a way of stopping scientific progress even within the Islamic community. Physics is no exception, for, "There was a notable controversy between supporters of the atomic theory of matter and the Aristotelianism of the Muslim theologians, who ultimately prevailed."[181] However, Aristotelianism did not prevail before some accomplishments came to fruition in physics:

> One of the earliest Arabic writers on physics was al-Kindi in the ninth century, who worked in Basra and Baghdad on optics, meteorology and the tides. He wrote a treatise summarizing the works of Euclid and Ptolemy, and also discussed the rainbow. At that time there was much interest in the various devices used for irrigation, water wheels and water clocks. Mathematics was applied to problems in statics and optics, and in the twelfth century al-Khazini wrote a treatise on mechanics and hydrostatics. Advances in optics were made by Ibn al-Haithan (Alhazen) in the tenth century. He discussed reflection and refraction, the propagation of light, colours, the rainbow and haloes, and experimented with magnifying glasses. The Persian al-Biruni, physician, astronomer, mathematician, physicist, geographer and historian, was one of the best-known among the scholars in what is known as the Islamic Golden Age.[182]

Being careful to note positive scientific contributions stemming from Islamic civilization, there still does not seem to be much evidence suggesting that Islam has ever helped toward creating a scientifically healthy society.

The evidence proffered here demonstrates that the Golden Age of Islam was not overly fruitful as far as science is concerned. Given the overwhelming amount of failure with respect to scientific originality and practice, one might suspect that any positive progress Islam made by way

---

179. Hodgson, *Theology and Modern Physics*, 44.
180. Hodgson, *Theology and Modern Physics*, 44.
181. Hodgson, *Theology and Modern Physics*, 44.
182. Hodgson, *Theology and Modern Physics*, 44–45.

of science was accomplished in spite of the Islamic worldview, and not because of it.

> In spite of all these great achievements, the Muslim civilization went into decline from the end of the fifteenth century onwards. The rate of decline varies from country to country; indeed as late as the fifteenth century there was still an active astronomical observatory at Samarkand. Generally speaking, however, from the twelfth century onwards the lead passed to the West, which soon surpassed the greatest achievements of the Islamic Empire. Modern science was born in the High Middle Ages, and came to maturity in the Renaissance. Nothing remotely similar occurred in the Muslim lands. The Muslim leaders were acute and intelligent men and they saw clearly what was happening but they did not know how to prevent it.[183]

What, specifically, prevents Islamic societies from being known as scientific societies? This crucial question will be more closely examined and answered in chapter 5 where it is argued that although a number of different causes for scientific failure obtain within an Islamic worldview, the inability to affirm a specifically Christian doctrine of divine providence with its implications for the laws of nature and induction is a main cause for the pervasive scientific failure of Islam.[184]

SCIENTIFIC IMPLICATIONS OF PROVIDENCE IN SCIENCE

If the quality and quantity of scientific discovery is any guide to discerning whether or not a worldview possesses a successful approach to science, then pagan, polytheistic, pantheistic, animistic, Buddhist, and Islamic approaches to science are obviously flawed. Hints are available from the cultural apologetic above as to how the aforementioned worldviews are methodologically flawed. Christian theologians and apologists have held

---

183. Hodgson, *Theology and Modern Physics*, 49. See also Lewis, *What Went Wrong?*.

184. Most of the objections to science stemming from a monistic or pantheistic metaphysic present in a system of thought like Buddhism can be applied to Hinduism with equal effect. Atheism and science are covered by implication in the secular responses to the problem of induction presented in chap. 4. As for the history of science, the fact that science arose in a Christianized society precludes the notion that it arose within Hindu or atheist societies.

that the doctrine of divine providence has scientific implications. If so, then rejecting a Christian doctrine of divine providence might very well lead to the sort of scientific failure illustrated in the previous section. Most Christian theologians and apologists would likely agree.

Is there any evidence that scientists themselves, whether Christian or non-Christian, have found the claims of the theologians and apologists true? Do scientists see any type of providential activity in their observations of nature and their positing apparent laws which describe the rational, orderly operations of the world? In order to answer these questions, one might pose yet another question. Where did modern science originate, and what type of society contributed to its progress? The answer is that a significant number of scientists would, in fact, agree with the observations of the theologians and apologists provided above, because those scientists were generally Christian. Moreover, there is evidence to show that a number of modern scientists who have not professed the Christian faith nevertheless have discerned something like a divine providence behind their work in the orderliness of nature.

The history of modern science is most often traced to medieval Christian society. Sociologist Alvin J. Schmidt writes,

> Alfred North Whitehead, the renowned philosopher of science, once said that "faith in the possibility of science, generated antecedently to the development of modern scientific theory, is an unconscious derivative from medieval theology." Similarly, Lynn White, the historian of medieval science, has stated that "the [medieval] monk was an intellectual ancestor of the scientist." And the German physicist Ernst Mach once remarked, "Every unbiased mind must admit that the age in which the chief development of the science of mechanics took place was an age of predominantly theological cast."[185]

This "theological cast" was Christian. One major difference between Christianity and paganism is the former's insistence upon rational monotheism.[186] That is, only one God exists, and he is a rational being. Some have been so bold as to state, "Without this Christian presupposition, there would be no science."[187] There are some difficulties with this bold claim. For example, belief in a single rational God is not exclusive

---

185. Schmidt, *How Christianity*, 218.
186. Schmidt, *How Christianity*, 219.
187. Schmidt, *How Christianity*, 219.

to Christianity, yet in the quote this belief is called a "Christian presupposition." Additionally, the claim that there would be no science apart from the aforementioned presupposition is an assertion without argument. One of the purposes of this book is to work toward filling out that argument, even if its conclusions are stated in terms of Christianity being the *best* candidate for sustaining the scientific enterprise, rather than the *only* one.

Schmidt writes, "The origin of science, said Alfred North Whitehead, required Christianity's 'insistence on the rationality of God.'"[188] In Christianity, not only is God rational, but human beings, who are created in his image, are rational as well. Thus Schmidt asks, "If God is a rational being, then may not human beings, who are made in his image, also employ rational processes to study and investigate the world in which they live?"[189]

> That question, of course, was answered in the affirmative when some Christian philosophers linked rationality with the empirical, inductive method. One such person was Robert Grosseteste (ca. 1168–1253), a Franciscan bishop and the first chancellor of Oxford University, who first proposed the inductive, experimental method, an approach to knowledge that was further advocated by his student Roger Bacon (1214–94), also a Franciscan monk, who asserted that "all things must be verified by experience." Bacon was a devout believer in the truthfulness of Scripture, and being empirically minded, he saw the Bible in the light of sound reason and as verifiable by experience. Another natural philosopher, also a Franciscan monk, was William of Occam (or Ockham, 1285–1347). He too, like Bacon, argued that knowledge needed to be derived inductively.[190]

Already at the mention of Christian presuppositions, specifically, the rationality of God and derivative rationality of people created in his image, the inductive method comes up. As the quotation explains, rationality was closely identified with an inductive approach to knowledge. This empirical approach to knowledge is commonsensical, taking for granted that our senses deliver information to us concerning the external world which is ordered by God. Grosseteste, Bacon, and Ockham spring boarded from

---

188. Schmidt, *How Christianity*, 219.
189. Schmidt, *How Christianity*, 219.
190. Schmidt, *How Christianity*, 219.

SCIENTIFIC IMPLICATIONS OF PROVIDENCE

their Christian presuppositions to a confidence in inductive reasoning that is generally thought to be necessary to the scientific endeavor.

These three Christian men were only partially responsible for introducing the inductive method into the world as it pertains to science. Schmidt explains:

> Almost three hundred years later another Bacon, Francis Bacon (1561–1626), gave further momentum to the inductive method by actually recording his experimental results. He has been called "the practical creator of scientific induction." In the context of rationality, he stressed careful observation of phenomena and collecting systematic information in order to understand nature's secrets. His scientific interests did not deter him from also devoting time to theology, for he also wrote treatises on the Psalms and on prayer.[191]

An indubitable link exists between Christianity and science, especially per the latter of the two Bacons mentioned above. Earlier, it was mentioned that the Greeks did not really contribute anything to a scientific worldview. The work of the men listed above is thus significant, because "By introducing the inductive empirical method guided by rational procedures, Roger Bacon, William Occam, and Francis Bacon departed to a considerable degree from the ancient Greek perspective of Aristotle (384–322 B.C.)."[192]

The creator-creature distinction of Christianity was mentioned in the previous section. God is the transcendent creator of the world, which is separate and distinct from him.[193] Denying this doctrine can lead to pantheism, or animism, which serve to virtually destroy the assumptions of science such as the laws of nature and induction.[194] Consider again, as above, the worldview of the Greeks, which contributed little in the

---

191. Schmidt, *How Christianity*, 219.

192. Schmidt, *How Christianity*, 219. Concerning Greek thought and practice, Schmidt explains, "Aristotelianism, which had a stranglehold on the world for fifteen hundred years, held that knowledge was only acquired through the deductive processes of the mind; the inductive method, which required manual activity, was taboo. As noted in chapter 7, physical activities were only for slaves, not for thinkers or freemen." Schmidt, *How Christianity*, 219–2. Aristotle is known as a taxonomist.

193. I say separate *and* distinct to call attention to the fact that creation is different, in many respects, from its creator.

194. I am trying to point out that the presuppositions of science are interrelated in systematic fashion such that a change or denial of one leads to change or denial of others.

way of scientific thought. This failure is inextricably linked to problems that were only alluded to before involving pantheism, animism, and the doctrine of the forms.

> Aristotelian philosophy, on the other hand, saw God (or the gods in Aristotle's pagan thinking) and the universe of nature intertwined. This posits a pantheistic, panemanationist conception of the world. Planets, for example, were seen as having an inner intelligence (*anima*) that induced them to move. This pantheistic view of planetary movement was first challenged by Jean Buridan (1300–1358), a Christian philosopher at the University of Paris. Also contrary to Christian theology, which said that "in the beginning God created the heavens and the earth" (Genesis 1:1), was Aristotle's theory that the world neither had a beginning nor was created by God (see his *On the Heavens* 279–84).[195]

Science simply was not successful in worldviews like those mentioned above because their underlying metaphysical positions did not comport with presuppositions of science like the laws of nature and the rational use of inductive reasoning. Animism makes for a relatively unpredictable world saturated with arbitrary independent causal agents and the doctrine of pre-existent matter ascribes all of the actions of nature to whatever the objects of the world just happen to do. These views are much less preferable to the view of Christian theism, which takes God to have created and governed the world since its inception.

Schmidt claims, "Continued resistance to the inductive method together with the failure to see Aristotle's pantheistic view of the physical world delayed not only the arrival of science but also its progress, because pantheism, like the anti-inductive approach to knowledge, is antithetical to science."[196] Why does Schmidt claim that pantheism is antithetical to

---

195. Schmidt, *How Christianity*, 220–21.

196. Schmidt, *How Christianity*, 221. Many did not immediately join with those advocating the inductive method over against the older Aristotelian errors. Schmidt explains, "Although Christianity very early in its existence condemned pantheism, its natural philosophers and scholastics for the longest time failed to see the pantheistic elements embedded in the Aristotelian philosophy that they used to explain the world of nature. Even after Roger Bacon and William Occam broke with Aristotle's perspective by advocating the inductive method, the natural philosophers and scholastics within Christendom clung to it contumaciously. Some—for example, the Franciscan order to which Bacon belonged—even saw Bacon's views as heretical, and in 1278 it imprisoned him for fourteen years." Schmidt, *How Christianity*, 221.

science?[197] In addition to the observation above concerning the systematic implications of pantheism for the inductive method, "Pantheism implies that the scientific method, which manipulates various elements within the physical universe, is sacrilegious and an affront to the divine within nature."[198] Schmidt thus makes a bold claim in conclusion:

> Thus, only in the Christian perspective, which sees God and nature as distinctively separate entities, is science possible. As has been rightly said, "Science could never have come into being among the animists of central or southern Africa or many other places in the world because they would never have begun to experiment on the natural world, since everything—whether stones or trees or animals or anything else—within it contained living spirits of various gods or ancestors."[199]

Here again, Schmidt may be overlooking the implications of his statement for the laws of nature. While his argument appears to pertain to the fear of people to tinker with objects that are to be held sacred, as they may contain various respectable spirits, the argument may be drawn out further to include the idea that an animistic worldview entails a potentially chaotic view of nature. Spirits acting in accordance with individual whims behind the surface of empirical reality really destroys the foundations of scientific inquiry, and it does so in virtue of the neglect of laws of nature.

Thankfully, gifted Christian men called the aforementioned assumptions into question, bringing modern science into sharper focus. Schmidt relates the story as follows:

> Had this major paradigm shift from Aristotle's pantheistic theory to a rational-inductive approach not occurred with men like Grosseteste, Buridan, the Bacons, William Ockham, and Nicholas of Oresme, and later with men like Copernicus, Vesalius, Kepler, and Galileo, who from their knowledge of Scripture knew they were not investigating the divine in nature, there would be no science today. They saw themselves as merely trying to understand the world that God had created and over which he told mankind to have "dominion" (Genesis 1:28 NKJV). This

---

197. Schmidt's use of "antithetical" is admittedly too strong for the context.
198. Schmidt, *How Christianity*, 221.
199. Schmidt, *How Christianity*, 221.

paradigm shift is another example of Christianity's wholesome impact on the world.[200]

Here is a strong piece of evidence for use in a cultural apologetic. Not only that, but this piece of evidence lends support to the understanding of the scientific achievements of societies being related to their understanding of the laws of nature which were, in turn, related to their understanding of theism. Schmidt is explicit at this point regarding the role of the laws of nature in the scientific endeavor, and their dependence upon a theistic, and perhaps even Christian theistic, view of the world.

> Belief in the rationality of God not only led to the inductive method but also led to the conclusion that the universe is governed rationally by discoverable laws. This assumption is vitally important to scientific research, because in a pagan or polytheistic world, which saw its gods often engaged in jealous, irrational behavior in a world that was nonrational, any systematic investigation of such a world would seem futile. Only in Christian thought, which posits "the existence of a single God, the Creator and Governor of the universe, [one that] functions in an orderly and normally predictable manner," is it possible for science to exist and operate.[201]

As mentioned earlier, when assembling information regarding scientific thought relative to the Christian doctrine of providence and its relation to laws of nature in particular, one must not miss the obvious. Though Christianity is sometimes thought of as opposed to the scientific endeavor, it is in fact an old friend of science. Modern science itself stems from a *Christian* context and not any other: "It was Christianized Europe that became the birthplace of modern science—there and nowhere else."[202] Why might it be the case that modern science would arise in such a context?

One reason might be that Christianity as a thoroughgoing view of the world provides certain assumptions heavily relied upon within the scientific realm. Such assumptions are posited prior to any actual scientific practice. Pearcey and Thaxton explain, "Scientific investigation depends upon certain assumptions about the world—and science is

---

200. Schmidt, *How Christianity*, 221.

201. Schmidt, *How Christianity*, 222.

202. Pearcey and Thaxton, *Soul of Science*, 21. Pearcey and Thaxton write, "That historical fact alone is suggestive." Pearcey and Thaxton, *Soul of Science*, 21.

impossible until those assumptions are in place."²⁰³ Pearcey and Thaxton point out that Alfred North Whitehead argued that belief in the very *possibility* of science must in the logical sense *precede* science itself.²⁰⁴ A belief in the possibility of science rests at least in part upon a belief in a regular, or lawful, natural world.

> This faith, Whitehead explains, rested on certain habits of thought, such as the lawfulness of nature—which in turn, he maintains, came from the Christian doctrine of the world as a divine creation. Whitehead did not mean that everyone living in Europe at the time of the scientific revolution was a committed Christian. But even those who rejected orthodox Biblical doctrines continued to live and think within the intellectual framework of the Biblical worldview. "I am not talking of the explicit beliefs of a few individuals," Whitehead says, but rather "the impress on the European mind arising from the unquestioned faith of centuries"—the "instinctive tone of thought and not a mere creed of words."²⁰⁵

Pearcey and Thaxton further explain, "To become an object of study the world must be regarded as a place where events occur in a reliable, predictable fashion."²⁰⁶ Pearcey and Thaxton describe this premise as a "legacy of Christianity."²⁰⁷ Melvin Calvin, a biochemist noted for his Nobel Prize in Chemistry, is quoted to the effect that a conviction of order in the universe is found in the ancient monotheistic Hebrews.²⁰⁸ Much like Calvin, Pearcey and Thaxton emphasize the *goodness* of God when they write, "Of course, the idea of order in nature rests not simply on the *existence* of a single God but also on the *character* of that God."²⁰⁹ They continue, "The God revealed in the Bible is trustworthy and dependable; the creation of such a God must likewise be dependable."²¹⁰

203. Pearcey and Thaxton, *Soul of Science*, 21.
204. Pearcey and Thaxton, *Soul of Science*, 21.
205. Pearcey and Thaxton, *Soul of Science*, 21.
206. Pearcey and Thaxton, *Soul of Science*, 24.
207. Pearcey and Thaxton, *Soul of Science*, 24.
208. Pearcey and Thaxton, *Soul of Science*, 25. Pearcey and Thaxton quote from Thomas Derr, a Presbyterian theologian, who contrasts the capricious gods of animism with the steadfast God of Christian creationism, and Melvin Calvin, a biochemist with a Nobel Prize, who emphasizes ancient Hebrew monotheism as the basis of modern science rather than the whimsical gods of polytheism. Pearcey and Thaxton, *Soul of Science*, 25.
209. Pearcey and Thaxton, *Soul of Science*, 25.
210. Pearcey and Thaxton, *Soul of Science*, 25.

Pearcey and Thaxton work from the thoughts of a theologian named Thomas Derr, who agrees that a *trustworthy* God leads to a world that is regular, dependable, and orderly.[211] According to Pearcey and Thaxton, Copernicus too derived his faith in the orderliness of the universe from his faith in the orderliness of the good creator.[212]

> The order of the reasoning here is important. The early scientists did not argue that the world was lawfully ordered, and *therefore* there must be a rational God. Instead, they argued that there was a rational God, and *therefore* the world must be lawfully ordered. They had greater confidence in the existence and character of God than in the lawfulness of nature.[213]

Even when nature did not appear regular, but random, those who believed in the doctrine of creation likewise held that the universe operated in accordance with some plan, and hence coherence would be found out beneath the chaos.[214] The universe operates in law-like fashion.

Little thought is given to the use of the word "law" in describing some of the workings of nature.[215] The word entails, naturally enough, some law-like efficacy in nature that is not present in many views of the world.[216] Where the language of law fits is an ancient Hebraic or Christian worldview where the Bible teaches that God is the creator, sustainer, and governor of everything. Pearcey and Thaxton write, "The Biblical God is the Divine Legislator who governs nature by decrees set down in the beginning."[217] Pearcey and Thaxton appeal to the thought of mathematician René Descartes as an example, "who said the mathematical laws

---

211. Pearcey and Thaxton, *Soul of Science*, 25.

212. Pearcey and Thaxton, *Soul of Science*, 25. Copernicus is provided as an example: "Copernicus tells us that, in his search for a better cosmology than that of Aristotle and Ptolemy, he first went back to the writings of other ancient philosophers. But he uncovered significant disagreement among the ancients regarding the structure of the universe. This inconsistency disturbed him, Copernicus said, for he knew the universe was 'wrought for us by a supremely good and orderly Creator.' His own scientific work became a quest for a better cosmology—one that would, in the words of theologian Christopher Kaiser, 'uphold the regularity, uniformity, and symmetry that befitted the work of God.'" Pearcey and Thaxton, *Soul of Science*, 25.

213. Pearcey and Thaxton, *Soul of Science*, 26–27.

214. Pearcey and Thaxton, *Soul of Science*, 26.

215. Pearcey and Thaxton, *Soul of Science*, 26.

216. Pearcey and Thaxton, *Soul of Science*, 26.

217. Pearcey and Thaxton, *Soul of Science*, 26. Note the similarities between the claims of Jaeger, Calvin, Pearcey, and Thaxton.

sought by science were legislated by God in the same manner as a king ordains laws in his realm."[218] According to Pearcey and Thaxton, the historian Carl Becker notes that most people did not think of nature as lawful prior to the scientific revolution, when biblical principles drove them to apply the goodness and rationality of God to nature, inferring that creation must also be, in some sense, both good and rational.[219] Again, this approach to the scientific endeavor did not begin with experience, but "was derived *prior* to observations from belief in the Biblical God."[220]

While Descartes, mentioned earlier, was not, strictly speaking, a scientist, he was a philosopher and mathematician. As a mathematician, he is categorized loosely as a modern scientist. Modern science relies heavily upon and uses mathematics.[221] But the application of mathematics through science to nature is likewise a feature of science that cannot be taken for granted.

> One of the most distinctive aspects of modern science is its use of mathematics—the conviction not only that nature is lawful but also that those laws can be stated in precise mathematical formulas. This conviction, too, historians have traced to the Biblical teaching on creation.[222]

Because God created everything from nothing and exercises total control over creation, "in its essential structure the universe is precisely what God wants it to be."[223] Not only is God *over* his creation, which is a feature of theology absent in any religion which takes its god or gods to merely mold pre-existent matter, but God acts in creation with *precision*.[224] This precision is exhibited in mathematical descriptions of and predictions about the world.[225]

218. Pearcey and Thaxton, *Soul of Science*, 26.
219. Pearcey and Thaxton, *Soul of Science*, 27.
220. Pearcey and Thaxton, *Soul of Science*, 27.
221. In my observations about Islam I cite mathematics negatively in terms of its relation to science. Deductive systems are often developed independently from the empirical world. This would seem to be the case with Muslims who worked with texts on mathematics. However, Muslims are credited with applying mathematics to the science of astronomy. Loosely categorized as a scientist, Descartes is credited with providing the precise analytical thought in mathematics that is then used in science to make predictions, measurements, and the like. He also posed various theories about the world, including his concept of aether.
222. Pearcey and Thaxton, *Soul of Science*, 27.
223. Pearcey and Thaxton, *Soul of Science*, 27.
224. Pearcey and Thaxton, *Soul of Science*, 27–28.
225. Pearcey and Thaxton, *Soul of Science*, 27–28.

For example, when the mathematician, astronomer, and astrologist Johannes Kepler found an imprecision of eight minutes pertaining to the orbit of Mars, he inferred that its orbit was not circular, but elliptical.[226] Pearcey and Thaxton argue, "If Kepler had not maintained the conviction that nature must be precise, he would not have agonized over those eight minutes and would not have broken through a traditional belief in circular orbits that had held sway for two thousand years."[227]

Thus the application of geometry and mathematics to the analysis of physical motion rests on the Christian doctrine of creation *ex nihilo*. The implication is that God is omnipotent; there is no recalcitrant matter to resist his will. In the words of physicist C.F. von Weizsacker:

> Matter in the Platonic sense, which must be 'prevailed upon' by reason, will not obey mathematical laws exactly: matter which God has created from nothing may well strictly follow the rules which its Creator has laid down for it. In this sense I called modern science a legacy, I might even have said a child, of Christianity.[228]

To state her point about mathematics in the starkest terms, Pearcey and Thaxton quote the succinct statement of a historian named R. G. Collingwood, "He writes: 'The possibility of an applied mathematics is an expression, in terms of natural science, of the Christian belief that nature is the creation of an omnipotent God.'"[229]

One of the hopes of Christian apologists, like those referenced in the previous section, is to present a compelling case for Christian theism, or at any rate some of its tenets. Though some scoff at the effectiveness of the apologetic endeavor, instances of skeptics coming to faith or agreement with particular tenets of Christian theism abound. One of the most recent skeptics to come to agree with Christians concerning at least one truth, the existence of God, is world-renowned (former) atheist philosopher Antony Flew.[230] Though some have attempted to discredit Flew's move from atheism to theism, Flew offered a number of well-reasoned

---

226. Pearcey and Thaxton, *Soul of Science*, 28.

227. Pearcey and Thaxton, *Soul of Science*, 28. According to Pearcey and Thaxton, "Kepler spoke gratefully of those eight minutes as a 'gift of God.'" Pearcey and Thaxton, *Soul of Science*, 28.

228. Pearcey and Thaxton, *Soul of Science*, 28.

229. Pearcey and Thaxton, *Soul of Science*, 28–29.

230. Flew and Varghese, *There Is a God*.

arguments detailing the thinking that led him to forsake his life's work.[231] Flew categorized at least two of these arguments as design arguments. He writes, "Although I was once sharply critical of the argument to design, I have since come to see that, when correctly formulated, this argument constitutes a persuasive case for the existence of God."[232] Often on the cutting-edge of philosophy and science, Flew notes two developments that led him to the conclusion that the design argument carries some force. Only the first of these two developments concerns the purpose of this book. Flew writes, "The first is the question of the origin of the laws of nature and the related insights of eminent modern scientists."[233] Flew's definition of the laws of nature is simple, "By *law*, I simply mean a regularity or symmetry in nature."[234]

The regularity or symmetry to which Flew refers is consistent with the observations of the theologians and apologists detailed above. However, Flew carries his observations regarding these regularities further than do the aforementioned commentators, theologians, and apologists. He wishes to press these regularities into use as a theistic evidence, and thus delves deeper into their character. Flew explains, "The important point is not merely that there are regularities in nature, but that these regularities are mathematically precise, universal, and 'tied together.'"[235] The reason this observation concerning the character of natural laws is such an important point is the question which arises from it. According to Flew, this question has motivated more than one reputable scientist throughout the course of history.[236] Commenting upon the mathematical precision, universality, and coherence of the regularities of nature, Flew notes the following:

---

231. For example, I witnessed in person famed "New Atheist" Richard Dawkins dismissing Flew's work when challenged by Will Honeycutt of Liberty University. This was regarding why Flew's work was relegated to a footnote in Dawkins' book, *The God Delusion*, when Dawkins spoke at (then) Randolph Macon Women's College in Lynchburg, Virginia.

232. Flew and Varghese, *There Is a God*, 95.

233. Flew and Varghese, *There Is a God*, 95. Flew writes, "The second is the question of the origin of life and reproduction." Flew and Varghese, *There Is a God*, 95.

234. Flew and Varghese, *There Is a God*, 96. Flew cites Boyle's law, Newton's first law of motion, and the law of the conservation of energy as examples of what he is referring to as law.

235. Flew and Varghese, *There Is a God*, 96.

236. Flew and Varghese, *There Is a God*, 96.

Einstein spoke of them as "reason incarnate." The question we should ask is how nature came packaged in this fashion. This is certainly the question that scientists from Newton to Einstein to Heisenberg have asked—and answered. Their answer was the Mind of God.[237]

Particularly interesting to note is not Flew's insistence upon the presence of this talk about the "Mind of God" in older, clearly theistic thinkers, but his insistence upon the occurrence of the language in prominent modern scientists as well.[238] The first example Flew cites is theoretical physicist, cosmologist, and author Stephen Hawking, who concludes his best-selling work, *A Brief History of Time*, with a statement that discovering a complete scientific theory, understood not only by scientists and philosophers, but everyone, and explaining why everything exists, would be to know God's mind.[239]

Flew argues similarly from Albert Einstein. While Einstein uses a great deal of explicit language about God and his relationship to the world and science, Flew previously argued that such language must not be taken too seriously, since Einstein had also expressed his agreement with Baruch Spinoza's concept of God, which identifies God with nature.[240] However, Flew changed his mind upon reading *Einstein and Religion*, a work by a friend of Einstein named Max Jammer.[241] In this work, Jammer demonstrates that Einstein was not terribly familiar with Spinoza, though both were determinists who were raised within the context of a Jewish background but had since left behind its religious

---

237. Flew and Varghese, *There Is a God*, 96.

238. Flew and Varghese, *There Is a God*, 96–97.

239. Flew and Varghese, *There Is a God*, 97. Regarding Hawking, Flew writes, "On the previous page he asked: 'Even if there is only one possible unified theory, it is just a set of rules and equations. What is it that breathes fire into the equations and makes a universe for them to describe?'" (Flew and Varghese, *There Is a God*, 97). Flew continues, "Hawking had more to say on this in later interviews: 'The overwhelming impression is one of order. The more we discover about the universe, the more we find that it is governed by rational laws.' And, 'You still have the question: why does the universe bother to exist? If you like, you can define God to be the answer to that question.'" Flew and Varghese, *There Is a God*, 97.

240. Flew and Varghese, *There Is a God*, 98. Flew explains his older reasoning: "Since for Baruch Spinoza the words *God* and *nature* were synonymous, it could be said that Einstein, in the eyes of Judaism, Christianity, and Islam, was unequivocally an atheist and that he was 'a spiritual father of all atheists.'" Flew and Varghese, *There Is a God*, 98.

241. Flew and Varghese, *There Is a God*, 98–99.

aspects.[242] Indeed, Einstein explicitly denied being an atheist or a pantheist.[243] According to Flew, following Jammer, like Maimonides and Spinoza, Einstein rejected belief in a personal God: "But unlike Spinoza, who saw the only logical consequence of the denial of a personal God in an identification of God with nature, Einstein maintained that God manifests himself 'in the laws of the universe as a spirit vastly superior to that of man, and one in the face of which we with our modest powers must feel humble.'"[244] Flew provides a number of quotes from Einstein that demonstrate, "Einstein clearly believed in a transcendent source of the rationality of the world that he variously called 'superior mind,' 'illimitable superior spirit,' 'superior reasoning force,' and 'mysterious force that moves the constellations.'"[245] The rationality, order, regularities, and law-like nature of the universe were so overwhelming to Einstein that he posited such language to describe it.

Other famous scientists on the cutting-edge of scientific discovery have held similar views to Einstein on the rationality of the universe and have used similar language to describe it. Flew points out, "The progenitors of quantum physics, the other great scientific discovery of modern times, Max Planck, Werner Heisenberg, Erwin Schrödinger, and Paul Dirac, have all made similar statements."[246] Flew also notes the following:

242. Flew and Varghese, *There Is a God*, 98–99. Flew explains, "Jammer shows that Einstein's knowledge of Spinoza was quite limited; he had read only Spinoza's *Ethics* and turned down repeated requests to write about Spinoza's philosophy." He continues, "In response to one request, he replied, 'I do not have the professional knowledge to write a scholarly article about Spinoza.'" Flew and Varghese, *There Is a God*, 98–99.

243. Flew and Varghese, *There Is a God*, 99. Flew's detailed defense of his claim is provided on pp. 99–100. Flew takes atheist Richard Dawkins to task for utilizing Max Jammer as a source for regarding Einstein as an atheist while ignoring important evidence. Flew explains, "Jammer observes, for instance, that 'Einstein always protested against being regarded as an atheist. In a conversation with Prince Hubertus of Lowenstein, for example, he declared, 'What really makes me angry is that they [people who say there is no God] quote me for support of their views.' Einstein renounced atheism because he never considered his denial of a personal God as a denial of God.'" Flew and Varghese, *There Is a God*, 99–100.

244. Flew and Varghese, *There Is a God*, 100–1. I have quoted the text as it appears in Flew, even though it seems Flew misplaced the quotation marks. Jammer begins "Unlike Spinoza" in Max Jammer, *Einstein and Religion: Physics and Theology* (Princeton: Princeton University Press, 1999), 148. Flew writes, "Einstein agreed with Spinoza that he who knows nature knows God, but not because nature is God, but because the pursuit of science in studying nature leads to religion." Flew and Varghese, *There is a God*, 101.

245. Flew and Varghese, *There is a God*, 101–3.

246. Flew and Varghese, *There is a God*, 103–6. Flew provides extensive evidence in

> This train of thought has been kept alive in the present time in the writings of many of today's leading expositors of science. These range from scientists like Paul Davies, John Barrow, John Polkinghorne, Freeman Dyson, Francis Collins, Owen Gingerich, and Roger Penrose to philosophers of science like Richard Swinburne and John Leslie.[247]

Flew highlights comments made by Paul Davies, in particular, in his Templeton address regarding the relationship between the laws of physics and God.[248]

> In his Templeton address, Paul Davies makes the point that "science can proceed only if the scientist adopts an essentially theological worldview." Nobody asks where the laws of physics come from, but "even the most atheistic scientist accepts as an act of faith the existence of a lawlike order in nature that is at least in part comprehensible to us."[249]

Davies is not the only Templeton Prize winning scientist to have made such comments. Flew notes, "John Barrow, in his Templeton address, observes that the unending complexity and exquisite structure of the universe are governed by a few simple laws that are symmetrical and intelligible."[250] Flew expresses his deep agreement with the aforementioned scientists on this particular point, writing, "the laws of nature pose a

---

the form of quotes to support his remark.

247. Flew and Varghese, *There is a God*, 106. Flew writes, "Davies and Barrow, in particular, have further developed the insights of Einstein, Heisenberg, and other scientists into theories about the relationship between the rationality of nature and the Mind of God. Both have received the Templeton Prize for their contributions to this exploration. Their works correct many common misconceptions while shedding light on the issues discussed here." Flew and Varghese, *There is a God*, 106–7.

248. Flew and Varghese, *There is a God*, 107–8.

249. Flew and Varghese, *There is a God*, 107. Flew writes, "Davies rejects two common misconceptions. He says the idea that a theory of everything would show that this is the only logically consistent world is 'demonstrably wrong,' because there is no evidence at all that the universe is logically necessary, and in fact it is possible to imagine alternative universes that are logically consistent. Second, he says it is 'arrant nonsense' to suppose that the laws of physics are our laws and not nature's. Physicists will not believe that Newton's inverse law of gravitation is a cultural creation. He holds that the laws of physics 'really exist,' and scientists' job is to uncover and not invent them." Flew and Varghese, *There is a God*, 107–8.

250. Flew and Varghese, *There is a God*, 108.

problem for atheists because they are a voice of rationality heard through the mechanisms of matter."[251]

> Those scientists who point to the Mind of God do not merely advance a series of arguments or a process of syllogistic reasoning. Rather, they propound a vision of reality that emerges from the conceptual heart of modern science and imposes itself on the rational mind. It is a vision that I personally find compelling and irrefutable.[252]

This vision fits well with the doctrine of divine providence.

The doctrine of providence, at least as it is found situated within the context of Christian theism, has been explained at some length in chapter 1 and chapter 2. Chapter 3 moves from theological and historical considerations to a more philosophical analysis of the laws of nature.

---

251. Flew and Varghese, *There is a God*, 111.
252. Flew and Varghese, *There is a God*, 112.

Chapter 3

Laws of Nature

THE LAWS OF NATURE are a recurring theme in discussions devoted to providence and science. In general, theologians and apologists believe the Christian doctrine of divine providence implies laws of nature. Conversely, scientists, whether Christian or not, have made a number of revealing statements about their sentiments regarding something like a divine providence behind the laws of nature and the scientific endeavor itself. Consistent with the aforementioned observations is the undeniable fact that science as we know it began in Christianized society. Before moving forward to examine the philosophical link between divine providence and laws of nature, the concept of the laws of nature must be more closely examined.

Philosophy is largely concerned with questions. Questions about knowledge, ethics, and the nature of reality are intended to bring the philosopher closer to the truth of things. In the case of knowledge and ethics, questions arise with respect to at least the frequency with which such topics enter our daily routines.[1] Even the nature of reality could become a topic of discussion. But how is the topic of the laws of nature related to everyday experience? Is the question of what it is to be a law of nature really so important as to merit the voluminous discussion that has surrounded the attempt to answer that question? What are the laws of nature?

---

1. Carroll, *Laws of Nature*, 4.

The question is a crucial one for a number of reasons. One significant sort of justification provided by some philosophers regarding the importance of the question is that the question plays a major role in the scientific endeavor.[2] Few would argue against the importance and presence of science in daily life.[3] Given the information in the previous chapter, there is no wonder why philosopher John T. Roberts writes, "Many of us believe that the scientifically informed common sense of our culture includes a particular striking idea."[4] This idea is what Roberts calls the *"law-governed world-picture."*[5] Regarding this view, I quote him at length as follows:

> Scientific inquiry has revealed to us a universe that is governed by laws of nature. It has also found out what some of those laws are. Or at least, it has made some very good guesses: it has found principles that are, under certain circumstances, very good approximations to the laws of nature. And there is no principled limit to how much better its guesses and approximations might get; so in principle, science can discover particular laws of nature, whether it has already done so or not.
>
> The laws of the land can be violated by those on whom they are binding, but doing so carries certain consequences, for there are enforcement mechanisms in place. Laws of nature, by contrast, have no enforcement mechanisms. None are required, for there are no violations.
>
> That doesn't mean that the laws of nature do not govern the universe at all, or that they 'govern' only in the figurative sense that nature does its elaborate dance *as if* it were obeying laws. The laws of nature govern the universe in the sense that the universe cannot but conform to them; their requirements are not merely required but also inevitable; with them, resistance is futile.
>
> This has important consequences for our understanding of the universe and what makes it go. The evolution of natural things is not wholly determined by some inscrutable fate;

---

2. Carroll, *Laws of Nature*, 4. Regarding more abstract philosophical concerns about the laws of nature, Carroll remarks, "it is the account of counterfactuals championed by Roderick Chisholm (1946, 1955) and Nelson Goodman (1947) that, I think, provoked much of the recent philosophical interest in laws of nature." Carroll, *Laws of Nature*, 4.

3. Carroll, *Laws of Nature*, 4.

4. Roberts, *Law Governed Universe*, 4–5.

5. Roberts, *Law Governed Universe*, 4–5.

it is not an inexplicable sequence of events, 'just one damned thing after another'; it is not a puppet show in which the action is directed by capricious gods according to fickle whims. It must proceed in a certain way because that way is determined by certain principles. Those principles can be grasped by reason, formulated in a language, and discerned by empirical inquiry. Just as a well-ordered state has a 'government of laws, and not a government of men,' this well-ordered universe has a government of laws, and not a government of unprincipled gods, or fairies, or demons, or fates, or what have you. Understanding of the natural universe and of the events it contains can be achieved only by understanding its laws.[6]

Roberts takes the view just described to be correct, but only if its content is properly explicated with reason for accepting it.[7] He continues, "It is easy for modern, scientifically educated Westerners to take the law-governed world-picture for granted, as if it were a truism, or part of the universal common sense of humanity."[8] The picture Roberts paints, and its acceptability in the West, seem generally correct. Hereafter, I will refer to the "law-governed world-picture" as "LGWP."

Historians are not united in their understanding of the LGWP set forth in the discussion above.[9] According to Roberts, "Zilsel argues that the concept emerged only in the seventeenth century; Ruby claims to find the modern concept of a scientific law already in the thirteenth century, in Roger Bacon's optical writings; Milton agrees that the idea of law-governed nature occurs earlier than the seventeenth century, but argues that it remains too vague to play a genuine role in scientific research until Descartes begins the search for the laws of motion."[10] Both Zilsel and Needham, also according to Roberts, argue that God was thought

---

6. Roberts, *Law Governed Universe*, 1–2. Roberts does not mean to rule out the possibility that some type of theism is involved in the account of the laws of nature. Roberts explains, "It just means that what goes on in the natural world goes on according to laws, and not according to the wills of lawless beings. If there are supernatural beings, then either they are themselves subject to the laws of nature whenever they attempt to intervene in the natural world, or else their influence on the natural world consists in having set up the laws of nature to begin with. (In the latter case, perhaps they have the power to suspend the laws on special occasions.)" Roberts, *Law Governed Universe*, 2n1.

7. Roberts, *Law Governed Universe*, 2.
8. Roberts, *Law Governed Universe*, 2.
9. Roberts, *Law Governed Universe*, 3.
10. Roberts, *Law Governed Universe*, 3.

of as imposing the laws of nature on his creation, but Ruby disagrees.[11] However, all of the historians above agree that, whether the LGWP was brought out in the thirteenth or the seventeenth century, it happened to arise in a specific context in history, rather than having always been around.[12] Not everyone has held the popular modern view. For example, neither the ancient Greeks nor the Chinese had such a concept.[13]

Another philosopher, Brian Ellis, corroborates the aforementioned idea in virtue of the historian A. R. Hall. Ellis writes, "According to A. R. Hall, the idea that nature is governed by laws does not appear to have existed in the ancient Greek, Roman, or the Far Eastern traditions of science (Hall, 1954, p. 171). Hall suggests that the idea arose as a result of a 'peculiar interaction between the religious, philosophical and legalistic ideas of the medieval European world.'"[14] Ellis believes other factors contributed to the rise of the concept of laws of nature.[15] He cites the geometry of Euclid and the statics of Archimedes and the subsequent attempt to apply these geometrical studies to mechanics.[16] In the opinion of Ellis, "These ancient works must have suggested to the medieval, as geometry had suggested to the ancient Greeks, that knowledge is structured, and the successes that were achieved in the early medieval period in solving problems of mechanical equilibrium, making use of such principles as the law of the lever and the principles of moments and virtual work would certainly have added substance to the idea that nature is governed by laws."[17] Regardless, "it is true that the laws of nature were conceived from medieval times as general principles of motion (in the sense of locomotion) and equilibrium—that is, as principles governing the kinds of changes that can occur in the world and the kinds of equilibrium states that can exist."[18] No one is suggesting, and Ellis certainly would agree, that the laws of nature have not undergone changes in terms of their theoretical nature. Additionally, it is granted that the concept of the laws

---

11. Roberts, *Law Governed Universe*, 3.
12. Roberts, *Law Governed Universe*, 3.
13. Roberts, *Law Governed Universe*, 3.
14. Ellis, *Scientific Essentialism*, 203.
15. Ellis, *Scientific Essentialism*, 203.
16. Ellis, *Scientific Essentialism*, 203.
17. Ellis, *Scientific Essentialism*, 203.
18. Ellis, *Scientific Essentialism*, 203.

of nature has been extended beyond the realm of mechanics, where it was most often present in medieval times.[19]

Psychologically speaking, the LGWP is received in different ways by different people, usually depending upon how they already view the world in other areas not directly related to the laws of nature. Roberts lists some of the different reactions to the concept he describes.[20]

> For some, the idea that science has revealed a law-governed universe is liberating: it releases us from the dreadful belief that we are at the mercy of capricious or vengeful powers, and brings with it the promise that we can learn the laws of nature and use this knowledge to control our destiny, at least to some degree. On the other hand, for some it brings with it the terrifying thought that we are cogs in a great machine that we are powerless to control. The idea of a law-governed universe can seem alienating, since the laws of nature are imposed on us from without and we have no say in them; but it can also make us feel at home in a universe that, like us when we are at our best, acts in accordance with principles that reason can grasp. To many, a universe governed by laws of nature necessarily implies a deity to serve as the supernatural lawmaker, since otherwise the power of the laws to govern would be inexplicable. But there is also the view that a law-governed universe is precisely the kind of universe that does not require a supernatural creator for its existence; having its own laws, it is self-sustaining and nothing from outside of it need be called on for any explanatory purpose—thus the line attributed to Laplace, 'Sire, I have no need of that hypothesis.' In short, it is clear that if we accept the law-governed world-picture, this must have a big effect on our world-view.[21]

Roberts takes the question of whether or not the LGWP is correct to be one of the most fundamental questions in the task of philosophy since it is so closely related to the fundamental metaphysical question of what reality is really like.[22] This realization is reason enough to study the laws of nature, but the topic is also closely related to many other important topics

---

19. Ellis, *Scientific Essentialism*, 203. Ellis writes, "The laws of nature are still widely thought of as governing nature—as imposing order and structure upon it—as if by the command of God." Ellis, *Scientific Essentialism*, 203.

20. Roberts, *Law Governed Universe*, 4.

21. Roberts, *Law Governed Universe*, 3–4.

22. Roberts, *Law Governed Universe*, 4.

in philosophy such as "causation, determinism, and explanation; there are interesting philosophical theories of things like induction, counterfactuals, explanation, reduction, and content which take the concept of a law of nature for granted, so that we won't really know what those theories say until we know what a law is; and so on."[23]

Of course, not everyone agrees with the LGWP, as Roberts explains:

> Some say that the very idea of a law of nature is a metaphysical holdover from a bygone age when science, theology, and metaphysics had yet to be properly distinguished from one another; the law-governed universe is not something that science has revealed to us, but an interpretative construct that we have illegitimately imposed on the output of science. By contrast, some agree that there really are such things as laws of nature, and empirical science is in principle capable of discovering them, but say that it is a mistake to think of these laws as 'governing' the universe in any but a thin metaphorical sense. For these philosophers, the laws are nothing more than a special set of exceptionless regularities—patterns in the great cosmic mosaic—which are privileged by their comprehensiveness and their simplicity. Others think that while the concept of a law of nature does play an important role in modern science, the laws do not govern the universe, and the universe does not even conform to them; they are principles we use in constructing models of the world, rather than a feature of the world itself.[24]

This chapter will include an examination of laws of nature as regularities, logical necessities, and natural necessities, in that order. For now, the quote from Roberts is helpful in introducing the fact of genuine disagreement between philosophers of science regarding the laws of nature. Why does this disagreement exist? One of the difficulties we face in speaking of the laws of nature is that we do not appear to possess any way

---

23. Roberts, *Law Governed Universe*, 4.
24. Roberts, *Law Governed Universe*, 4–5.

of perceiving them directly.[25] One means of attempting to answer this concern, and others like it, is to provide a philosophical definition of "law of nature."[26]

Like Roberts, philosopher David Armstrong takes the question of the definition of a law of nature to be one of the main questions in the philosophy of science.[27] However, the question about the character of laws of nature extends beyond science into epistemology and metaphysics in general.[28] Armstrong believes traditional natural science is concerned with no less than three tasks of finding out the geography of the universe as well as its history, finding out the sorts of things and properties that exist, and finally stating the laws in virtue of which the aforementioned things operate in the geography and history of the universe.[29] Armstrong writes, "The third task is to state the laws which link sort of thing with sort of thing, and property with property."[30]

While it is obvious that learning about the world grants science its importance, it is not as obvious that discovering the laws of nature is one of the three main tasks of science.[31] And if discovering laws of nature is so important to the scientific endeavor, then one of the chief tasks of the philosophy of science should be to discover the character of the laws of nature.[32] Armstrong points out, again, that this concern is much broader than the particular redemptive aspect of its answer for science.[33] Arm-

---

25. Roberts, *Law Governed Universe*, 4–5. Roberts describes the messiness of this situation: "Given the mood set by logical positivism, many philosophers from the middle part of this century onward have viewed laws and counterfactuals with a certain amount of suspicion. There are several notoriously slippery issues that sustain their doubts. The most significant is a thoroughly epistemological concern. Hume's argument against the idea of necessary connection, though largely of a semantic nature involving—it is safe to say—suspect semantic assumptions, contained an important and still plausible epistemological premise. This premise points out our lack of 'direct perceptual access' to causal connections: All events seem entirely loose and separate. One event follows another, but we never can observe any tie between them." Roberts, *Law Governed Universe*, 4–5.

26. Roberts, *Law Governed Universe*, 5.
27. Armstrong, *What is a Law?*, 3.
28. Armstrong, *What is a Law?*, 3.
29. Armstrong, *What is a Law?*, 3.
30. Armstrong, *What is a Law?*, 3.
31. Armstrong, *What is a Law?*, 4.
32. Armstrong, *What is a Law?*, 4.
33. Armstrong, *What is a Law?*, 4.

strong appeals to Hume, who said that "the *only* relation which enables us to infer from observed matters of fact to unobserved matters of fact is the relation of cause and effect."[34]

> Hume spoke little of laws. Nevertheless, it can be said that he held a law theory of cause and effect. Setting aside the mental component which he found in our concept of cause, he conceived of the relation between cause and effect as a law-like relation. (The law in turn he conceived of as a mere regularity.) We can therefore invoke his authority to say that inferences to particular matters of unobserved fact would not be reliable inferences if there were no laws of nature.[35]

Scientists are not the only people who depend upon laws of nature.

> As Hume understood and emphasized, inference from the observed to the unobserved is central to our whole life as human beings. We have just seen, however, that if there were no laws (whatever a law is, be it regularity or something else), then such inferences would not be reliable. Hence the notion of law is, or should be, a central concept for epistemology. If so, we will also want to enquire into its ontology. We will want to know what a law of nature *is*.[36]

This inquiry should begin with some general notion of what a law of nature is as known through its commonsensical utilization in the sciences and everyday life and move to "an articular, explicit and reasoned grasp of what an X is."[37]

According to Armstrong, "It is perfectly possible, epistemically possible, that we do not know a single law of nature."[38] However, Armstrong offers two responses to the aforementioned observation. The first is that our current scientific theories do appear to at least *approximate* true laws, "For if our theories did not nearly grasp the truth at many points, it would be inexplicable that they should permit so much successful prediction."[39]

---

34. Armstrong, *What is a Law?*, 4.
35. Armstrong, *What is a Law?*, 4.
36. Armstrong, *What is a Law?*, 4–5. Some philosophers insist there are no laws of nature, or that laws of nature are mere regularities. Armstrong does not think such views are capable of answering the problem of induction. The problem of induction is discussed in chap. 4.
37. Armstrong, *What is a Law?*, 5.
38. Armstrong, *What is a Law?*, 6.
39. Armstrong, *What is a Law?*, 6.

Indeed, those generalizations which pertain to our survival appear to approximate the truth, lest we die.[40] The second is, "even if we know no laws, we do know the *forms* which statements of law take."[41] Armstrong explains with the following formulas:

1. It is a law that Fs are Gs
2. It is a law that an F has a certain probability (>0,<1) of being a G
3. It is a law that the quantities P and Q co-vary in such a way that Q is a certain function of P ($Q=f(P)$).[42]

These basic formulas should be sufficient to the philosophical task of further delineating laws of nature.[43] This *philosophical* approach to laws of nature must be contrasted with the *scientific* approach to laws of nature. The scientific approach to laws of nature is to discover examples of the laws of nature.[44] One might counter that a valid approach to defining a term is by way of example. While true, merely providing examples of laws of nature is not only scientific in nature, as already pointed out, and not only rather involved as regarding a more informed view of the details of the scientific discipline, but would not bring much clarity to the concept

---

40. Armstrong, *What is a Law?*, 6. Armstrong reasons, "Theoretical calculations which can return men from the moon with split-second accuracy can hardly be mere fantasies. We may make an 'inference to the best explanation' from the predictive success of contemporary scientific theory to the conclusion that such theory mirrors at least some of the laws of nature over some part of their range with tolerable accuracy." Armstrong, *What is a Law?*, 6.

He continues, "Actually, it seems that even the rough-and-ready generalizations of pre-scientific practical wisdom represent a reasonable degree of approximation to genuine laws. Consider Hume's examples: fire burns, bread nourishes, water suffocates. If there were not laws to which these generalizations represent some rough approximation, then we should all be dead." Armstrong, *What is a Law?*, 6.

41. Armstrong, *What is a Law?*, 6.

42. Armstrong, *What is a Law?*, 6.

43. Armstrong, *What is a Law?*, 7. Armstrong suggests, "Our abstract formulae may actually exhibit the heart of many philosophical problems about laws of nature, disentangled from confusing empirical detail." Armstrong, *What is a Law?*, 7.

44. Armstrong, *What is a Law?*, 7. Armstrong defends this claim, "After all, it is not as if philosophers can expect to make any serious contribution to the *scientific* project of establishing what in fact the laws of nature are!" He also writes, "If more concrete examples are required, then we can take them from current or earlier science. We now know that Newton's Law of Universal Gravitation is not really a law. Yet we also know that Newton's formula approximates to the truth for at least a wide range of phenomena. Its predictive power would be inexplicable otherwise. So it makes a very good stand-in for a paradigm of a law of nature." Armstrong, *What is a Law?*, 7.

of a law of nature. Clarifying the character of the laws of nature is a task of philosophy of science, since in general the task of the philosophy of science is to identify, explain, and critique the presuppositions of science. One major assumption behind the overall argument of this book is that as the character of the laws of nature becomes clearer, so do the theological underpinnings of the philosophy of science, and hence science itself. The object is to show good reason to suspect that those theological underpinnings are Christian theistic.

As with most other areas in philosophy, when it comes to the task of explaining the philosophical concept of the laws of nature, virtually everyone disagrees. This disagreement applies no less to establishing an agreed upon taxonomy of disagreements about the character of the laws of nature than it does to the actual disagreements themselves. For the purposes of this chapter, different views of the laws of nature are divided into three basic categories. As noted above, this chapter will include an examination of laws of nature as regularities, logical necessities, and natural necessities, in that order. There are other, more nuanced understandings of the laws of nature that may or may not fit into each of these categories, but for the most part these three categories capture the essence of the debate over the character of the laws of nature. In this chapter, each category for understanding the laws of nature will be addressed in turn. At the same time, it will be argued that laws of nature are best understood as natural necessities, the third category mentioned above. Once the laws of nature have been more clearly explained, the hope is to show how reliance upon the concept of the laws of nature as natural necessities in science, induction, and everyday life best fits with reliance upon a theistic metaphysic. After arguing in chapter 4 that this understanding of the laws of nature equips the theist to answer the problem of induction in a way that secularists cannot answer the problem of induction, I return to the theistic metaphysic of Islam in order to demonstrate that relevant differences between the theistic systems of Christianity and Islam make Christianity a much better theistic worldview from which to carry out the scientific endeavor.

LAWS OF NATURE AS REGULARITIES

When it comes to the laws of nature, philosophers differ a great deal as to how they are to be construed. Not all philosophers agree that natural laws or causation exhibit the characteristic of objective necessity.[45] Objective necessity might be thought of as necessary relations that obtain outside of or apart from observers. Rejection of the element of objective necessity in accounts of laws of nature has become popular ever since the work of philosophers David Hume and Immanuel Kant.[46] Most interpreters of Hume agree that he attempted to reduce the "objective content of causal relations to constant conjunctions."[47] Some disagree with the traditional interpretation of Hume on this point. Nevertheless, the theory that was developed from what it is thought that Hume was stating is known as "Regularity Theory" (hereafter "RT").[48] RT identifies laws of nature with mere regularities. This section provides an explanation and critique of RT.

Before critiquing RT, Armstrong provides some brief remarks about the popularity of RT:

> The credit of this theory does not stand as high as it used to. But, although somewhat battered, it is still orthodoxy among analytic philosophers. In particular, there are still many who would *like* it to be true. While this liking persists, we can expect it to have a powerful, if not always acknowledged, influence. So it is still important to work through the theory in detail, and see just how unsatisfactory it is.[49]

Ellis agrees that the Humean metaphysic is a widely held position.[50] This position was extremely popular during the seventeenth and eighteenth centuries, and posits that matter is essentially passive, a theme to which Ellis returns in his critique of RT.[51]

The RT of causation stems from a strong empiricism. Some would no doubt count this close affinity with empiricism as a positive point of acceptance in its favor. According to RT, what is typically thought of as a "cause" and what is typically thought of as an "effect," in the context of some event, are empirically discerned.[52] For example, the first billiard

---

45. Beauchamp, *Philosophical Problems*, 36.
46. Beauchamp, *Philosophical Problems*, 36.
47. Beauchamp, *Philosophical Problems*, 36.
48. Beauchamp, *Philosophical Problems*, 36.
49. Armstrong, *What Is a Law?*, 9.
50. Ellis, *Scientific Essentialism*, 7.
51. Ellis, *Scientific Essentialism*, 7.
52. Beauchamp, *Philosophical Problems*, 36.

ball strikes ("cause") the second billiard ball, which moves ("effect"). But all that is observed are the striking action of the first billiard ball and the moving action of the second billiard ball. There is no third "thing" evident to the senses.[53]

Why might someone be interested in discerning some third thing through the senses? Because some believe that cause and effect operate as they do in various circumstances in virtue of some type of "necessity." In the case of the billiard balls above, if there is any "necessity" involved in the cause and effect relationship between the first billiard ball striking the second billiard ball, it is indiscernible through empirical means.[54] What follows from the realization that cause and effect relationships are indiscernible?

When a causal statement is made about some event like the one exemplified in the billiard ball illustration, the statement corresponds to a more general statement of causation.[55] For example, it seems the statement, "The first billiard ball struck the second billiard ball, *causing* the movement of the second billiard ball as an *effect*," is related to the more general causal statement, "Billiard balls move when struck by other billiard balls."[56]

What does RT look like without the specific example of billiard balls provided above? Any given causal statement is analyzed in virtue of "regularities."[57] Any given causal statement is an *instance* of regularity.[58] On RT, laws of nature are synonymous with regularities. Thus any causal statement is understood in terms of regularities, *and serves to corroborate* regularities.[59] Beauchamp summarizes the matter, "In this view, to regard an individual sequence as causal is to regard it as an instance of a general law, and to confirm that a sequence is causal is to confirm a causal law."[60]

---

53. Beauchamp, *Philosophical Problems*, 36.
54. Beauchamp, *Philosophical Problems*, 36.
55. Beauchamp, *Philosophical Problems*, 36.
56. Obviously, there is more than one way of construing the aforementioned type of statements, but they suffice to illustrate the point being made. Not only might the aforementioned causal statements be stated differently, but each *particular* causal statement might correspond, not just to *one* more general causal statement, but to others as well.
57. Beauchamp, *Philosophical Problems*, 36.
58. Beauchamp, *Philosophical Problems*, 36.
59. Beauchamp, *Philosophical Problems*, 36.
60. Beauchamp, *Philosophical Problems*, 36.

Beauchamp explains, "Since this theory requires that a logical connection be present between individual and general causal statements, it is easily identifiable as a *conceptual* version of Hume's *psychological* thesis that causal inference depends on a constant conjunction and mental association between ideas."[61] The concept of objective necessity has no place in the RT. RT draws attention, rather, to the *universality* of regularities, or laws of nature.[62] Universality is implicit in causal statements.[63] Faithful analysis of the laws of nature in RT regards the laws as "true, contingent, universal generalizations which are omnispatially and omnitemporally unrestricted in scope."[64] The RT account of laws of nature precludes identifying objective necessity in regularities and causal statements.[65]

Ellis similarly contends that Humean Supervenience is "the thesis that all modal properties (for example, natural necessity, natural possibility, objective probability, and so on) supervene on non-modal properties."[66]

> This thesis derives its plausibility from the Humean conception of reality as consisting of "atoms in the void"—of self-contained atomic objects or states of affairs that are located in space and time, and succeeding one another in ways determined by the laws of nature. The intuition to which this conception naturally gives rise is that if one can say which objects possessing what intrinsic qualities exist at which points in space and time, then one can describe the world completely. Therefore, any properties that describe what a thing must or might do in given circumstances must supervene on those that describe things as they are in themselves. That is, there could not be two worlds that are identical in respect of all non-modal properties that nevertheless differed in respect of modal properties.[67]

---

61. Beauchamp, *Philosophical Problems*, 36.
62. Beauchamp, *Philosophical Problems*, 36.
63. Beauchamp, *Philosophical Problems*, 36.
64. Beauchamp, *Philosophical Problems*, 36.
65. Beauchamp, *Philosophical Problems*, 36.
66. Ellis, *Scientific Essentialism*, 4.
67. Ellis, *Scientific Essentialism*, 4–5.

In RT, it is difficult to define modal properties.[68] The problem of explaining the truth of statements about the modal properties of things is heightened in RT.[69]

> Some Humeans have gone to quite extraordinary lengths to accommodate them, interpreting all modal statements as claims about relationships holding between possible worlds. But since every possible world, according to Humeanism, is a world without modal properties, it is hard to see how this is supposed to solve the problem. A universe of worlds without modalities is a universe without causal powers.[70]

Ellis tends to think of the Humean account of the world as "an agglomeration of logically independent states of affairs or self-contained atoms."[71]

Ellis spells out the remaining premises of this view as follows:

1. That causal relations hold between logically independent events.
2. That the laws of nature are behavioral regularities of some kind that could, in principle, be found to exist in any field of inquiry.
3. That the laws of nature are contingent.
4. That the identities of objects are independent of the laws of nature.
5. That the dispositional properties of things are not genuinely occurrent properties—which would have to be the same in all possible worlds—but are somewhat phoney world-bound properties that depend on what the laws of nature happen to be.[72]

Ellis is careful to explain that what a thing *is* and what a thing *does* on the Humean scheme are two very different, or at any rate independent or separate, things.[73] Identity is separate from "causal powers, capacities, and propensities."[74]

---

68. Ellis, *Scientific Essentialism*, 5.
69. Ellis, *Scientific Essentialism*, 5.
70. Ellis, *Scientific Essentialism*, 5. Of his own view which is discussed in the following section of this chapter, Ellis writes, "Scientific essentialists simply reject the Humean conception of reality, and the Supervenience Thesis that it entails." Ellis, *Scientific Essentialism*, 5.
71. Ellis, *Scientific Essentialism*, 5.
72. Ellis, *Scientific Essentialism*, 5.
73. Ellis, *Scientific Essentialism*, 283.
74. Ellis, *Scientific Essentialism*, 283.

> The dispositions of things are supposed to depend on the laws of nature, which might be different in different worlds. Thus, things that are constituted very differently might be disposed to behave in exactly the same way, if the laws of nature were sufficiently different (cf. the Catholic doctrine of transubstantiation), while things that have precisely the same constitutions might not, or might not always, be disposed to behave in the same ways in the same circumstances. In Hume's philosophy, the ways in which things are disposed to behave are supposed to depend, not on their intrinsic natures or constitutions, but on what the laws of nature happen to be. Therefore, for a neo-Humean, there is no solution to Hume's problem to be found by considering what sorts of things exist in the world.[75]

Ellis claims that the Humean account of the nature of reality precludes "genuine causal powers."[76] Though some items in the world do appear to possess causal powers insofar as they interact with other entities, "this is not due to any powers they may have by nature, or may have acquired, but to how they are required to behave by the laws that govern them."[77]

In defining RT, Armstrong offers a set of premises which are similar to those offered by Ellis above. Working from philosopher George Molnar, Armstrong relays the following information concerning RT,

> Molnar defines the Naive Regularity theory by using the device of semantic ascent. He says:
>
> p is a *statement* of a law of nature if and only iff:
> i. p is universally quantified
> ii. p is [omnitemporally and omnispatially] true
> iii. p is contingent
> iv. p contains only non-logical empirical predicates, apart from logical connectives and quantifiers.[78]

Armstrong contends the point of the above definition is "to pick out the *unrestricted* or *cosmic* uniformities from all other uniformities in nature, I will call them *Humean* uniformities, for obvious reasons."[79] These

---

75. Ellis, *Scientific Essentialism*, 283–84. Ellis refers to the problem of induction, discussed at length in chap. 4.

76. Ellis, *Scientific Essentialism*, 284.

77. Ellis, *Scientific Essentialism*, 284.

78. Armstrong, *What Is a Law?*, 12.

79. Armstrong, *What Is a Law?*, 12.

uniformities, as Armstrong calls them, are (as before with regularities) synonymous with laws of nature.[80]

RT defenders insist "that lawlikeness is explicable in terms of the type of support which unrestricted factual statements receive."[81] Beauchamp adds, "Scientific contexts, where laws have direct inductive confirmation as well as support from other laws, are thought to be especially important."[82] Beauchamp does an excellent job of explaining the nuances of this view:

> The general direction of thought about casual necessity by modern defenders of this Regularity Theory may be described as follows: In causal contexts, the word "necessity" does not function to describe or to convey information about the facts as such. Rather, it marks a distinction between laws and accidental generalizations (segregating laws from non-laws), which is needed for certain activities that involve the use of predictive and subjunctive expressions. The facts referred to by both sorts of generalization do not differ in that only one sort refers to a modal fact; on the contrary, the two types of generalization differ primarily in the strength of our commitment to their unrestricted universality. General causal statements are not initially used for prediction because they are recognized by empirical study as distinctively lawlike; rather, general statements are recognized as lawlike because they draw our confidence by faithfully serving predictive functions. There are, then, pragmatic reasons for employing the notion of necessity, but there are no physical or metaphysical grounds for supposing that some objective feature of nature is denoted.[83]

Lange notes that Humean philosophers, who hold to the RT of laws of nature, make the aspect of necessity in natural laws appear much less significant than what it really is.[84] In RT, "no profound metaphysical gap separates laws from accidents."[85]

While all sides admit that laws of nature most often manifest in regularities, it does not follow from this concession that the laws of nature

---

80. Armstrong, *What Is a Law?*, 12.
81. Beauchamp, *Philosophical Problems*, 74.
82. Beauchamp, *Philosophical Problems*, 74.
83. Beauchamp, *Philosophical Problems*, 74.
84. Lange, *Laws and Lawmakers*, xii. David Lewis is mentioned as an example.
85. Lange, *Laws and Lawmakers*, xii.

are *nothing more* than the aforementioned regularities.[86] RT is related to causal theory, but in evaluating the theory the focus falls on the RT understanding of laws.[87] The status of causal connections is not overly important with respect to the evaluation of RT. Focusing on the aspect of RT which holds regularities to constitute laws; two opportunities for attacking RT present themselves. The first is to argue that regularities are not *sufficient* for statements to count as laws, and the second is to argue that regularities are not *necessary* for statements to count as laws.[88] However, this section focuses on objections to RT that go beyond the two aforementioned concerns.

Regarding the concern that regularities are not sufficient for statements to count as laws, one problem facing the RT is how to distinguish between regularities, which are law, and universal generalizations, which are accidental.[89] According to Beauchamp, philosopher William Kneale "argues that the only appropriate way to distinguish lawlike generalizations from mere universal generalizations of fact is by resorting to the notion of natural necessity."[90] The difference between statements that exhibit nomological necessity and those that do not is a difference between being expressed modally or categorically.[91]

As Kneale sees the matter, laws are at least statements about what is empirically possible.[92]

> Nomological generalizations are properly expressed as modal statements, Kneale contends, while de facto universals are properly expressed as categorical statements. Defenders of the Regularity Theory have attempted to distinguish laws from non-laws by arguing that the former are expressed through universals of fact which are spatio-temporally unrestricted in scope, while the latter are merely universals of fact restricted to a limited range of instances. Kneale regards this device as insufficient. He agrees that laws are not established a priori and are not experientially

86. Armstrong, *What Is a Law?*, 12.
87. Armstrong, *What Is a Law?*, 12.
88. Armstrong, *What Is a Law?*, 12–13.
89. Beauchamp, *Philosophical Problems*, 36.
90. Beauchamp, *Philosophical Problems*, 36. Beauchamp notes, "Kneale does not confine his attention to any one species of laws of nature, but his thesis is quite clearly intended to cover both causal laws in general and the Regularity Theory in particular." Beauchamp, *Philosophical Problems*, 36.
91. Beauchamp, *Philosophical Problems*, 36.
92. Beauchamp, *Philosophical Problems*, 36–37.

certain, but he also contends that one of the essential functions of laws is to express a boundary on empirical possibility.[93]

Laws of nature are therefore statements of factual necessity, namely, that factual necessity which obtains in the relation between two things, X and Y. Beauchamp puts Kneale's understanding of true nomological statements as "'Whenever X, Y *must* ensue.'"[94]

Regarding counterfactuals, Armstrong suggests, "The statement that it is a law that Fs are Gs supports the counterfactual that if *a*, which is not in fact an F, were to be an F, then it would also be a G."[95] The difficulty for RT, once again, is that statements of Humean uniformity will not work to support counterfactuals as just explained.[96] Armstrong provides an example:

> Suppose it to be a mere uniformity that everybody in a certain room at a certain time is wearing a wrist-watch. There will be no particular reason to assert that if *a*, who was not in the room at the time, had been in the room, then *a* would have been wearing a wrist-watch.[97]

The illustration is designed to show that Humean uniformity, the mechanism that does the trick on RT, is incapable of supporting counterfactuals.[98] Laws are not synonymous with uniformities.[99] This critique is especially devastating for RT in the current context, because RT is not in a position to help with the scientific endeavor.

When pressed, RT defenders must, "reconsider the basis for the distinction between universals of fact and nomological generalizations

---

93. Beauchamp, *Philosophical Problems*, 36–37.
94. Beauchamp, *Philosophical Problems*, 37.
95. Armstrong, *What Is a Law?*, 146.
96. Armstrong, *What Is a Law?*, 146.
97. Armstrong, *What Is a Law?*, 46–47. Armstrong states an important qualification, "Notice that it is not part of this argument that law-statements are the only sort of statement which support counter-factuals. All the soldiers in a certain place at a certain time may be in uniform. Furthermore, this may be no accident. Orders may have been given which ensure that soldiers who are in that place at that time are all in uniform. Under these circumstances, the counterfactual statement 'If a soldier *a* had been in that place at that time, then he would have been wearing uniform' may well be accounted true. But it is not a law of nature that soldiers in that place at that time are wearing uniform." Armstrong, *What Is a Law?*, 47.
98. Armstrong, *What Is a Law?*, 47.
99. Armstrong, *What Is a Law?*, 47.

and also to explain the relation between laws and the counterfactual conditionals they support."[100] Regarding the first consideration, I take it that "nomological" here does not have anything to do with necessity, since that is the very aspect of law the Humean rejects. Nomological generalizations are, on RT, simply regularities, as explained above. Whether these regularities consist of frequent "connections" in the mind or in nature is not terribly important to the question of their necessity. Humeans will reject the claim that there is anything nomologically or naturally necessary about them.[101] How is it, on RT, that mere factual universals are distinguished from what RT wishes to label as law? That is one difficulty for RT. Another difficulty is to explain how what qualifies as law supports counterfactual conditionals.

The sufficiency of regularities for making statements count as laws is also plagued by what Armstrong calls "extensional difficulties."[102] These difficulties work against RT by beginning with a clear explanation of what Humean regularities (or "uniformities") are and then showing that it is possible some of these regularities exist but are not laws. This procedure establishes that a regularity is not necessarily a law, hence being a regularity is not a sufficient condition for also being a law.[103]

In thinking about RT, it is helpful to separate two distinct forms of statements from one another. There are "two types of logically contingent universal statements, namely, (1) factual statements which express constant conjunctions and (2) nomological generalizations which express empirically necessary connections."[104] Some non-Humeans take the modal component of necessity in statements of the second type as irreducible, or incapable of further explanation.[105] This irreducibility thesis is wrong. There is further explanation for nomic necessity in the Christian worldview because the triune God imposes his rational will upon creation as explained in the first two chapters. This "nomic necessity" is the very same idea of necessity that Hume sought to discredit in

---

100. Beauchamp, *Philosophical Problems*, 74.

101. But why? A lack of evidence for nomological necessity is not an evidence of lack of nomological necessity. Nevertheless, it is the empiricist preference to reject those beliefs not based upon any empirical evidence.

102. Armstrong, *What Is a Law?*, 13.

103. Armstrong, *What Is a Law?*, 13.

104. Beauchamp, *Philosophical Problems*, 37.

105. Beauchamp, *Philosophical Problems*, 37.

the midst of offering his version of the RT.[106] Kneale regards this concept of necessity, "an embarrassment to regularity analyses of causation."[107] The trouble here with the RT is prevalent in the literature. Beauchamp explains that some "stronger ingredient is needed to distinguish causal laws from accidental generalizations."[108] Regularities are not *sufficient* for statements to count as laws.

Regularities are not necessary conditions for laws of nature either. This proposition is argued for by offering examples of laws of nature which do not exist omnitemporally or omnispatially, and offering examples of laws of nature which are probabilistic.[109] Since temporally and spatially limited laws of nature, as well as probabilistic laws of nature, do not fulfill the conditions set forth by Armstrong per Molnar in (i) and (ii) above, it is not necessary to a law of nature to also be a Humean regularity or uniformity.[110]

How have Humeans typically responded to these apparent difficulties? According to Beauchamp, "Modern regularity advocates have generally agreed that these problems are genuine and that elucidation of the concept of lawlikeness merely in terms of 'unrestricted universals of fact' is inadequate, whether the context is a scientific one or an ordinary context involving causal generalizations."[111]

Ellis takes a different approach to arguing against RT. He argues not just against the RT of law, but *any* position that posits the nature of things in this world as essentially passive. Ellis's argument is that any view which takes the world to be passive cannot solve the problem of induction.

> Metaphysically, things in the world are to be thought of as puppets pushed around by the forces of God or nature. They are not themselves actors on the stage. Induction is therefore a problem for the broad philosophical tradition that has its roots in seventeenth and eighteenth century mechanism. It is not just a problem of empiricism. It is a problem for anyone who believes that the laws of nature are superimposed on a world that

---

106. Beauchamp, *Philosophical Problems*, 37.
107. Beauchamp, *Philosophical Problems*, 37.
108. Beauchamp, *Philosophical Problems*, 37.
109. Armstrong, *What Is a Law?*, 13.
110. Armstrong, *What Is a Law?*, 13.
111. Beauchamp, *Philosophical Problems*, 74.

is essentially passive, and that these laws are contingent, and not knowable *a priori*.[112]

Again, Ellis has expanded his attack beyond RT, since he speaks of such things as governing laws and God, and he believes his attack applies to any view which takes the world to be essentially passive in nature. Ellis's alternative view will be examined and evaluated shortly, and the problem of induction is the subject of chapter 4 of this book. There, I will agree with Ellis that the RT is incapable of providing a solution to the problem of induction, but not for the reason Ellis thinks; that is, not because reality is proposed as essentially passive on RT. What should nevertheless be gleaned from Ellis here are his remarks concerning the nature of the world on RT, and also his observation that RT stands in no position to answer the problem of induction.

Disregarding these two arguments against RT, consider a statement of RT such that "It is a law that Fs are Gs if and only if all Fs are Gs, where the latter is a Humean uniformity."[113] Armstrong rightfully points out, "The content of the law and the content of the uniformity are identical."[114] Why is this a difficulty for RT? Because "there appear to be cases where a law and its manifestation are not related in this straightforward way."[115] One potential example is found in probabilistic laws.[116] A second is found in functional laws.[117] The best way to describe the problem is as Armstrong does, "A gap can open up between law and manifestation of law."[118]

112. Ellis, *Scientific Essentialism*, 284.
113. Armstrong, *What Is a Law?*, 13.
114. Armstrong, *What Is a Law?*, 13.
115. Armstrong, *What Is a Law?*, 13.
116. Armstrong, *What Is a Law?*, 13. Armstrong explains, "Probabilistic laws *permit* distributions which do not reflect the probabilities involved. They are therefore not logically supervenient upon, they are logically independent of, particular matters of fact. *Prima facie*, probabilistic laws cannot be accommodated by the Regularity theory." Armstrong, *What Is a Law?*, 32.
117. Armstrong, *What Is a Law?*, 32. Armstrong explains at length, "We have already considered the possibility that a functional law might hold, but that there might be missing, that is, uninstantiated, values of the function (Ch. 2, Sec. 7). Suppose now that a functional law appears to hold, but that the instantiated values of the function do not suffice to determine the function uniquely. Many possible functions, perhaps infinitely many, are logically compatible with the instantiated values." Armstrong, *What Is a Law?*, 37–38. He continues, "The difficulty for the Naive Regularity theory is this. It seems natural to think that, although many possible functions are compatible with the data, there is in fact just one function which constitutes the law which actually governs the situation. But the relevant set of Humean uniformities do not logically determine what that function is." Armstrong, *What Is a Law?*, 37–38.
118. Armstrong, *What Is a Law?*, 37–38.

Finally, so-called "intensional difficulties" also plague the RT. Armstrong explains as follows:

> Suppose that there is a Humean uniformity to which a law does correspond, and suppose that the content of the uniformity is the same as the content of the law. Even so, there are a number of reasons for thinking that the law and the uniformity are not identical. For the law has properties which the manifestation lacks.[119]

It can be granted that particular things, even the same sorts of things in general, can act in different ways depending upon their contexts. It does not follow, of course, that the laws of nature are not in place in such circumstances. This does not follow because, in fact, the laws of nature are precisely that which account for the things acting the way they do, given these different contexts, or sets of conditions. However, some philosophers have suggested that the laws of nature themselves could, in theory, be different depending upon place or time. Armstrong explains, "The suggestion is rather that the same sorts of thing may behave differently at different places and times, although the conditions which prevail are not different *except* in respect of place and time."[120] One might quibble over whether or not arbitrarily varying scientific laws are even possible, but there is no need.[121] This is because regardless of our inclinations regard-

---

119. Armstrong, *What Is a Law?*, 37–38. Armstrong discusses these problems more in chap. 4 of his own work.

120. Armstrong, *What Is a Law?*, 24. According to Armstrong, "One philosopher who held such a view was Whitehead. He believed that the laws of nature might be different in different 'cosmic epochs.' (see 1933, Ch. 7, Sec. 5. Further references are given in Beauchamp 1972.)." Armstrong, *What Is a Law?*, 24. Armstrong also makes an important qualification via the observations of philosopher Michael Tooley, "As Michael Tooley has pointed out to me, however, there are two possibilities which can be distinguished here. It might be that, although irreducibly different laws obtain in different cosmic epochs, these laws are governed by a single second-order law. This second-order law determines that, for any time t, if the laws at time t are L, then, given a time $g(t)$ which is a certain function of t, the laws at $g(t)$ will be a certain function, f, of L. The second possibility is that there is no such higher-order law. It is the second possibility which most clearly poses problems for the Regularity theory, and is the possibility which I wish to consider." Armstrong, *What Is a Law?*, 24–25.

121. Armstrong, *What Is a Law?*, 25. Armstrong did not initially consider the existence of arbitrarily varying scientific laws a possibility, but changed his mind. He explains, "If laws of nature are relations of universals, as I shall be arguing in the latter half of this book, it seems not to be a possibility. However, a case of Michael Tooley's, to be discussed in the next section, suggests that laws which essentially involve particulars must be admitted as a logical possibility. If so, the possibility of arbitrarily

ing the possibility of laws of nature arbitrarily varying at different places and times, the adherent to RT is not really in a position to reject this possibility.[122]

> The reason for this is that only a rather small conceptual gap separates cosmic, that is, Humean, uniformities from large-scale uniformities which are less than cosmic. Suppose that there are no cosmic uniformities at all, but that there are large-scale regularities of the sort we are envisaging. This supposition is logically compatible with all our observational evidence. How should the Regularity theorist describe the situation? 'There are no laws, but there are large-scale regularities' or 'There are laws, but they do not have cosmic scope'? The latter seems far closer to the pragmatic and positivist spirit which animates the Regularity analysis.[123]

The Humean has no empirical evidence to offer against the possibility that regularities are not cosmic, but are large-scale. If regularities are merely large-scale, then, of course, there are laws of nature which do not exhibit the property of Humean uniformity. And if there are laws of nature on RT that are not Humean uniformities, then RT faces what Armstrong calls the "paradox of the heap."[124]

> Where, in the gamut of possible cases, do laws of limited scope end and merely accidental collocations begin? Presumably it will have to be said that there is no conceptually sharp dividing line. Laws fade off into states of affairs which are not laws.[125]

The problem gets even worse for the RT adherent because, "It seems logically possible that even a small-scale, local, possibility could be a

---

different laws in different cosmic epochs will have to be allowed, and the theory of laws modified to admit the possibility." Armstrong, *What Is a Law?*, 25.

122. Armstrong, *What Is a Law?*, 25.

123. Armstrong, *What Is a Law?*, 25.

124. Armstrong, *What Is a Law?*, 25. This is also known as the "sorites paradox." The term comes from the Greek word for sand, which one might think of as existing in a heap.

125. Armstrong, *What Is a Law?*, 25. Armstrong suggests that if cosmic epochs are possible, then RT is pressed toward anti-Realism. He explains, "What constitutes a law of nature becomes a bit more arbitrary and conventional." Armstrong, *What Is a Law?*, 26.

LAWS OF NATURE   119

law or manifestation of a law."[126] All versions of RT fall prey to this fatal objection.[127]

> The theory cannot claim that every local uniformity is a law. That would be madness. But if some *untested* local uniformities can be laws, how is the theory to mark off those local uniformities which are laws from those which are not?[128]

This argument should serve as a decisive refutation of RT.

One can also argue against RT upon the basis of intuitions about necessity and laws. One more stab at RT runs, "Suppose it to be a law of nature that Fs are Gs, and that this law issues in the (actually instantiated) uniformity that each F is a G."[129] (It is hard to imagine a more ideal set of assumptions for RT.)

> Suppose it to be a law that Fs are Gs, and suppose there to be a plurality of Fs. Consider one of these: *a*. By hypothesis, it is a G. We can say that *a*'s being F nomically necessitates *a*'s being G.[130]

What Armstrong writes here is confusing until one realizes that Armstrong is working from a view of law that includes necessity. The nomic necessitation above is at home in a theory of the laws of nature that appeals to some concept of necessity outside of the empirical experience required by RT. Recall that necessity is by definition not a part of RT. If RT is in view in the instance of the affairs described above, then the necessity which obtains cannot be in virtue of the actual state of affairs. The nomic necessity Armstrong has in mind here apparently obtains in virtue of the deductive relationships between the terms in question, at least from the perspective of RT. So, Armstrong asks his readers to think of the instance described above from the perspective of the RT.

> What does the theory postulate to obtain? Nothing but the two states of affairs: *a*'s being F, and *a*'s being G. Yet such a mere conjunction of states of affairs can obtain where there is absolutely no nomic connection between the states of affairs

126. Armstrong, *What Is a Law?*, 26
127. Armstrong, *What Is a Law?*, 27.
128. Armstrong, *What Is a Law?*, 27. Armstrong believes his own view avoids the consequences of this argument because "the theory that laws of nature are relations between universals can be generalized in what I find a rather unintuitive way." Armstrong, *What Is a Law?*, 27. But this generalization will not work in RT.
129. Armstrong, *What Is a Law?*, 39.
130. Armstrong, *What Is a Law?*, 39.

> involved. For the Regularity theory, the essence of the nomic connection is not to be found in the two states of affairs and any dyadic relation which holds just between them. Rather, *a*'s being F nomically necessitates *a*'s being G only because *the other Fs are also all of them Gs*. That the conjunction of states of affairs is a case of nomic necessitation is a *purely relational property* of the conjunction.[131]

The conjunction just so *happens* to involve nomic necessity. This revelation offends our intuitions. For certainly, "We think that if *a*'s being F is nomically to necessitate *a*'s being G, then at least part of what must exist is some direct, dyadic relation holding between the two particular states of affairs."[132] But there is no necessary relation between the states of affairs.

Armstrong describes a second, similar case. This time, instead of there being an actual uniformity in terms of every F being G, as above, there is only one instance of F.

> Suppose now that *a* is the only instance of an F in the whole history of the universe, and that it is still a G. In this case the Naive Regularity theory, at least, is forced to say that it is a law that Fs are Gs. *a*'s being F necessitates *a*'s being G. But this also is unintuitive. For it is natural to say that, given *a* is F and is G, and given that this is the only F, it is still a further question whether or not a relation of nomic necessitation holds between the two states of affairs.[133]

The second example reveals what may have been hidden by the first example. It runs against intuition to describe something as "law" when the ultimate relations that law appeals to in order to set it apart as law exhibit no necessity. The relations appear to be accidental. Intuition guards us against accepting RT with cases of instantiated *and* uninstantiated uniformities. In addition to the aforementioned difficulty, one wonders why the single instance of *a* as F and G should be considered a regularity anyway.

---

131. Armstrong, *What Is a Law?*, 39.

132. Armstrong, *What Is a Law?*, 40. Armstrong explains, "This is part of what Hume was saying when he demanded a necessary connection between particular cause and particular effect over and above the fact that they instantiate a regularity." Armstrong, *What Is a Law?*, 40.

133. Armstrong, *What Is a Law?*, 40.

The sticky situation of RT becomes even clearer in Armstrong's next hypothetical. Assume, again, the law "Fs are Gs."[134] If this statement is an expression of an actual law in a non-RT sense, that is, if it exhibits some form of necessary relation, then it also possesses explanatory value. For example, imagine a scenario where, "a number of Fs have all been observed, and that each is a G."[135] Additionally, "No F that is not a G has been observed."[136] This state of affairs leads to questions about why it might be the case that this state of affairs has, up until now, consistently rendered the same results. In other words, intuitively, we begin to sift for an answer as to why this relationship continues to obtain in states of affairs. The non-RT law above that "Fs are Gs" *explains* the situation.[137] Not so with RT. Armstrong states the difficulty as follows:

> Suppose, however, that laws are mere regularities. We are then trying to explain the fact that all observed Fs are Gs by appealing to the hypothesis that all Fs are Gs. Could this hypothesis serve as an explanation? It does not seem that it could. That all Fs are Gs is a complex state of affairs which is in part *constituted* by the fact that all observed Fs are Gs. 'All Fs are Gs' can even be rewritten as 'All observed Fs are Gs and all unobserved Fs are Gs.' As a result, trying to explain why all observed Fs are Gs by postulating that all Fs are Gs is a case of trying to explain something by appealing to a state of affairs part of which is the thing to be explained. But a fact cannot be used to explain itself. And that all *unobserved* Fs are Gs can hardly explain why all observed Fs are Gs.[138]

There may be, of course, *good reason* to suspect that "all Fs are Gs," since every F that has been observed up until now is a G.[139] Yet this observation does not explain *why* it is the case that every F that has been observed until now is a G. That question is only answered with further insight into the nature of the relationship between Fs and Gs. The presence of apparent uniformities or regularities seems acceptable evidence for the belief that laws are involved, but this presence of regularity does not *explain* the

---

134. Armstrong, *What Is a Law?*, 40.
135. Armstrong, *What Is a Law?*, 40.
136. Armstrong, *What Is a Law?*, 40.
137. Armstrong, *What Is a Law?*, 40. Armstrong opines, "If such a law really holds, then the explanation will be quite a good one." Armstrong, *What Is a Law?*, 40.
138. Armstrong, *What Is a Law?*, 40.
139. Armstrong, *What Is a Law?*, 40.

laws.[140] Armstrong illustrates the point with an analogy. He writes, "The presence of smoke is a good reason for thinking that fire is present. But it is not an explanation of the presence of fire."[141] It should be pointed out that "Laws, however, explain regularities."[142] The RT does not at all include nomic necessity in the laws of nature. In fact, the fruit of RT is circularity.

> Even if we take the Humean uniformity itself, that all Fs are Gs, it seems to be an explanation of this uniformity that it is a law that Fs are Gs. But, given the Regularity theory, this would involve using the law to explain itself. We need to put some 'distance' between the law and its manifestation if the law is to explain the manifestation.[143]

The RT lacks intuitive appeal, explanatory value, and ends in circularity.

Humean uniformities are "statements of unrestricted, universally quantified, material implication."[144] If one is content to attempt the confirmation of the aforementioned statements, then the problems associated with RT are not really problems for the Humean, unless he or she happens to be persuaded by Armstrong's appeals to intuition. However, the problems do still apply to RT. Armstrong's arguments pose difficulties for RT when they are applied to the task of confirming statements like, "It is a law of nature that Fs are Gs."[145] In those cases, "statements of mere Humean uniformity will have a property which statements of purported laws of nature lack."[146]

The constant worry for RT is that so-called "laws of nature" are mere accidents. A number of arguments were offered above to show just how pressing a concern this is for RT. If laws in RT are merely accidental, then they cannot serve as scientific assumptions. Traditionally, laws of nature are contrasted with accidents.[147] The meaning of the term "accident" in the context of the laws of nature must not be confused with

---

140. Armstrong, *What Is a Law?*, 40. As Armstrong notes, "But a good reason for P is not necessarily an explanation of P." Armstrong, *What Is a Law?*, 40.

141. Armstrong, *What Is a Law?*, 40.

142. Armstrong, *What Is a Law?*, 41.

143. Armstrong, *What Is a Law?*, 41.

144. Armstrong, *What Is a Law?*, 41.

145. Armstrong, *What Is a Law?*, 41.

146. Armstrong, *What Is a Law?*, 41.

147. Lange, *Laws and Lawmakers*, 4.

what is meant by the term in non-philosophical, common discourse. Philosopher Marc Lange asks, "Please do not confuse it with the ordinary meaning of 'accident'—what I mean when I say to you, 'Our meeting here was no accident; I was looking for you,' or when the owner of a car dealership confidentially informs us, 'It is no accident that every car in my showroom smells so fresh; I put the same chemical in each of them, to give them all that fabled 'new car' smell.'"[148] This ordinary sense of accident means something like unintentional, coincidental, or sharing no common explanation.[149] This sense of accident is not the philosophical sense of the term relevant to this discussion.

> An "accident" in that sense is simply a truth that does not follow from the natural laws (and the "broadly logical" truths) alone. In other words, an accident could have failed to hold without any violation of the natural laws. For example, no natural law has to be violated for the showroom to contain a car without the "new car" smell.[150]

Having attempted to define "accident" as used here, it may still be helpful to present another illustration of the concept. Lange does so as follows:

> Take another example: suppose that many apples are hanging on the tree in my backyard, and all of them are now ripe. Their ripeness is an accident, since even if some of them were not ripe, the laws of nature could still have all held. If the warm weather had arrived a few weeks later, for instance, then the apples would not yet have been ripe, though the natural laws would have been no different. Nevertheless, it is no coincidence that every single one of those apples is ripe today. Their ripeness resulted from the recent weather conditions, the levels at which various plant hormones have been flowing through the tree, and so forth. Since each of these factors was common to every one of those apples, they all ripened together. Certain laws of nature governing chemical reactions are also responsible for the apples' ripeness. These laws determined how the weather, the plant hormones, and so forth influenced the rate at which the apples ripened. Again, that there are laws and other conditions explaining why all of those apples are now ripe does not keep this fact from qualifying as an accident. Those other conditions are themselves accidental; there is no explanation of the ripeness of any of those

---

148. Lange, *Laws and Lawmakers*, 4.
149. Lange, *Laws and Lawmakers*, 4–5.
150. Lange, *Laws and Lawmakers*, 5.

apples that appeals to no accidents at all, but exclusively to laws of nature.[151]

Are Humean uniformities, or regularities, merely accidents in the Regularity Theory of laws of nature? It would seem so. And while much more could be said on the topic of why philosophers continue to hold something akin to the RT, and why others so vehemently disagree with the picture of the world presented in RT, it should suffice, given the considerations of this section, to look elsewhere for a sustainable view of the laws of nature.

LAWS OF NATURE AS LOGICAL NECESSITIES

While the laws of nature are to be contrasted with accidents, they should also be contrasted with what are known as "broadly logical" truths.[152] Broadly logical truths are logically necessary truths. Consider the account of logical necessity offered by philosopher Alfred Tarski, "A statement is logically necessary, according to Tarski, if and only if it is deductible from a statement function which is satisfied by every model."[153] Beauchamp notes, "Such universally valid statement functions are true in all possible worlds."[154] A brief description of possible worlds semantics may be helpful here. A "possible world" is just one of many, many (potentially infinite) ways the actual world might have been.[155] There are some things in the actual world which could have been other than what they are, logically speaking, and these things which could have been different are conceptualized along with all of the other relevant contingent features of the hypothetical and labeled a possible world.[156]

Mathematical, conceptual, logical, and metaphysical truths can be considered broadly logical truths. Lange provides an illustration to help discern what is meant by a truth being broadly logical, or logically necessary. He explains the following:

---

151. Lange, *Laws and Lawmakers*, 5.
152. Lange, *Laws and Lawmakers*, 4.
153. Beauchamp, *Philosophical Problems*, 38.
154. Beauchamp, *Philosophical Problems*, 38.
155. Nash, *Life's Ultimate Questions*, 212.
156. Nash, *Life's Ultimate Questions*, 212.

A broadly logical truth possesses a kind of *necessity* that is possessed neither by natural laws nor by accidents. For instance, one kind of broadly logical truth consists of the mathematical truths, such as the fact that there is no way to divide 23 evenly by 3. There does not merely *happen* to be no integer that added to itself, and then added again, equals 23—in the way that there merely happens to be no gold cube larger than a cubic mile (and even in the way that like charges merely happen to repel rather than to attract). Rather, there *couldn't* have been an integer that added to itself, and then added again, equals 23. That it is *impossible* to divide 23 evenly by 3 explains why no one has ever succeeded in figuring out a way to do so, no matter how much mathematics she knows—and why every time someone tries to divide 23 objects evenly into thirds, she fails. None of these efforts could have succeeded. They all fail because they must; their failure was inevitable. Analogous considerations apply to other kinds of broadly logical truths, such as conceptual truths (for example, "All sisters are female"), narrowly logical truths ("Either all emeralds are green or some emerald is not green"), and metaphysical truths ("Red is a color" or perhaps "Water is $H2O$").[157]

The explanation by way of examples from Lange provides some insight into the character of logical necessity. Although Lange claims that this type of necessity is not of the sort enjoyed by laws of nature, some philosophers disagree, arguing that laws of nature *are* logically necessary.[158]

For example, Ellis holds a minority position on the laws of nature he calls "Scientific Essentialism" (hereafter SE).[159] According to Ellis, a modern science wants to say that our world "is a dynamic world consisting of more or less transient objects which are constantly interacting with each other, and whose identities would appear to depend on their roles in these processes."[160] In this view, there is very little "gap" between what an entity *is*, and what it *does*. More than that, the gap between appearance and reality is collapsed, making it "impossible—metaphysically impossible—for

---

157. Lange, *Laws and Lawmakers*, 5–6.

158. Lange is of course aware of this disagreement. He is just expressing his disagreement in the quote that's provided.

159. Ellis, *Scientific Essentialism*, 1. Ellis explains, "It is not a view that has been widely accepted in modern times. One has to go all the way back to Aristotle to find a truly notable defender of essentialism." Ellis, *Scientific Essentialism*, 1.

160. Ellis, *Scientific Essentialism*, 2.

a proton or any other fundamental particle to have a causal role different from the one it actually has."[161] Ellis suggests the following:

> The assumption is plausible, I suggest, because a proton would appear to have no identity at all apart from its role in causal processes. If this is right, then the laws concerning the behavior of protons and their interactions cannot be just accidental—that is, laws which could well have been otherwise. On the contrary, it is essential to the nature of a proton that it be disposed to interact with other things as it does. Its causal powers, capacities, and propensities are not just accidental properties of protons, which depend on what the laws of nature happen to be, but essential properties, without which there would be no protons, and which protons could not lose without ceasing to exist (or gain without coming into being).[162]

Notice, as already mentioned that the identity of a thing, in this example a proton, is bound up with its disposition. Presumably if something does not *act* like a proton is "supposed" to behave, then that thing is not a proton.[163] Contingency is not a feature of the laws of nature in Ellis's scheme because the way things behave is essential to the nature of those things.[164] Ellis summarizes his view, "According to scientific essentialism, therefore, all of the laws of nature, from the most general (for example, the conservation laws and the global structural principles) to the more specific (for example, laws defining the structures of molecules of various kinds, or specific laws of chemical interaction) derive from the essential properties of the object and events that constitute it, and must hold in any world of the same natural kinds as ours."[165] As metaphysically necessary, the laws of nature in this view are broadly logical truths.

161. Ellis, *Scientific Essentialism*, 2.

162. Ellis, *Scientific Essentialism*, 2.

163. This explanation does not, however, solve the difficulty of explaining how the thing we believe to be a proton should act, but rather diverts attention away to the meanings of words in what is known as the "No True Scotsman" fallacy. Musgrave, *Common Sense*, 166–69.

164. The notion that the behavior of things is essential to their natures is counterintuitive and inhospitable to the reality of change.

165. Ellis, *Scientific Essentialism*, 4. Ellis writes, "The possible displays of any given causal power are all processes that are essentially similar in their structure and that differ from each other only in ways that lie within the permitted range variation for the kind of process concerned. The causal powers of an object are thus the real essences of the causal processes that can occur when that object acts causally. The gravitational mass of an object, for example, is the dispositional property it has that determines

Ellis considers another example of a particle. Assuming this particle "has a certain mass and a certain charge essentially, then it must generate such fields in any world in which it might exist, and have precisely the same effects on things of just the same kinds."[166] One of the implications for this view important to the current discussion is as follows:

> First, it implies that these laws of nature are metaphysically necessary. Since they are immanent in the world, the laws of nature cannot be changed, without the world itself being changed. And things of the kinds that do exist in this world could not exist in any other world in which the laws of nature affecting them are supposed to be different.[167]

The implication of Ellis's view that it renders the laws of nature metaphysically necessary is not lost on Ellis.[168]

> There are natural dispositional properties that are genuinely occurrent, and which therefore act in the same ways in all possible worlds. These include the causal powers of the most fundamental kinds of things, so that things of these same kinds, existing in any other world, would be disposed to behave in just the same ways.[169]

Aside from broadly logical truths stemming from metaphysical necessity, Ellis affirms the place of certain *logically necessary* truths in his account of the laws of nature, truths which would obtain *in every possible world*.

Ellis's account of the laws of nature is well-crafted, though obscure. Nature itself is contingent, and so the idea that the laws of nature are broadly logically necessary is counterintuitive. But for those who are unconvinced by such a seemingly arbitrary assertion, there have been some philosophical objections leveled at the view in question. Ellis

---

its causal role in generating gravitational fields, and hence the effects it has on other objects immersed in these fields. The charge on an object is the dispositional property it has that determines its causal role in generating electromagnetic fields, and hence the effects it has on other objects that are in or moving through these fields." Ellis, *Scientific Essentialism*, 6.

166. Ellis, *Scientific Essentialism*, 6.
167. Ellis, *Scientific Essentialism*, 6.
168. Ellis, *Scientific Essentialism*, 7. He explicitly states, "The laws of nature are not contingent, but metaphysically necessary." Ellis, *Scientific Essentialism*, 7.
169. Ellis, *Scientific Essentialism*, 8.

himself references a serious objection "from the theory of counter-factual conditionals."[170]

> The objection is this: If truth conditions for such conditionals are to be based on real possibilities, rather than just epistemic possibilities, as surely they should be, then the truth conditions for some perfectly ordinary, and highly assertible, conditionals will turn out to be problematic. I have to admit the soundness of this objection.[171]

This objection serves as one example that SE has not gone unchallenged.

Lange understands that the laws of nature in scientific essentialism are necessary in a metaphysical sense.[172] He proposes a counterfactual to call attention to a significant weakness in the SE view. Lange asks us to consider the counterfactual statement, "Had I worn an orange shirt, then there would still have been gravity (rather than, for example, a force varying with the inverse-cube of the distance)."[173] Gravity is an inverse-square force. Recall that, according to SE, gravity *must* act as an inverse-square force. This "must" is a must of *metaphysical necessity*. Laws are dispositions necessarily connected to essences or identities. But does it follow that "gravity would still have been one of the universe's forces, had I worn

---

170. Ellis, *Scientific Essentialism*, 12.

171. Ellis, *Scientific Essentialism*, 12. Ellis admits this objection presents a serious difficulty for his position on the laws of nature, but also believes he may have an answer to it, which he offers later in his book. He writes, "But then I never did think that one could provide adequate truth conditions for counter-factual conditionals, and I have always thought that 'possible worlds' semantics for such conditionals and other modal claims were phoney. For such conditionals, and indeed for logic generally, I argued (Ellis, 1979) that what is needed is not a theory about their truth conditions, but a theory about their acceptability conditions, and that we should stop thinking of logic as the theory of truth preservation, and begin to think of it, as subjective probability theorists always have, as part of the theory of rationality." Ellis, *Scientific Essentialism*, 12–13.

172. Lange, *Laws and Lawmakers*, 82. Lange writes, "According to scientific essentialism, laws are metaphysically necessary: for example, being electrically charged essentially involves having the power to exert and to feel forces in accordance with certain particular laws, such as Coulomb's law and Heaviside's equation. Essentialism takes counterfactuals, such as 'Had I worn an orange shirt, then gravity would still have declined with the square of the distance,' to be grounded in essences (in this case, gravity's)." Lange, *Laws and Lawmakers*, 82.

173. Lange, *Laws and Lawmakers*, 82.

an orange shirt"?[174] The question is proposed with respect to a counterfactual state of affairs, rather than with respect to gravity *qua* gravity.

Lange begins his critique of SE by claiming that, in response to counterfactuals like the one in question, "some essentialists have maintained that our *world's* essence determines what natural kinds of things exist."[175] This is an interesting move to be sure, but it seems to only push the potential difficulty back a step. Lange quotes extensively from Ellis in an attempt to fairly represent how an SE adherent would think through the potential difficulty encapsulated in the aforementioned counterfactual. Lange's concerns are quoted at length.

> Brian Ellis, for instance, says that a world of the same natural kind as the actual world must also have the same basic ontology of kinds of objects, properties, and processes. It must, for example, be a physical world made up of particles and fields of the same fundamental natural kinds as those that are fundamental in this world. If electrons and protons are such fundamental natural kinds in this world, then they must also exist in every similar world.
>
> Thus, it is a metaphysical necessity that any world of the same kind as the actual world possesses gravity and lacks a similar inverse-cube force. Ellis writes:
>
> Could there be fundamental natural kinds of objects, properties, or processes existing in worlds similar to ours that do not exist in our world? In other words, could a world of the same natural kind as ours have a richer basic ontology? I think not. A world with an ontology otherwise like ours, which included some extra ingredients, could . . . not be a world of the same specific natural kind as ours . . . Worlds with different basic ontologies cannot be essentially the same.
>
> Therefore, since the counterfactual supposition "Had I worn an orange shirt" supposes a world of the same kind as the actual world, there would still have been gravity rather than a similar but inverse-cube force.[176]

Lange does not appear at all satisfied with this response from Ellis. I find myself in general agreement with Lange's criticisms of the move the SE advocate has taken.

---

174. Lange, *Laws and Lawmakers*, 82.
175. Lange, *Laws and Lawmakers*, 82–83.
176. Lange, *Laws and Lawmakers*, 83.

Lange offers four reasons for rejecting what Ellis offers in defense of SE. First, the SE advocate is only positing an "essence" of the *world* in order to justify a law that has just come under attack. It is not at all clear that there is something like an "essence" to a world.[177] Second, the counterfactual in question does not require the supposition of a world like unto the actual (or instantiated) world. The idea that another world the same as the one we find ourselves in is included in or implied by the counterfactual statement is simply false.[178] Third, the claim that a world that is "the same natural kind" as the actual (or instantiated) world is the most similar possible world where the antecedent of the counterfactual statement obtains (the wearing of an orange shirt) is an unsubstantiated assertion.[179] Fourth and finally, on SE, all sets of nomically necessary laws are the same, and cannot differ as to strength.[180] This final concern with SE is especially troublesome to Lange, who believes that laws exhibit themselves in strata.

Two theories of laws of nature have been offered thus far. The first was RT. For all of its popularity, there are enough objections to RT for one to look elsewhere when it comes to understanding the laws of nature. The second was SE. Though SE is somewhat obscure, being found mostly in Aristotle and a small number of modern day defenders, it too faces numerous difficulties like RT. A viable theory of laws seems to lie somewhere in between RT and SE. The next section reviews the categories of accidents and necessities. Two more critiques are offered, one of RT and one of SE. Then a popular theory is proposed wherein laws of nature exhibit *nomic* or *natural* necessity. This theory is offered as the theory of laws of nature that is most consistent with the theology of chapter 1 and chapter 2 and most accommodating to philosophical concerns.

LAWS OF NATURE AS NATURAL NECESSITIES

A number of arguments were offered against the RT and SE theories of laws of nature. These arguments serve to corroborate two more arguments offered here. The first argument is against RT, and the second is against SE. However, each of these two arguments assumes that something like

---

177. Lange, *Laws and Lawmakers*, 83.
178. Lange, *Laws and Lawmakers*, 83–84.
179. Lange, *Laws and Lawmakers*, 84.
180. Lange, *Laws and Lawmakers*, 85.

the Christian theism spelled out in earlier chapters is true. For this reason, these arguments are not likely to be persuasive to a non-Christian. Rather, these two arguments grant insight into the way Christians might think consistently about laws of nature. That having been stated, these two arguments *could* still maintain some persuasiveness for the non-Christian in terms of their coherence with an exhaustive view of the debate over the character of laws of nature, and in virtue of what merely serve as corroborative arguments for the Christian.

First, against RT, or Humean Regularities is the thesis that Scripture implies such things as nomic necessities imposed on creation by God. Second, against SE or scientific essentialism it is asserted that these aforementioned nomic necessities must not be true in every possible world, lest the freedom of God be impinged upon by these logically necessary relations in every possible state of affairs. Consider briefly the principles of logic in their relation to God. The person who believes that principles of logic are not *necessarily* true would most likely grant that laws of nature are likewise not *necessarily* true in a modal sense, as they are in SE. And yet, even the person who grants that principles of logic *are* necessarily true, true in every possible world, would still likely think that the laws of *nature* are nevertheless only contingently true. There seem to be relevant differences between the way the laws of logic and the laws of nature work. The laws of nature might not be the same in other possible worlds. Each of these persons would, then, agree that God is nowise *bound* by the laws of nature, whatever type of necessity they exhibit. It follows that the laws of nature are *contingent*, rather than *necessary* in a broadly logical sense. This is the second argument from theological presuppositions concerning Christian theism. If God is free with respect to the laws of nature, then the laws of nature are not the same in every possible world. God is free with respect to the laws of nature (as he is free with respect to all of his creation). Therefore, the laws of nature are not the same in every possible world, and SE appears to be false. Again, some may wish to press this argument into the realm of other broadly logical necessities like principles of logic, universals, properties, possible worlds, and the like, but that is another argument for another time. These arguments presupposing Christian theism are corroborated by the independent arguments against Humean Regularities and Scientific Essentialism examined earlier.

The laws of nature must be distinguished from accidents. The RT theory of laws appears to leave no room for distinguishing laws from accidents. However, the laws of nature must also be distinguished from broadly logical truths. The SE theory of laws appears to leave no room for distinguishing laws from broadly logical truths. If the laws of nature are not accidents and are not broadly logical truths, then what are they? Lange explains, "Laws of nature have traditionally been thought to possess a distinctive species of necessity (dubbed 'natural' necessity)."[181] What does this species of necessity, which sets laws of nature apart from both accidents and broadly logical truths, look like? Lange provides an example:

> For example, take the fact that any two positive (or negative) electric charges repel each other. Because this regularity holds as a matter of natural law, it is inevitable, unavoidable—necessary. An exception to it is (naturally) impossible. Any two like charges not only as a matter of fact *do* repel each other—they *must*. Yet the laws are also thought to be contingent truths; unlike the broadly logical truths, the laws of nature could have been different from the way they actually are.[182]

Admittedly, this way of putting the matter is rather strange. What exactly is it to be both *necessary* and *contingent*?

Lange provides some definitional insight into the aforementioned difficulty. Lange explains, "Whatever natural necessity is, it must deserve the name by truly being a variety of *necessity*—a species of the same genus as the variety (or varieties) of necessity possessed by broadly logical truths."[183] Lange makes the following important qualification, "Although the laws are necessary, they are not *as necessary as* the truths possessing logical, conceptual, mathematical, metaphysical, or moral necessity."[184] Thus, "Natural necessity is a weaker variety of necessity."[185] The difficulty of understanding the character of natural laws as necessary is not lost on most philosophers. However, it is worth pointing out that since other views of the laws of nature face significant difficulties, as with RT and SE, one is left attempting to make sense of how laws of nature are both necessary and contingent.

181. Lange, *Laws and Lawmakers*, xi.
182. Lange, *Laws and Lawmakers*, xi–xii.
183. Lange, *Laws and Lawmakers*, 45.
184. Lange, *Laws and Lawmakers*, 45.
185. Lange, *Laws and Lawmakers*, 45. Past events are also necessary but not in a logical or metaphysical sense.

Plantinga views this problem of understanding the necessity of laws of nature as the very place Christian theism is most helpful with respect to laws of nature in general and a thoroughgoing philosophy of science.[186] To help illustrate the difference between accidents and necessities in the relevant sense needed for understanding laws of nature, Plantinga asks his readers to note that "not just any true universal statement is a law."[187] He provides three examples of true universal propositions that are nevertheless not laws. The three examples are, "Everyone in my house is over 50 years old,"[188] "Every sphere made of gold is less than ½ mile in diameter,"[189] and "No provost of a large university climbs at the 5.12 level."[190] Plantinga explains, "While these propositions are true and universal in form, they aren't laws. Why not? One answer: because they are merely *accidentally* true. They are accidentally true universal generalizations; laws, however, are not accidentally true."[191] Plantinga has a point, and the point is intuitively plausible. Laws are not merely accidentally true. If laws are not merely accidentally true, then laws are in some sense necessary.

Plantinga is helpful here as well. He offers several examples that seem to show that laws are in some sense necessary, with a major qualification.

> However, it seems that laws are not *logically* necessary; it seems logically possible that, for example, there may be a pair of particles that do not attract each other with a force inversely proportional to the square of the distance between them, even if Newton's inverse square law is indeed a natural law. It seems possible that God accelerate an object from a speed slower than c, the speed of light, to a speed greater than c. Still, that this doesn't happen seems necessary in some way—*causally* necessary, as people say, or *nomologically* necessary. But what kind of necessity is that? Logical necessity we know and love: but what is this causal or nomological necessity?[192]

---

186. Plantinga, *Where Conflict Really Lies*, 278. Plantinga writes, "There is still another important way in which theism is hospitable to science: theism makes it much easier to understand what these laws are like. The main point here has to do with the alleged *necessity* of natural law." Plantinga, *Where Conflict Really Lies*, 278.

187. Plantinga, *Where Conflict Really Lies*, 278.

188. Plantinga, *Where Conflict Really Lies*, 278.

189. Plantinga, *Where Conflict Really Lies*, 278.

190. Plantinga, *Where Conflict Really Lies*, 278.

191. Plantinga, *Where Conflict Really Lies*, 278.

192. Plantinga, *Where Conflict Really Lies*, 278–79. Plantinga writes, "All we're

While Plantinga's illustrations are helpful, thus far he has taken this matter no further than Lange and others who have thought about it in great detail. One philosopher who has given attention to the laws of nature is Armstrong, as seen above. However, Armstrong's own theory of laws leads to a dead end when it comes to explaining the feature of necessity he posits as obtaining in laws of nature. Another philosopher who has thought about the laws of nature, David Lewis, critiques Armstrong on this very point, as seen in the following quote from Plantinga.

> The philosopher David Armstrong at one time spoke of laws as involving a necessitating relationship among universals: a law is just the expression of a certain necessary relationship between universals. But, as David Lewis pointed out, naming this relation "necessity" doesn't tell us much. It also doesn't mean that it really *is* necessity—anymore, said Lewis, than being named "Armstrong" confers mighty biceps.
>
> Armstrong added that the class of propositions necessary in this sense is larger than the class of logically necessary propositions, but smaller than that of true propositions. But this too is no real help: any class of true propositions that includes all the logically necessary propositions, but doesn't include all true propositions, meets this condition. (For example, the class of true propositions minus the proposition *China is a large country* meets this condition: but obviously this tells us nothing about the intended sense of "necessary.") Armstrong later decided that the laws of nature are logically necessary after all, prompted no doubt by the difficulty of saying what this other brand of necessity might be. It is also this difficulty, one suspects, that prompts others who hold that the laws of nature, despite appearances to the contrary, are logically necessary.[193]

Plantinga references theism as providing "important resources."[194] He points out that natural laws limit technology.[195] For example, it is a natural

---

ordinarily told is that this necessity is weaker than logical necessity (the laws of nature are not logically necessary), but still stronger than mere universal truth (not all true universal generalizations are necessary in this sense). But what *is* this necessity? What is its nature? This is the real rub. It seems impossible to say what it is." Plantinga, *Where Conflict Really Lies*, 279.

193. Plantinga, *Where Conflict Really Lies*, 279–80.

194. Plantinga, *Where Conflict Really Lies*, 280. He claims, "we can think of the necessity of natural law both as a consequence and also as a sort of measure of divine power." Plantinga, *Where Conflict Really Lies*, 280.

195. Plantinga, *Where Conflict Really Lies*, 280.

law that "c, the velocity of light, is an upper limit on the relative velocity of one body with respect to another."[196] Again, there is necessity to the laws of nature.

Here Plantinga offers insight into how theism is helpful with respect to solving the difficulty of explaining why, how, and what it means for the laws of nature to be necessary in this way.

> From a theistic perspective, the reason is that God has established and upholds this law for our cosmos, and no creature (actual or possible) has the power to act contrary to what God establishes and upholds. God is omnipotent; there are no non-logical limits on his power; we might say that his power is infinite. The sense in which the laws of nature are necessary, therefore, is that they are propositions God has established or decreed, and no creature—no finite power, we might say—has the power to act against these propositions, that is, to bring it about that they are false. It is as if God says: "Let c, the speed of light, be such that no material object accelerates from a velocity less than c to a velocity greater than c"; no creaturely power is then able to cause a material object to accelerate from a velocity less than c to one greater than c. The laws of nature, therefore, resemble necessary truths in that there is nothing we or other creatures can do to render them false. We could say that they are *finitely inviolable*.[197]

Still, theism provides the conceptual equipment to explain more than just the necessity of laws of nature. It can also help explain their contingency. The laws of nature are not necessary truths. Plantinga appeals to theism to explain as follows:

---

196. Plantinga, *Where Conflict Really Lies*, 280. Plantinga clarifies, "Natural laws, obviously enough, impose limits on our technology. We can do many wonderful things: for example, we can fly from Paris to New York in less than four hours. No doubt our abilities along these lines will continue to expand; perhaps one day we will be able to travel from Paris to New York in under four minutes. Even so, we will never be able to travel to the nearest star, Proxima Centauri, in less than four years. That is because Proxima Centauri is about 4.3 light years from us, and c, the velocity of light, is an upper limit on the relative velocity of one body with respect to another. That it *is* such an upper limit, we think, is a natural law. But the distance to *Proxima Centauri* is such that if I were to travel there (in a spaceship, say) in less than four years, my velocity with respect to the earth would have to exceed that limit. And if, indeed, this restriction on the relative velocities of moving objects *is* a law of nature, we won't be able to manage that feat, no matter how hard we try, and no matter how good our technology."

197. Plantinga, *Where Conflict Really Lies*, 280–81.

> Though these laws are finitely inviolable, they are nevertheless contingent, in that it is not necessary, not part of the divine nature, to institute or promulgate just *these* laws. God could have created our world in such a way that the speed of light should have been something quite different from *c*; he could have created things in such a way that Newton's laws don't hold for middle-sized objects. As we saw in chapter 7 on fine-tuning, there are many physical constants that are finitely inviolable (*we* can't change them) but could have been different and are therefore contingent. The natural laws are finitely inviolably, but not necessarily true.[198]

It turns out that the laws of nature are not only consistent with the Christian understanding of the doctrine of divine providence, but may actually depend upon the doctrine of providence for their intelligibility. While it is far beyond the scope of this book to argue against every non-theistic (and especially every non-Christian-theistic) precondition of the laws of nature, a basic outline of how the laws of nature function in accord with a Christian theistic understanding of the relationship between God and the universe has been provided. Additionally, the regularity and predictability of the universe allowed for in the Christian theistic worldview are most easily described in terms of laws which God imposes upon his creation.[199] Not only are such laws a necessary component of scientific inquiry, they are *discoverable* by human beings and scientifically *describable*.[200]

The so-called laws of nature can be understood in at least three ways. They can be understood as accidental, logically necessary, or nomically necessary. In the final analysis, one wishes to find something that is stronger than mere universality, but weaker than logical necessity.[201]

---

198. Plantinga, *Where Conflict Really Lies*, 281.

199. Plantinga echoes the commentators in chap. 2 of this book, "This constancy and predictability, this regularity, was often thought of in terms of *law*: God sets, prescribes laws for his creation, or creates in such a way that what he creates is subject to, conforms to, laws he institutes." Plantinga, *Where Conflict Really Lies*, 274–75.

200. Plantinga, *Where Conflict Really Lies*, 276. Plantinga writes, "On this conception, part of the job of science is to discover the laws of nature; but then of course science will be successful only if it is possible for us human beings to do that. Science will be successful only if these laws are not too complex, or deep, or otherwise beyond us. Again, this thought fits well with theistic religion and its doctrine of the image of God; God not only sets laws for the universe, but sets laws we can (at least approximately) grasp. This thought also traces back to the beginnings of modern science." Plantinga, *Where Conflict Really Lies*, 277.

201. Plantinga, *Where Conflict Really Lies*, 279–80.

This nomic necessity is easily accounted for in theistic terms, for God preserves and governs his creation as he pleases, and the creation does nothing contrary to his rational will.[202] Perhaps this necessity is just the kind needed to answer the problem of induction. The topic of the problem of induction is picked up in the next chapter.

---

202. Plantinga, *Where Conflict Really Lies*, 280–81. Thus nomic necessity is a subset of what theologians call decretal necessity.

Chapter 4

Problem of Induction

A CONSIDERATION OF SCIENTIFIC law would not be complete without a discussion of the implications of laws of nature for inductive reasoning. Inductive reasoning is to be distinguished from deductive reasoning. Deductive reasoning rests on deductive arguments. Valid deductive arguments must have true conclusions if all of their premises are true.[1] When a valid deductive argument also has all true premises, it is a sound deductive argument.[2] The following is a popular example of a sound deductive argument:

> All men are mortal.
> Socrates is a man.
> Therefore, Socrates is mortal.

The argument is stated in valid deductive form. The first premise appears to be true. All men are subject to death, or will die, which is what it means to be mortal.[3] The second premise likewise appears to be true. Socrates, the famous philosopher of Ancient Greece written about by Plato, is, or

---

1. Copi and Cohen, *Essentials of Logic*, 330. Copi and Cohen write, "It is impossible for the conclusion of a valid deductive argument to be false if its premises are true."

2. Copi and Cohen, *Essentials of Logic*, 330. According to Copi and Cohen, "So a sound deductive argument allows you to assert its conclusion with certainty."

3. Whether one takes "men" to refer to male humans only or male and female humans does not matter in this context.

was, a man.[4] But then, the conclusion must also be true. Since all men are mortal, and Socrates is a man, it follows that Socrates is mortal. Thus Richard Swinburne writes,

> An argument or inference proceeds from one or more premises to a conclusion. An argument is a valid deductive argument if all that it does is to reach a conclusion tacitly contained in the premises, that is a conclusion such that it would be self-contradictory to assert the premises but to deny the conclusion. In such a case we say that the conclusion follows deductively from the premises. Arguments which purport to be deductively valid are assessed as valid or invalid. An argument is valid if the conclusion does indeed follow deductively from the premises, invalid if it does not.[5]

Inductive reasoning rests on inductive arguments; inductive arguments, in contrast to deductive ones, are not deductively valid.[6]

Deductive validity ensures the conclusion of an argument to be true when the premises of that argument are true. By contrast, when the premises of an inductive argument are true, it does not follow that the conclusion of that argument is also true.[7] The following is an example of an inductive argument, based loosely on the example above.

> Man 1 was mortal.
> Man 2 was mortal.
> Therefore, all men are mortal.

The argument is stated in inductive form. Assume the first premise is true. Man 1 was subject to death. Man 2 was likewise subject to death. To strengthen the argument, assume that both of these men were not only subject to death, but are actually dead, empirically verifying that they were, in fact, subject to death. Does it follow that all men are subject to death? No.[8] It does not follow from the fact that the first man and second man died that all men will die. It does not even follow that a third man will die. Not until after all men died could one affirm that all men

---

4. Socrates was both male and human.
5. Swinburne, *Justification of Induction*, 1.
6. Copi and Cohen, *Essentials of Logic*, 330.
7. Copi and Cohen, *Essentials of Logic*, 330.
8. Unless, of course, "mortal" is just a definitional aspect of "man," but the purpose of the hypothetical inductive argument is to inductively verify the proposition that all men are mortal.

are mortal, if the statement is to be demonstrated inductively (of course, no one would be alive to affirm the statement).

The first premise of the deductive argument appears to be a contingent statement. The statement pertains to a matter of fact that is supposed to obtain in the empirical world. The same may be said of the second premise of the deductive argument. That Socrates is, or was, a man is a contingent statement.[9] It is not necessarily the case that Socrates be a man. The fact that Socrates is a man is a part of the contingent realm of history. Such truths about the world, contingent truths, are known through induction.[10] It follows that much, even most, of our reasoning concerning matters of fact in the world relies upon inductive arguments, regardless of whether or not these arguments are explicitly recognized or stated.[11] If the natural world is to be known through induction, then science, too, relies upon induction.[12] Far from an abstract, uninteresting facet of reasoning, induction is immensely practical in important ways.[13]

While deductive arguments submit themselves to a more rigorous evaluation with respect to the criteria for determining whether or not an argument is deductively valid, and hence leading one to be able to make a better judgment about whether or not those arguments are also sound, inductive arguments may not be subjected to such evaluative criteria.[14] However, inductive arguments can be evaluated as stronger or weaker in terms of the evidence they provide for their conclusions.[15] Recall the inductive argument from above. Adding additional observa-

---

9. However, see *The Stanford Encyclopedia of Philosophy*, s.v. "Rigid Designators," http://plato.stanford.edu/archives/sum2011/entries/rigid-designators. Some argue the actual referent of "Socrates" could not have been other than a man, which can be conceded without affecting the point, so long as the first premise of the argument is contingent.

10. Copi and Cohen, *Essentials of Logic*, 330.

11. Copi and Cohen, *Essentials of Logic*, 330.

12. Copi and Cohen, *Essentials of Logic*, 330.

13. Copi and Cohen, *Essentials of Logic*, 330.

14. Copi and Cohen, *Essentials of Logic*, 330.

15. Copi and Cohen, *Essentials of Logic*, 330. Copi and Cohen explain, "As we have seen, in the case of *deductive* arguments there are criteria that allow us *to determine conclusively* whether or not an argument form is valid. If an argument form is *invalid*, it might provide *some* evidence, but it cannot provide conclusive evidence for the truth of its conclusion. Some inductive arguments provide better evidence for the truth of their conclusions—they are *stronger*—than others. The criteria for evaluating inductive arguments are criteria that *tend to show* that an inductive argument is strong or weak." Copi and Cohen, *Essentials of Logic*, 330.

tions of men who were mortal as premises to the argument would serve to strengthen the likelihood of the conclusion being true. This feature of inductive arguments is closely related to the concept of *sample*. Copi and Cohen define a sample as "a limited collection of objects of the kind under investigation."[16] The idea for building a strong inductive argument is to collect as large a sample size, with as much diversity, as feasible, and to state the conclusion proportionately to the evidence acquired.[17] A stronger conclusion requires less evidence by way of inductive counterexample to demonstrate the conclusion false.[18] Copi and Cohen write, "An inductive counterexample is a case that is sufficient to show that the conclusion of an inductive argument is false."[19] Copi and Cohen nicely summarize inductive criteria, given the previous discussion:

> So, we may summarize the criteria for evaluating inductive arguments by enumeration as follows:
>
> 1. As the number of objects taken into account increases, the generalization is strengthened.
> 2. The more diverse the sample is, the better the basis for the generalization is.
> 3. The stronger the conclusion is, the weaker the argument is.[20]

As already alluded to, inductive arguments are not completely impractical. Indeed, "One of the reasons inductive arguments are important is that we use them to predict what will happen in the future."[21] Copi and Cohen illustrate as follows:

> One of the reasons inductive arguments are important is that we use them to predict what will happen in the future. When you were a kid, you might have touched a hot stove a couple times, felt pain, and concluded that if you touched the stove again, you'd feel pain again. You've avoided stoves ever since—much to the glee of fast-food restaurants. Or you might have read several of J.K. Rowling's *Harry Potter* books, found each enjoyable, and looked forward to the release of the next one since you inferred

---

16. Copi and Cohen, *Essentials of Logic*, 331.
17. Copi and Cohen, *Essentials of Logic*, 331–32.
18. Copi and Cohen, *Essentials of Logic*, 332.
19. Copi and Cohen, *Essentials of Logic*, 332.
20. Copi and Cohen, *Essentials of Logic*, 332.
21. Copi and Cohen, *Essentials of Logic*, 332.

that it would be enjoyable, too. Could you have been wrong? Sure.[22]

And yet, it is *unlikely* that you would be wrong, given a proper sample and properly stated conclusion. However, there is an extremely important assumption present, not only in all of the examples of inductive reasoning provided here, but in all inductive reasoning. This assumption "is that, at some level, the future will resemble the past."[23] Here is how the assumption appears in the earlier inductive argument, if explicitly stated:

> Man 1 was mortal.
> Man 2 was mortal.
> *The future will resemble the past.*
> Therefore, all men are mortal.

Copi and Cohen refer to this assumption as the "Principle of the Uniformity of Nature."[24] Examining this principle reveals a significant cause for concern regarding all inductive arguments.

The concern was popularized when, "Over 250 years ago, the Scottish philosopher David Hume (1711–1776) asked whether the principle of the uniformity of nature can be known to be true."[25]

> He argued that the principle of the uniformity of nature is not self-evidently true: You can at least imagine what it would be like for one event to occur and not that which regularly follows it. Arguments from experience *assume* that the principle of the uniformity of nature is true. So, any argument from experience to support the principle of the uniformity of nature begs the question. All arguments are either arguments from self-evident premises or arguments from experience. Therefore, there is no argument showing that the principle of the uniformity of nature is true. Hence, there is no way to know that the principle is true. Hence, any inductive argument contains an implicit premise (the principle of the uniformity of nature) that is not known to be true. Notice, the principle of the uniformity of nature might

---

22. Copi and Cohen, *Essentials of Logic*, 332.
23. Copi and Cohen, *Essentials of Logic*, 332.
24. Copi and Cohen, *Essentials of Logic*, 333. Uniformity need not be thought of as absolute, as though it precludes, for example, catastrophism.
25. Copi and Cohen, *Essentials of Logic*, 333.

be true, but it cannot be known to be such. So, there are grounds to doubt any inductive argument.[26]

Copi and Cohen note that the principle in question is always assumed to be true, since "life would be virtually impossible if we didn't."[27] However, Copi and Cohen's comment might not be a sufficient response to the highlighted concern.

PROBLEM OF INDUCTION AS A SKEPTICAL CONCERN

According to Jonathan L. Cohen, "The classical paradox about induction arose as a by-product of empiricist epistemology in the late seventeenth and early eighteenth centuries."[28]

> It was hinted at in Locke's *Essay* and elsewhere and explicitly formulated for the first time in Hume's *Treatise* though neither Locke nor Hume used the term 'induction' at all in this context. The paradox was generated by the fact that, according to an empiricist, the premises of our factual knowledge were all particular, distinct perceptual experiences, not general principles of any kind, whereas the content of our factual knowledge seemed to include many causal laws and other generalizations about natural processes. A rationalist could claim that such general conclusions were deducible, in accordance with standard logical rules, from even more general premises that Providence had kindly made self-evident. But there was no way that these general conclusions, with their implications about the as yet unperceived, could be so deduced from premises about particular past events.[29]

Apparently, for all the particular premises in the world, one could not draw a certain conclusion. More than that, one could not draw a conclusion from particular principles at all. The conclusion could still be false, even when all inductive premises were true. Nothing is illogical or contradictory about taking the conclusion to an inductive argument to be

---

26. Copi and Cohen, *Essentials of Logic*, 333.
27. Copi and Cohen, *Essentials of Logic*, 333.
28. Cohen, *An Introduction to Philosophy*, 176–77.
29. Cohen, *An Introduction to Philosophy*, 177.

false even when all of its premises are true.[30] This now public realization was more than a little problematic for the scientific endeavor.

> So just at the very period at which the scientific revolution seemed to have produced its greatest theoretical achievement—Newtonian mechanics—the triumph of empiricist over rationalist epistemology seemed to imply, if Hume was right, that this achievement had no rational foundation. No valid inference was possible from the past to the future, or from what is in sight to what is out of sight. Nor was it any use trying to rescue the situation by an appeal to some overarching principle about the uniformity of nature, whereby, in relevant respects, the future might be guaranteed to be like the past and unseen instances of a property like seen ones. With such a principle as a major premiss, Hume thought, the requisite deductions would be forthcoming. But, he pointed out, the truth of that major premiss would itself be at least as impossible to substantiate by formallogically sanctioned deduction from the ultimate premisses of experience.[31]

What would become known as the infamous problem of induction had apparently undermined science.[32]

The problem of induction is a skeptical problem in epistemology prompted by any metaphysic that essentially calls into question the alleged *necessity* of the relationship between that which is thought to be a *cause* and that which is thought to be an *effect*, though there are various interpretations of the difficulty. As far as logical necessity is concerned, it is *logically possible* to affirm any given cause without its effect or *vice versa*. Or to state the claim the other way around, there is no logical difficulty involved in *denying* any given cause without denying its effect or *vice versa*. So far as anyone knows, causes and effects are independent from one another or possess no necessary connection.[33]

---

30. Cohen, *An Introduction to Philosophy*, 177.

31. Cohen, *An Introduction to Philosophy*, 177–78.

32. Philosopher Immanuel Kant writes, "I openly confess that my remembering David Hume was the very thing which many years ago first interrupted my dogmatic slumber and gave my investigations in the field of speculative philosophy a quite new direction." Kant, *Prolegomena*, 5.

33. Although the problem is traditionally attributed to the Scottish skeptic David Hume, it was noted by others long before Hume was ever even born. For example, the Muslim philosopher Al-Ghazali wrote, "The connection between what is customarily believed to be a cause and what is believed to be an effect is not necessary, according to our opinion; but each of the two [namely, cause and effect] is independent of the

Moreover, causation is not discernible through empirical means. The very language of cause and effect is not available in virtue of sensory experience alone. Thus it will not help to claim that the aforementioned problems regarding cause and effect are resolved through merely defining one's terms. According to this philosophical problem, there is no discernible necessary connection between alleged causes and effects, and there are no discernible causes or effects.[34] The difficulty here seems one of conflating *correlation* with *causation*.[35] Finally, people typically act upon propositions which pertain to objects and events they have not yet experienced and reason in an inductive fashion by making singular predictive inferences and generalizations. But such reasoning is based upon the very cause and effect relationships called into question by the problem of induction. Thus it seems that insofar as people reason inductively at all, they do so in an irrational fashion.[36]

A number of clarifications should be made concerning the nature of the problem of induction. Recall Copi and Cohen's statement that "the principle of the uniformity of nature might *be* true, but it cannot be known to be such."[37] Copi and Cohen admit that this aforementioned

---

other." Al-Ghazali, "Incoherence of Philosophers," 283. He continues, "The affirmation of one does not imply the affirmation of the other, nor does the denial of one imply the denial of the other; the existence of one does not necessitate the existence of the other, nor does the non-existence of one necessitate the non-existence of the other." Al-Ghazali, "Incoherence of Philosophers," 283.

34. Hume will bring further clarity to this observation, but it is important to note that Al-Ghazali also thought that causation is not discoverable through empiricism since, "observation only proves that one occurs together with the other, but it does not prove that one occurs through [the agency of] the other." Al-Ghazali, "Incoherence of Philosophers," 284. Al-Ghazali is quick to state his alleged solution to these philosophical difficulties, claiming, "the connection of these occurs because the decree of God preceded their being created in this sequence not because the existence [of this connection] is necessary in itself, not receptive of separation." Al-Ghazali, "Incoherence of Philosophers," 284. He likewise believes that in the second case, "there is no other cause but God." Al-Ghazali, "Incoherence of Philosophers," 284. Note that Al-Ghazali famously affirms a form of occasionalism.

35. Buildings that burn down tend to have more fire trucks at the scene than buildings that do not. There is a correlation between the severity of a fire and the number of fire trucks at the scene. It does not follow that fire trucks cause buildings to burn down. (However, one might argue that the severity of the fire causes more fire trucks to arrive on the scene.)

36. Musgrave, *Common Sense*, 154–55. Musgrave is using "irrational" in the sense of a lack of reasoned philosophical justification.

37. Copi and Cohen, *Essentials of Logic*, 333.

observation grants us grounds for doubt regarding inductive arguments, but also note the impossibility of life were it not for the assumption of the uniformity of nature.[38] With this assumption in place, Copi and Cohen go on to address inductive arguments more fully. Copi and Cohen are correct regarding the consequences of the skeptical concerns regarding the inductive principle. After hearing skeptical arguments against the uniformity of nature, people will continue to live their lives as though it is true. Copi and Cohen's comments are thus sufficient for their purposes. However, given the skeptical worries above, not only is doubt admissible in any inductive argument, but if the uniformity of nature turns out to be false, then there is no positive reason for accepting any inductively inferred belief or conclusion. It is not as though deductive arguments are capable of granting people certainty whereas inductive arguments grant only probabilistic conclusions. Not even probabilistic conclusions can be inferred from independent premises if the inductive principle is not justified.

Hume points out in his book, *An Enquiry Concerning Human Understanding*, that humans commonly assert and act upon propositions pertaining to that of which they have no experience. Humans frequently and necessarily reason by way of singular predictive inferences and inductive generalizations. As noted above, this kind of reasoning is not valid in the way that deductive reasoning is valid. Thus it would seem that humans are irrational creatures.[39] This chapter will examine some of the many attempts to solve this problem of induction and explain their shortcomings. At the very least Hume sheds light on some very serious problems with our method of thinking about the empirical world.

Hume famously divides the contents of reason into relations of ideas and matters of fact.[40] Relations of ideas may be known prior to and apart from experience of the empirical world and are either intuitive or demonstrative. Good examples are the truths of mathematics. Hume writes, "Propositions of this kind are discoverable by the mere operation of thought, without dependence on what is anywhere existent in the universe."[41] A more specific example is three multiplied by five being

---

38. Copi and Cohen, *Essentials of Logic*, 333.
39. Which conclusion is, of course, irrational.
40. Hume, *An Enquiry*, 24.
41. Hume, *An Enquiry*, 24.

equivalent to fifteen.[42] This proposition cannot be other than what it is; it is impossible to conceive of three multiplied by five ever being equivalent to fourteen without generating a contradiction. This characteristic makes the first kind of objects of human reasoning mentioned by Hume different from the second kind of objects of human reasoning. Matters of fact are the second type of reason and can be conceived of as being completely opposite what they are without generating any contradiction.[43]

A potential question about reasoning concerning matters of fact is brought to the surface by the aforementioned consideration, namely, "What is the nature of that evidence which assures us of any real existence and matter of fact, beyond the present testimony of our senses, or the records of our memory"?[44] Philosophers predating Hume raised this question as well, but Hume wishes to publicly carry it further.[45] He does so by addressing the relationship of cause and effect, claiming that "The hearing of an articulate voice and rational discourse in the dark assures us of the presence of some person: Why? because these are the effects of the human make and fabric, and closely connected with it."[46] Hume's point is that an inference is drawn from what is known via the senses and memory to what cannot be known through either. So in this example, it is inferred that a person is with the voice because people are the causes of the effects of voices. Indeed, "All reasonings concerning matter of fact seem to be founded on the relation of Cause and Effect. By means of that relation alone we can go beyond the evidence of our memory and senses."[47]

The cause and effect relation cannot initially be found in objects themselves since "No object ever discovers, by the qualities which appear to the senses, either the causes which produced it, or the effects which will arise from it; nor can our reason, unassisted by experience, ever draw

42. Hume, *An Enquiry*, 24.

43. Hume, *An Enquiry*, 24–25. Thus Hume, "The contrary of every matter of fact is still possible; because it can never imply a contradiction, and is conceived by the mind with the same facility and distinctness, as if ever so conformable to reality. That the sun will not rise to-morrow is no less intelligible a proposition, and implies no more contradiction than the affirmation, that it will rise."

44. Hume, *An Enquiry*, 25.

45. Hume, *An Enquiry*, 25.

46. Hume, *An Enquiry*, 26.

47. Hume, *An Enquiry*, 26. Hume reasons, "If we would satisfy ourselves, therefore, concerning the nature of that evidence, which assures us of matters of fact, we must enquire how we arrive at the knowledge of cause and effect."

any inference concerning real existence and matter of fact."[48] Whenever anyone is new to an object, that person is unable to know causes and effects of the object and unable to discover them through any reason. It is experience only which makes discovery of these possible to an observer and makes knowledge of cause and effect possible. *A priori* reasoning is not a means to discovering the relation of cause and effect either. Rather, "all the laws of nature, and all the operations of bodies without exception, are known only by experience."[49] The realization that cause and effect are drawn from experience alone places great weight upon the authority of experience.

Hume appears to have established that, so far as anyone knows, causes and effects are separate and unrelated. He summarizes his reasoning thus far.

> In a word, then, every effect is a distinct event from its cause. It could not, therefore, be discovered in the cause, and the first invention or conception of it, *a priori*, must be entirely arbitrary. And even after it is suggested, the conjunction of it with the cause must appear equally arbitrary; since there are always many other effects, which, to reason, must seem fully as consistent and natural. In vain, therefore, should we pretend to determine any single event, or infer any cause or effect, without the assistance of observation and experience.[50]

All reasoning about matter of fact is based upon the relation of cause and effect, which is in turn based upon experience. Hume goes a step further and asks what experience is based upon, and this question leads his readers into the heart of his argument concerning induction.[51]

> When it is asked, What is the nature of all our reasonings concerning matter of fact? the proper answer seems to be, that they are founded on the relation of cause and effect. When again it is asked, What is the foundation of all our reasonings and conclusions concerning that relation? it may be replied in one word,

---

48. Hume, *An Enquiry*, 27.

49. Hume, *An Enquiry*, 28. Hume explains, "This proposition, that causes and effects are discoverable, not by reason but by experience, will readily be admitted with regard to such objects, as we remember to have once been altogether unknown to us; since we must be conscious of the utter inability, which we then lay under, of foretelling what would arise from them." Hume, *An Enquiry*,27.

50. Hume, *An Enquiry*, 30.

51. Hume, *An Enquiry*, 32.

Experience. But if we still carry on our sifting humour, and ask, What is the foundation of all conclusions from experience? this implies a new question, which may be of more difficult solution and explication.[52]

The main thrust of his argument is to show that a few possible foundations for reasoning concerning matter of fact fail. This line of thought leads to the conclusion that reasoning about matters of fact is founded on nothing and thus operates in an intellectual void.[53] Hume does later on provide a psychological explanation as to why people reason in this manner even though such reasoning appears to be unfounded, at least in terms of a justificatory account.[54]

Hume illustrates his point using the example of bread. Bread is taken to be nourishing because at certain times in the past, the sensible qualities it exhibits have been found with nourishment. It does not necessarily follow that anytime bread with the same sensible qualities is found it must also be nourishing, or that just because something has sensible qualities similar to or the same as those found in the past that the secret powers of the objects must also be the same. There is, nevertheless, an inference drawn from like sensible qualities to like sensible powers.[55]

> The bread, which I formerly eat, nourished me; that is, a body of such sensible qualities was, at that time, endued with such secret powers: but does it follow, that other bread must also nourish me at another time, and that like sensible qualities must always be attended with like secret powers? The consequence seems nowise necessary. At least, it must be acknowledged that there is here a consequence drawn by the mind; that there is a certain step taken; a process of thought, and an inference, which wants to be explained.[56]

Like objects are found with like effects in past experience, which is not the same as like objects being found with like effects in future instances. Inferences are constantly made from the former to the latter. Hume is questioning how the reasoning behind such inferences is justified. Inductive

---

52. Hume, *An Enquiry*, 32.

53. Which is to say nothing of the experiential facts of sense data such as the apparent certainty that one is "appeared to treely," for example.

54. Hume, *An Enquiry*, 33.

55. Hume, *An Enquiry*, 34–35.

56. Hume, *An Enquiry*, 34–35.

reasoning, which involves both singular predictive inferences and inductive generalizations, does not appear to be a valid form of reasoning.[57]

Musgrave takes a strong approach to the explication of Hume's problem, writing, "His objection is that inductive arguments are logically invalid: the truth of the premises does not guarantee the truth of the conclusion, it is possible for the conclusion to be false even though all the premises are true, the conclusion does not follow from the premises."[58] Reasoning invalidly is not reasonable at all—it is irrational. However, everyone reasons inductively. The apparent conclusion, according to Musgrave's understanding of Hume, is that humans are irrational. Hume summarizes this whole endeavor.

> In reality, all arguments from experience are founded on the similarity which we discover among natural objects, and by which we are induced to expect effects similar to those which we have found to follow from such objects. And though none but a fool or madman will ever pretend to dispute the authority of experience, or to reject that great guide of human life, it may surely be allowed a philosopher to have so much curiosity at least as to examine the principle of human nature, which gives this mighty authority to experience, and makes us draw advantage from that similarity which nature has placed among different objects. From causes which appear similar we expect similar effects. This is the sum of all our experimental conclusions.[59]

Hume's conclusion seems wrong, but if there is an error in his argument, it is not as obvious as philosophers of science might want it to be.

Swinburne reinforces what is established through Hume's problem of induction, and restates Hume's "answer" to the problem of induction,

> Hume's answer is that we have no justification for believing that things will continue to behave as they have behaved. We do believe this and act on this supposition as a matter of animal habit, but there is no justification for our doing so.
>
> We have seen that inductive inference is a somewhat more complicated matter than Hume supposed, but it is easy enough to phrase Hume's problem in a way which allows for this. We use certain criteria by which we judge purported inductive

---

57. Musgrave, *Common Sense*, 154–55.
58. Musgrave, *Common Sense*, 152.
59. Hume, *An Enquiry*, 36–37.

arguments correct. What justifies us in using these criteria rather than any others and so making the particular inductive inferences which we do? What grounds have we got for supposing that a conclusion reached by the criteria which in practice we use is in fact true?[60]

Philosopher Colin Howson refers to Hume's argument as "metaphorically, dynamite."[61]

> Its famous conclusion, that there is no justification for regarding what has been observed to happen in the past as any sort of reliable guide to the future, subverted the prevailing methodology of observation and experiment on the back of which rode the new mathematical sciences that seemed at the time Hume wrote to have attained an extraordinary degree of success, and have gone on doing so. Yet no uncontroversial definitive answer has ever been forthcoming to Hume, and most people have followed his own example of behaving as though nothing had happened. I find this extraordinary, and I believe it is time to face up to the unpalatable possibility revealed by Hume that all of our hard-won factual knowledge is not secured by any process of demonstrably sound reasoning (and I mean sound reasoning in general, not merely deductive) to an empirical base, and see whether that is true and, if so, what follows from it.[62]

Howson argues Hume's problem, even though it seems absurd, is correct, but the consequences which follow are often exaggerated.[63] Nevertheless, Howson admits Hume's problem sharply redefines popular thoughts regarding the scientific endeavor.[64] Various responses to the problem of induction are examined in the next section.

---

60. Swinburne, *Justification of Induction*, 9–10.
61. Howson, *Hume's Problem*, 1.
62. Howson, *Hume's Problem*, 1.
63. Howson, *Hume's Problem*, 2. By Howson's reckoning, "The argument is deservedly one of the great classics of philosophy: Hume, no mean wielder of crushing arguments, produced in this one possibly the most crushing of them all. And not only crushing, but apparently attended by the gravest consequences for our standards of justified belief. But just as the force of Hume's argument is usually underestimated, so the devastation it is supposed to bring in its wake is usually exaggerated, and my supplementary thesis is that there is none the less a positive solution to Hume's problem."
64. Howson, *Hume's Problem*, 4–5.

Cohen rightly believes that Hume responded to the problem of induction with a healthy philosophical skepticism. Hume did not believe induction is rationally justified.

> Hume's own way of handling the problem was to accept the sceptical conclusion. On his view human beings, like animals, have a natural inclination to believe in the existence of a causal connection between one kind of event and another, whenever they have observed events of the one kind uniformly followed in their experience by the events of the other. And the inclination becomes proportionately stronger, according as the events in question resemble the hitherto observed ones more closely. This natural inclination suffices for all the practical purposes of life. So the absence of any rational justification for the belief is a matter of concern only to philosophers, and the latter can dispel their worries at any moment by leaving their studies and indulging their natural inclinations.[65]

Of course, if Hume's problem is a concern for philosophers, it is also a concern for philosophers of science. As Howson notes,

> It is a commonplace that our scientific knowledge far exceeds the observational basis on which it is grounded. It seems equally commonplace that a good part of it is securely grounded on careful observation. The inferential process by which observation, suitably controlled, is regarded as conferring an affidavit of reliability on what in a strict logical sense extends beyond it philosophers have traditionally called *induction*.[66]

Howson mentions the history of Francis Bacon and the logic of induction and claims, "In short, what was lacking was a set of prescriptions

---

65. Cohen, *An Introduction to Philosophy*, 179–80. Cohen goes after Hume's skeptical response. He attacks the response on three fronts. First, Cohen claims that people do not believe in uniformities like scientists, who seek what underlies the causal connections they experience. Second, Cohen notes that Hume posits a psychological law of sorts which describes a universal human experience of belief in the uniformity of nature, but if Hume is correct, then there is no rational justification for positing this law, which is itself a manifestation of the uniformity of nature. Third, Hume does not provide any explanation for why it is that people in general, and scientists in particular, still believe they are operating rationally in communicating with one another regarding "what the laws of nature are and what the strength of evidence is for their existence." Cohen, *An Introduction to Philosophy*, 180. None of these points fully answers Hume, however.

66. Howson, *Hume's Problem*, 6.

accompanied by a convincing explanation of why they should be regarded as sound."[67]

> Unfortunately progress in this direction failed to match that of the contemporary science itself, a success which, ironically, the development of an inductive logic was supposed to facilitate. People went on cheerfully interrogating nature, weighing the answers, and forming judicious conclusions with outstanding success even if no one seemed to be able to offer a convincing explanation why. What was wrong? For a start there was always perceived to be something not quite right, if not seriously defective, with every candidate system for such an explanation. Worse was the fact that not only were the philosophers unable to do the decent thing and uncontroversially sanctify inductive practice (though not for want of trying), they were not even able to counter an apparently absurd argument put forward two and a half centuries ago by the philosopher David Hume: that *there is no good reason to suppose that inductive practice should have been successful at all.* Thus the initial problem of how to justify induction—"the problem of induction"—difficult enough in itself as it began to turn out, became modulated into the far more serious *Hume's Problem*, the problem of reconciling the continuing failure to rebut Hume's argument with the undoubted fact that induction not only seemed to work but to work surprisingly well. The Cambridge philosopher C. D. Broad's famous aphorism that induction is "the glory of science and the scandal of philosophy" was both a tribute to Hume and a token of the exasperation that Broad felt at the stubborn resistance of Hume's argument to refutation (1952: 143).

> And so that argument has stood since it was first presented, a philosophical classic, not really believed but withstanding all attempts to overturn it. The continuing failure suggests that it might actually be correct. I believe that, for all its apparent absurdity, it is.[68]

Any inference from what is observed to what is not yet observed is not deductive, but more importantly, no such inference is justified as even *probable* unless the aforementioned observation entails the inference, even if the inference is more loosely based on the observational data.[69] Howson restates the argument yet another way:

67. Howson, *Hume's Problem*, 9.
68. Howson, *Hume's Problem*, 10.
69. Howson, *Hume's Problem*, 10–11.

> The argument can be put in a manner possibly more familiar to modern ears. Let P be the conjunction of all factual statements known to be true. Suppose that the inference from P to a statement Q describing some event not known to be true is not deductive (establishing that this is so where P stands for 'past' and Q for 'future' is the first part of Hume's argument). It follows immediately from the definition of deductive validity that in some subset W of all the possible worlds in which, like ours, P is true and Q is false. The second part of Hume's argument can be imagined as arising from trying to answer the question: what further information could be appealed to which would make it more likely that our world is not in W? Well, the only world we know is this one, so the information must presumably be about some aspect of this world. But the only information we have about this world that is known to be true is already in P. In other words, there is no further information. All we know is that in our world Q may be true or it may be false: nothing more. Hence any principle claiming to justify the inference from P to the truth *or even the probable truth* of Q must beg the question.[70]

Howson is hopeful regarding the effectiveness of the Humean skeptical argument against induction. He clarifies, "If I am correct, Hume's argument does not presuppose that the only form of justification is deductive: his argument is the very simple and effective one that any evidence that we take to indicate that our world is likely to be among those in which some general assertion is true requires some additional assumption to the effect that it is indeed evidence."[71]

> The argument is so effective just *because* it makes no assumption about what exactly constitutes valid reasoning—deductive,

---

70. Howson, *Hume's Problem*, 11–12. Philosopher Samir Okasha explains the difficulty of attempting to use subjective probability to solve Hume's problem, "Suppose John believes that the sun will rise tomorrow and Jack believes it will not. They both accept the evidence that the sun has risen every day in the past. Intuitively, we want to say that John is rational and Jack isn't, because the evidence makes John's belief more probable. But if probability is simply a matter of subjective opinion, we cannot say this. All we can say is that John assigns a high probability to 'the sun will rise tomorrow' and Jack does not. If there are no objective facts about probability, then we cannot say that the conclusions of inductive inferences are objectively probable. So we have no explanation of why someone like Jack, who declines to use induction, is irrational. But Hume's problem is precisely the demand for such an explanation." Okasha, *Philosophy of Science*, 37.

71. Howson, *Hume's Problem*, 14.

probabilistic, or whatever. Entirely simple and informal, Hume's argument is one of the most robust, if not the most robust, in the history of philosophy. David Miller (1994, ch. 6) has compared its impact with that of Gödel's great limitative results this century in logic, that put paid to Hilbert's Programme for so-called absolute proofs of consistency for mathematics. According to Miller, Hume's argument has the same devastating force vis-à-vis Bacon's programme for founding the sciences inductively on experiment that Gödel's had on Hilbert's.[72]

However, as Howson points out, Hume's skeptical worry seems to have not worried a soul. Hume's argument followed a scientific revolution that saw Isaac Newton at the helm, and science even now flourishes despite the difficulty highlighted by Hume.[73] Nevertheless, "If Hume is correct, then it seems to follow that we have no grounds for believing that science is any more reliable than soothsaying as a predictor of the future behaviour of the systems it studies."[74] So while scientists and others have seen very few practical consequences in Hume's problem of induction, philosophers have set their hands to solve the skeptical worry.

PROBLEM OF INDUCTION AND SECULAR RESPONSES

A number of secular responses to the problem of induction have become popular. By "secular" is meant a response that does not refer to Christian theology at all in a philosophical solution to the problem of induction.[75] Hume attempted a secular solution of sorts to his own problem that essentially ignored it, "For having advanced the sceptical case with such force and single-mindedness, he then continued his philosophical investigations as if there was no problem."[76] Karl Popper also conceded the problem and attempted a rather ingenious response to be evaluated shortly.

Not all philosophers are like Hume and Popper in conceding the difficulty. Most want to try their best to answer it instead. Of course, other problems present themselves within induction, even assuming that

72. Howson, *Hume's Problem*, 14–15.
73. Howson, *Hume's Problem*, 15.
74. Howson, *Hume's Problem*, 15.
75. Excluding the occasional *negative* reference to Christianity.
76. Foster, *Divine Lawmaker*, 8.

the problem of induction itself is resolved. But this need not worry the inductive apologist.

> All the defender of induction is committed to claiming is that inductive inferences are rational when they satisfy the appropriate conditions. In effect, he is committed to claiming that, *other things being equal*, the holding of a regularity over the examined cases provides evidential support for the conclusion that it will continue to hold for the unexamined cases, and that, *when the relevant conditions are satisfied*, this support is sufficiently strong to justify a belief or expectation that things will turn out that way. The sceptic, of course, is insisting that there are no circumstances in which such beliefs or expectations are justified or have any degree of rational support.[77]

However, many attempts at explaining away the difficulty are problematic. Foster offers three of these attempted solutions, which he labels "nonstarters."

One attempt to justify induction comes by way of citing the past success of induction. This approach is simple enough, and usually the first response offered, "The argument is that induction, appropriately employed, has served us well as a method of prediction in the past, and, on this basis, we are entitled to expect it to serve us well in future."[78] The difficulty here is that an inductive inference is used to justify inductive inference in general. This response begs the question, or assumes the very thing it intends to prove.[79]

Another shot at justifying induction comes from Hans Reichenbach, who proposes induction be justified pragmatically, an attempt Foster claims reminds one of Pascal's wager.[80] The pragmatic attempt to justify induction begins with an assumption of ignorance regarding whether or not the universe exhibits uniformity.[81]

> But if it does, or if its workings are at least *predominantly* uniform, then induction, it is claimed, promises to be a generally successful method of inference. And if it does not, then no method of inference from examined to unexamined cases has

---

77. Foster, *Divine Lawmaker*, 12.
78. Foster, *Divine Lawmaker*, 12.
79. Foster, *Divine Lawmaker*, 12–13.
80. Foster, *Divine Lawmaker*, 13.
81. Foster, *Divine Lawmaker*, 13.

any prospect of success. So we have much to gain and nothing to lose by employing induction.[82]

Reichenbach's solution carries an initial appeal, but it faces a number of difficulties. For one, it does not follow from the fact that the universe is not uniform, that no methods of inference exist which might allow one to advantageously move from the examined to the unexamined.[83] But more damaging is the fact that this response is not even really addressing the problem at hand, as it supposedly offers a practical account of why one might continue to use induction, "But it is not offering us any grounds for believing that induction will continue to be successful, nor grounds for believing, in any particular instance, that a regularity which has held for the examined cases will continue to hold for some unexamined case or group of cases."[84]

A final (in Foster's words) non-starter attempts to merely define inductive inferences as rational at the outset, given that they meet appropriate criteria.

> The argument here is that what we *mean* by saying, of an inference from the examined to the unexamined, that it is 'rational', is precisely that it is sanctioned by our ordinary inductive criteria—by our standard ways of deciding what is an acceptable form of inference from an inductive standpoint. And if this is so, then, in challenging the rationality of inferences which are thus sanctioned, the sceptic is showing that he has failed to grasp the meaning of the term 'rational'—the content of the concept of rationality—as it applies in this area. He has failed to notice that, once it is known that the evidence provides adequate support for the conclusion by the standards which are internal to our inductive practice—standards which concern such factors as the number of cases examined, the range of types of circumstance from which they are drawn, the proportion of such cases that have the relevant feature, and the strength of the conclusion inferred—there is no further issue of rationality that can be coherently raised.[85]

Foster replies here by merely claiming that the type of rational justification in view when it comes to the problem of induction is a normative

---

82. Foster, *Divine Lawmaker*, 13.
83. Foster, *Divine Lawmaker*, 13.
84. Foster, *Divine Lawmaker*, 13.
85. Foster, *Divine Lawmaker*, 13–14.

rationality. He writes, "To speak of an inference as *rational* is to imply that it is *worthy of endorsement*, that it *ought to be accepted*."[86] This normative view of rationality has come under attack in the literature. Foster seems to be aware of this alternate view of rationality, but makes the following comment in response.

> Nor, of course, could the argument be salvaged by introducing a new concept of rationality that was free of any normative element and guaranteed to apply to inferences of the relevant sort. For it is precisely the normative issue that the sceptic is addressing. His claim is not that inductive inferences cannot pass the test of acceptability by reference to our ordinary inductive criteria, but that these criteria themselves have no objective warrant, and that, because they have no objective warrant, the inferences they license are not ultimately worthy of acceptance.[87]

According to the inductive skeptic, the burden of proof is upon those who claim induction is rational.[88] The skeptic can be met with some rational justification as attempted in the examples above, or the skeptic can be resisted through claiming induction is simply taken for granted as a basic form of reasoning akin to deductive reasoning, which also, in one sense, stands in need of rational justification.[89] This second way of response is tempting given the utter failure of philosophers to come up with a decent rational justification for induction, and given that inductive reasoning is such a native part of our everyday psychological experience and reasoning.[90]

Recall that, according to Hume, reasoning is divided into "demonstrative reasoning, or that concerning relations of ideas, and moral reasoning, or that concerning matter of fact and existence" and that demonstrative arguments cannot be used in answering the problem he has raised because "it implies no contradiction that the course of nature may change, and that an object, seemingly like those which we have experienced, may be attended with different or contrary effects."[91] Nature may very well change and we may intelligibly conceive of it doing

---

86. Foster, *Divine Lawmaker*, 14.
87. Foster, *Divine Lawmaker*, 14.
88. Foster, *Divine Lawmaker*, 15.
89. Foster, *Divine Lawmaker*, 15.
90. Foster, *Divine Lawmaker*, 16.
91. Hume, *An Enquiry*, 35–36.

so in an indefinite number of ways without implying any contradictions whatsoever. Demonstrative reasoning or abstract reasoning is out of the picture as far as dealing with this problem.[92] A potential answer proposed by Hume is to base "solid and satisfactory" reasoning about matters of fact using past experience as the standard of future judgment through the "supposition that the future will be conformable to the past."[93] There is a very serious problem with this supposition though; it begs the question.

> We have said that all arguments concerning existence are founded on the relation of cause and effect; that our knowledge of that relation is derived entirely from experience; and that all our experimental conclusions proceed upon the supposition that the future will be conformable to the past. To endeavour, therefore, the proof of this last supposition by probable arguments, or arguments regarding existence, must be evidently going in a circle, and taking that for granted, which is the very point in question.[94]

Presupposing that the future will resemble the past and then proceeding to make judgments about the future based on past experience will not suffice as an answer to Hume. Hume proposes it himself and refutes it without any trouble, because the very point in question is as to whether or not we have some basis for believing that future experiences will resemble past experiences.

> All inferences from experience suppose, as their foundation, that the future will resemble the past, and that similar powers will be conjoined with similar sensible qualities. If there be any suspicion that the course of nature may change, and that the past may be no rule for the future, all experience becomes useless, and can give rise to no inference or conclusion. It is impossible, therefore, that any arguments from experience can prove this resemblance of the past to the future; since all these arguments are founded on the supposition of that resemblance.[95]

It does not matter that in the past there have been regularities in nature, what matters is whether or not we have reason to believe that it will continue to possess them in the future. Hume is adamantly opposed to

---

92. Hume, *An Enquiry*, 36.
93. Hume, *An Enquiry*, 36.
94. Hume, *An Enquiry*, 36.
95. Hume, *An Enquiry*, 38.

using past experience of any sort in an attempt to rationalize expectations about future experiences. An appeal to the past regularity of nature is no solution to the problem, nor is an appeal to the properties of objects, for these properties may change without warning from their sensible qualities. Hume notes, "This happens sometimes, and with regard to some objects: Why may it not happen always, and with regard to all objects?"[96]

Hume foresees the objection that he obviously does not have doubts about such things because he still practices inductive reasoning, but he explains that this is to miss the point, because while he agrees that he does use induction along with the rest of humanity, he wants to philosophically inquire into the foundation of such reasoning.[97] He writes, "I cannot find, I cannot imagine any such reasoning. But I keep my mind still open to instruction, if any one will vouchsafe to bestow it on me."[98]

It seems completely reasonable to expect that future experiences will resemble past experiences. Supposing that a presupposition or premise may be added to our inductive reasoning which is strong enough to lead us rationally to our conclusions but weak enough that it allows for some variation in the course of things, a seemingly commonsensical and reasonable way to answer Hume exists. Speaking of such seemingly reasonable expectations, philosopher Bertrand Russell writes, "It is to be observed that all such expectations are only *probable*; thus we have not to seek for a proof that they *must* be fulfilled, but only for some reason in favour of the view that they are *likely* to be fulfilled."[99] This is a version of the probabilistic answer to Hume. Just because a black swan or two turns up does not mean, based on past experience of swans, that the next swan will not most likely be white. In fact, this description of how someone would reason seems to fit the facts better. Surely most people do not claim to know for certain what future experiences hold, but they do claim to know, based on past experience, what is probable.

This view of probability really is no answer to Hume though. This view falls prey to one of the main problems with Hume's proposed presupposition about the uniformity of nature. Believing that future experience will *probably* resemble past experience, or that nature is *probably* uniform does fix the problem of being easily disproved by counter examples. The

---

96. Hume, *An Enquiry*, 38.
97. Hume, *An Enquiry*, 38–40.
98. Hume, *An Enquiry*, 37.
99. Russell, "Problems of Philosophy," 1161.

principle is incapable of being proven wrong by exceptions, but the response does not go far enough. Russell explains,

> The inductive principle, however, is equally incapable of being *proved* by an appeal to experience. Experience might conceivably confirm the inductive principle as regards the cases that have been already examined; but as regards unexamined cases, it is the inductive principle alone that can justify any inference from what has been examined to what has not been examined. All arguments which, on the basis of experience, argue as to the future or the unexperienced parts of the past or present, assume the inductive principle; hence we can never use experience to prove the inductive principle without begging the question. Thus we must either accept the inductive principle on the ground of its intrinsic evidence, or forgo all justification of our expectations about the future.[100]

Ultimately the use of probability, which assumes that the future will probably resemble the past, fails as an answer to Hume's problem of induction for the same reason that the presupposition of the uniformity of nature fails: it begs the question.

Foster clarifies, "The sceptic about induction is calling in question the legitimacy of the extrapolative mode of inference—the mode of inference whereby we reach conclusions about certain unexamined cases by extrapolating from how things are known to have been with respect to the examined cases."[101] One common mistake of those attempting to respond to the problem of induction is assuming that the worry stems from a lack of certainty concerning unexamined cases. While conclusions about unexamined cases are uncertain, they are nevertheless probable, and this is thought to serve as a proper response to the problem of induction.

> Now it is easy to suppose, particularly when one is first introduced to the topic, that what is at issue here is whether we have, on the basis of this kind of inference, the right to be *sure*—to be *certain*—about the outcome in these unexamined cases. Thus it might be thought that what the sceptic is pointing out and underlining is that there is a *logical gap* between the knowledge we have about the examined cases and the conclusions which we ordinarily reach about the unexamined cases, and that, just because of this gap, we cannot be sure that these conclusions are

---

100. Russell, "Problems of Philosophy," 1163.
101. Foster, *Divine Lawmaker*, 7.

correct. However strong the evidence from an inductive standpoint, we have to allow for the possibility that the unexamined cases may turn out differently from the examined, and so we ought, to that extent, to keep an open mind about the outcome. We should settle for merely claiming that there are *grounds for believing* that the unexamined cases will turn out the same way as the examined, and, with increasing inductive evidence, increasingly strong grounds for belief. What is in principle beyond our reach, it might be thought the sceptic is claiming, is rationally based *certainty*.[102]

While there are many things of which we are not certain, this is not at all what the skeptic is proposing about induction. According to Foster, "What he is claiming, much more strongly, is that, with respect to these outcomes, there is no rational basis for any kind of expectation at all."[103] Howson explains the attempt to answer Hume on the basis of probability as well, and why it fails:

> We can flesh out the argument thus: mathematical, indeed any, definitions say nothing about matters of fact ('It is indeed evident, that we can never, by the comparison of mere ideas, make any discovery which can be of consequence in this affair' (ibid.)). In order for them to do so special assumptions are required. Not only will these beg the question of their truth in general, but in view of the fact that 'the course of nature may change', and in very different ways, any extrapolation sanctioned by a probabilistic argument will beg the question of why that particular way should be regarded as a probable one. In fact, Hume's circularity thesis applies to arguments from mathematical probability as much as it does to any sort of non-deductive 'probable inference', and we shall see later how inductive arguments constructed within the mathematical theory of probability fully corroborate it.[104]

Presupposing the inductive principle is no way to answer Hume. Probabilistic arguments do not appear to be of much help to the philosopher who wishes to save induction from the skeptic either.

One particularly noble attempt at solving Hume's problem of induction and saving science is offered by Karl Popper in his hypothetico-deductivism. Popper thinks it is easy to confirm a theory if events that are

102. Foster, *Divine Lawmaker*, 7.
103. Foster, *Divine Lawmaker*, 8.
104. Howson, *Hume's Problem*, 14.

PROBLEM OF INDUCTION   163

incompatible with the theory are either not thought of or are ignored.[105] This oversight is essentially one of Hume's worries. The solution Popper proposes is unique because it sidesteps induction altogether.[106] Rationality is to be found in reasoning concerning matters of fact and in science through the use of deduction rather than induction. According to Popper, not only is it unnecessary to use induction, but we most often do not. Rather, we typically make conjectures or jump to conclusions and, "having formed beliefs or expectations in this non-inductive way, we employ them in perfectly valid deductive arguments in order to anticipate the future."[107] The claim is that leaps are made to belief in conclusions then deductive inferences are drawn from these conclusions. Falsifiable propositions which emerge unfalsified by rigorous testing are considered reasonable to believe. If this view is true, then it refutes the conclusion Hume comes to regarding the irrationality of humans.

Popper thinks falsifiability is the distinguishing factor between science and non-science, but for the purposes of this discussion it is only necessary to understand what is *meant* by "falsifiable." Popper's proposed solution to Hume will mostly be in terms of scientific reasoning, since this is Popper's main concern. According to Popper, scientific theories must be falsifiable; otherwise they are separate from the world and cannot yield any information about it. Philosopher A. F. Chalmers explains, "An hypothesis is falsifiable if there exists a logically possible observation statement or set of observation statements that are inconsistent with it, that is, which, if established as true, would falsify the hypothesis."[108] A simple example of a falsifiable statement is, "It never rains on Wednesdays," and an example of a non-falsifiable statement is, "Either it is raining or it is not raining."[109] It is clear that a statement like "Either it is raining or it is not raining" has little to do with the empirical world. The absolute best hypotheses make many claims about the world, making them more easily falsifiable while withstanding tests that are intended to falsify them.

---

105. Chalmers, *What Is This Thing?*, 68.

106. Popper is not misunderstanding or ignoring Hume's problem, but effectively parrying it by theorizing that induction is not all that important to the scientific endeavor after all.

107. Musgrave, *Common Sense*, 171.

108. Chalmers, *What Is This Thing?*, 62.

109. Chalmers, *What Is This Thing?*, 62–63.

With this understanding of falsification we move on to see how falsification relates to hypothetico-deduction. When theories are proposed in the manner already described, they are not proposed as true statements or probably true statements as is the case when conclusions from induction are proposed. Rather, these theories are conjectures. The purpose of a conjecture is to solve a problem or problems that a previous conjecture could not solve. For example, theories often fail to account for some observation or they cannot account for the result of some experiment. Laws or similar statements which have been proposed and refuted by even one observation or experiment are shown to be false. This is the tie between falsifiability and the hypothetico-deductive method. Notice also that induction has no role, since this method is based on deductive logic. Chalmers explains, "The falsity of universal statements can be deduced from suitable singular statements. The falsificationist exploits this logical point to the full."[110]

Popper and his followers would submit that induction is not to be used in science, thus the problem of induction is really no problem at all when it comes to scientific endeavors. By extension, this same reasoning can be applied to everyday activities regarding matters of fact. Hypotheses are proposed and have their falsity deduced from observations and experiments inconsistent with the hypotheses. A wild theory can be proposed as long as the language used in the theory is clear so as not to avoid falsification and as long as it describes something about the world.[111] Of course even then rigorous testing and immediate rejection of the theory if it is falsified are necessary.[112] Following this method, it is presumably possible to know that a theory is better than the ones which have preceded it; therefore it is the best theory available at the time that is proposed and tested. This is how science proceeds, moving closer to the truth with each refutation. Chalmers writes, "Because of the logical situation that renders the derivation of universal laws and theories from observation statements impossible, but the deduction of their falsity possible, falsifications become the important landmarks, the striking achievements, the major growing-points in science."[113]

---

110. Chalmers, *What Is This Thing?*, 61.
111. Chalmers, *What Is This Thing?*, 68.
112. Chalmers, *What Is This Thing?*, 67.
113. Chalmers, *What Is This Thing?*, 67.

Popper's proposition is nothing short of brilliant. However, some concerns are worth raising related to the overall theory itself. For example, it is rather easy to satisfy Popper's condition of falsifiability, as any prediction about the world can be made regardless of how absurd it might be.[114] Thus astrologers and scientists look alike when they hold onto accepted theories which require modification to avoid apparent contradictions with observation and experiment.[115] More fundamental than this, the idea of falsifiability itself, and of degrees of falsifiability, is initially vague and relative.[116] There is no objective standard available to make judgments about whether or not a theory is a good one, as Chalmers points out, "An absolute measure of falsifiablility cannot be defined simply because the number of potential falsifiers of a theory will always be infinite."[117]

Further problems plague Popper. When a theory contradicts an observation or experiment, it is not logically necessary that the *theory* is incorrect; the *observation* or *experiment* might just as well be. Determining which is incorrect when contradiction occurs could be extremely difficult. It could be that the observation or experiment is erroneous while the theory is not. Of course, this state of affairs assumes that a scientific statement can be put into clear enough language that it may be known whether or not it is falsified. This is also difficult because scientific theories are often extremely complex. Many other factors like assumptions, laws, instruments, and initial conditions go into the testing of a hypothesis. Some of these factors cannot be known to be true according to Popper's own method. It may be thought likely that something else has gone wrong when an observation or experiment contradicts a theory, in fact a "theory can always be protected from falsification by deflecting the falsification to some other part of the complex web of assumptions."[118] Chalmers writes, "It may be the theory under test that is at fault, but alternatively it may be an auxiliary assumption or some part of the description of the initial conditions that is responsible for an erroneous prediction."[119]

---

114. Chalmers, *What Is This Thing?*, 102.
115. Chalmers, *What Is This Thing?*, 102.
116. No doubt Popper's defenders would make some effort to more carefully delineate what is meant by falsifiability.
117. Chalmers, *What Is This Thing?*, 102.
118. Chalmers, *What Is This Thing?*, 91.
119. Chalmers, *What Is This Thing?*, 89.

There are often too many factors present in actual situations in science to make a judgment about if a theory is falsified. There could be another factor at fault which makes the theory look false when actually it is not.

According to this method, "The enterprise of science involves the proposal of highly falsifiable hypotheses, followed by deliberate and tenacious attempts to falsify them."[120] Scientific theories can never be thought of as true or probably true, which goes against a traditional sense of "justification."

> Faced with the problems surrounding the degree of definiteness with which theories can be falsified, Popper admits that it is often necessary to retain theories in spite of apparent falsifications. So although ruthless criticism is recommended, what would appear to be its opposite, dogmatism, has a positive role to play too. One might well wonder what is left of falsificationism once dogmatism is allowed a key role. Further, if both a critical and a dogmatic attitude can be condoned, then it is difficult to see what attitudes are ruled out. (It would be ironic if the highly qualified version of falsificationism became so weak as to rule out nothing, thereby clashing with the main intuition that led Popper to formulate it!)[121]

Again, Popper makes a noble attempt at answering Hume, but his methodology is problematic and leaves many questions to be answered.

With Popper's solution it is allegedly reasonable to believe particular propositions whether or not these propositions are known to be true or false and without justification for them. Hume would likewise think that adherence to unjustified conclusions is far from reasonable, at least according to philosopher Alan Musgrave.

> Hume would say that it is not reasonable to believe a prediction about the unobserved unless (what is not the case here) that prediction can be shown to be true or be shown to be highly probable. Let us say that a proposition has been justified if it has either been shown to be true or been shown to be probable (more likely to be true than not). Then Hume would insist that it is only reasonable to believe justified propositions. He would insist, further, that the invalidity of induction means that we cannot justify general hypotheses or propositions about

---

120. Chalmers, *What Is This Thing?*, 66.
121. Chalmers, *What Is This Thing?*, 103.

unobserved cases. It follows that we cannot reasonably believe any general hypothesis or proposition about the unobserved.[122]

We may, following what Musgrave speculates about Hume's response to Popper, find that Popper does not really answer Hume's problem so much as he offers a different set of standards from what Hume uses.[123]

Popper's proposal is only acceptable at the expense of empirical knowledge. That is, it can never be known whether or not the conclusions we hold are true. Certainty is not the issue here; we cannot even state that things are *probably* true. Popper seeks to show that it is reasonable to believe particular propositions whether or not those propositions are true or false and without justification for them. We only know which propositions are false when they are falsified, but never before. Empirical knowledge is no more possible on this view than on Hume's. Though hypothetico-deductivism is an elaborate and clever approach to saving science from the problem of induction, it does not address some of the most troubling concerns about the problem of induction.

In the end, Popper's solution rests upon the inductive principle anyway. Foster offers a lengthy, but clear example of why Popper's method does not escape the need for inductive logic:

> The point where, it seems to me, induction is needed is in deciding what kind of theory to choose as a replacement for one which has been shown, by the failure of one of its predictions, to be mistaken. Thus suppose we are provisionally entertaining the theory that whenever an A-type particle meets a B-type particle, they produce a C-type particle. This has held good in all the situations so far investigated. We then put the theory to the test in a further situation, which we may think is not significantly different from the others, and the predicted result does not occur. We check very carefully on what has happened, and cannot avoid the conclusion that, on this occasion, there was a genuine meeting of a genuine A-type particle and a genuine B-type particle, with no resulting C-type particle. So we are forced to acknowledge that the original theory is mistaken. But where do we go from there? Well, Popper would say, as any *scientist* would say, that we should try to find some relevant difference between the situation where the prediction failed and all the others where it succeeded, and then come up with a unitary theory

---

122. Musgrave, *Common Sense*, 174.

123. Perhaps Hume's standards are just wrong, but then why is all the fuss over the specifics of empirical knowledge really necessary?

which covers both types of result—a theory which represents the world as behaving in a uniform way after all. But an alternative response would just be to accept that the world is not wholly regular, and that, on this particular occasion, for no interesting reason, there was a different result. In other words, we might just replace the original theory by one which claims that whenever an A-type particle meets a B-type particle, they produce a C-type particle *except on that occasion*. Now, of course, if we were to put forward such a theory as our new provisional hypothesis, it would immediately invite a retesting of it in the same kind of conditions (the conditions in which the original theory failed), and no doubt when that retest was done, the same negative result would emerge, forcing us to reject the new theory too. But, in the face of any such refutation, we could always respond in the same conservative way, by retaining the original theory, and simply expanding the class of specified exceptions. Now, from a scientific standpoint, such a procedure would be seen as just perverse—something designed to lock us into an unending series of refutations, without making any theoretical progress. But notice, that the assumption underlying this scientific verdict is that nature is *uniform*, and that once the original hypothesis has been found to fail on one occasion, we should expect it to fail again when exactly the same type of situation recurs. And if we could not rely on this assumption of uniformity, then, as far as I can see, there is no way, except by arbitrary stipulation, in which the perverse procedure could be ruled out. But our only grounds for accepting that nature is uniform are that it has been found to be uniform over the cases so far examined; and these grounds will only entitle us to expect uniformity over the unexamined cases if we can rely on the rationality of induction. So if science is to have a principled way of excluding the envisaged procedure—which I assume that Popper himself would think crucial—it has to rely, at this point, on the rationality of induction, contrary to what Popper supposes.[124]

Some of the more popular attempts at answering Hume have been offered, including presuppositionalism, probabilism, and deductivism. Each attempts to answer Hume's problem in a slightly different way. Hume offers his own skeptical "solution" to the problem of induction, but it is of a very different nature than the potential solutions already discussed.

Nelson Goodman, the author of the "Grue Problem," which is also known as the "New Riddle of Induction," reviews Hume's problem of

124. Foster, *Divine Lawmaker*, 10–11.

induction before presenting his new version. Goodman claims that what "is commonly thought of as the Problem of Induction has been solved, or dissolved."[125] Goodman does not appear to think he is presenting a new or different solution to Hume's problem, but rather what Hume has already presented himself. In fact, Goodman calls the position that "Hume's account at best pertains only to the source of predictions, not their legitimacy" a "righteous position" and believes that "this seems to point to the awkward conclusion that the greatest of modern philosophers completely missed the point of his own problem."[126] Goodman explains, "All this seems to me quite wrong. I think Hume grasped the central question and considered his answer to be passably effective. And I think his answer is reasonable and relevant, even if it is not entirely satisfactory."[127]

Goodman defines Hume's problem as the "problem of justifying induction" only when it is divorced from Hume's description of "how induction takes place."[128] To clarify, Goodman understands what he refers to as Hume's problem, which has already been discussed, to be just as problematic to philosophers and laypersons as Hume describes, but finds that this is only because they fail to understand that Hume's solution is actually sufficient.[129] Goodman writes, "The typical writer begins by insisting that some way of justifying predictions must be found; proceeds to argue that for this purpose we need some resounding universal law of the Uniformity of Nature, and then inquires how this universal principle itself can be justified."[130] As already discussed, there are numerous problems with attempting to justify induction in the aforementioned manner. Goodman describes the typical philosopher's next step, and continues, "At this point, if he is tired, he concludes that the principle must be accepted as an indispensable assumption; or if he is energetic and ingenious, he goes on to devise some subtle justification for it. Such an invention, however, seldom satisfies anyone else; and the easier course of accepting an unsubstantiated and even dubious assumption much more sweeping

---

125. Goodman, *Fact, Fiction, and Forecast*, 59.
126. Goodman, *Fact, Fiction, and Forecast*, 61.
127. Goodman, *Fact, Fiction, and Forecast*, 61.
128. Goodman, *Fact, Fiction, and Forecast*, 61.
129. Goodman, *Fact, Fiction, and Forecast*, 61–62.
130. Goodman, *Fact, Fiction, and Forecast*, 61.

than any actual predictions we make seems an odd and expensive way of justifying them."[131]

Goodman's point is that the philosopher is typically rather frustrated by the problem of induction. Perhaps then, there is something else to this problem. Perhaps it is not properly posed or it makes no sense to bring it up. However, when Goodman asks, "Come to think of it, what precisely would constitute the justification we seek?" he disallows some possible answers to Hume.[132] Musgrave points this out:

> The problem of induction can be formulated as follows: can Hume's irrationalist conclusion be avoided? (Popper 1962: Chapter I, 1972: Chapter I). This is not the only way to formulate the problem, nor is it the usual way it is formulated; but it is the best way to formulate it. Common formulations like 'Can induction be justified?' or even 'How can induction be justified?' beg the question against some of the possible responses to Hume.[133]

Goodman's understanding of the question posed by Hume's discussion of induction forces Goodman into finding out what the question about justifying induction actually means, or what kind of answer the question entails.

Goodman is led to use analogical reasoning, asking what justifies *deduction*. He hopes that this will clarify what is being sought after in terms of justifying *induction*. After a brief, and very basic, explanation of the justification of deductive inferences, Goodman comes to an interesting conclusion.

> When a deductive argument has been shown to conform to the rules of logical inference, we usually consider it justified without going on to ask what justifies the rules. Analogously, the basic task in justifying an inductive inference is to show that it conforms to the general rules of *induction*. Once we have recognized this, we have gone a long way towards clarifying our problem.[134]

Goodman goes on to ask and answer where the justification for valid deductive inferences lies.

---

131. Goodman, *Fact, Fiction, and Forecast*, 61–62.
132. Goodman, *Fact, Fiction, and Forecast*, 62–63.
133. Musgrave, *Common Sense*, 153.
134. Goodman, *Fact, Fiction, and Forecast*, 63.

Their validity depends upon accordance with the particular deductive inferences we actually make and sanction. If a rule yields inacceptable inferences, we drop it as invalid. Justification of general rules thus derives from judgments rejecting or accepting particular deductive inferences.[135]

The circularity of Goodman's thesis does not appear to bother him. Goodman proposes that this circularity is a "virtuous circle" where rules and inferences are made to agree with each other. This understanding of the justification of deduction is then applied to induction, and he writes, "An inductive inference, too, is justified by conformity to general rules, and a general rule by conformity to accepted inductive inferences. Predictions are justified if they conform to valid canons of induction; and the canons are valid if they accurately codify accepted inductive practice."[136]

This unique answer to the problem of induction is not without its problems, and it is probably not the sort of thing Hume has in mind when he proposes his solution to the problem of induction. It seems more likely than not that Goodman is here proposing his own solution to the problem of induction and then ascribing it to Hume, for he holds that the "traditional smug insistence upon a hard-and-fast line between justifying induction and describing ordinary inductive practice distorts the problem."[137] It is suggested that we owe apologies to Hume, as though he has been misread for all of this time, "For in dealing with the question how normally accepted inductive judgments are made, he was in fact dealing with the question of inductive validity. The validity of a prediction consisted for him in its arising from habit, and thus in its exemplifying some past regularity."[138] This explanation leaves Goodman at a point where he can go on to write about confirmation theory and his "New Problem of Induction," for he views the problem of induction not in the traditional sense, but as a need to develop a system as elaborate and well-established as that of deduction, clearly defining what is valid and invalid when it comes to predictions.[139] However, Goodman's interpretation does not fit well with Hume's text.

135. Goodman, *Fact, Fiction, and Forecast*, 63–64.
136. Goodman, *Fact, Fiction, and Forecast*, 64.
137. Goodman, *Fact, Fiction, and Forecast*, 64.
138. Goodman, *Fact, Fiction, and Forecast*, 64–65.
139. Goodman, *Fact, Fiction, and Forecast*, 65.

Hume proposes a skeptical solution to his problem, but it is not intended to solve the problem in such a way that rational inductive inferences are secured. Rather, it further develops the skeptical view Hume holds. Hume has concluded that the mind takes a step in reasoning based on past experience from which reason and argument are absent. His curiosity leads him (ironically, due to the propensity to reason inductively and expect causes with effects) to inquire why the mind makes one unjustified leap rather than another and what authority other than reason can lead humans to think and behave the way they do with respect to matters of fact.[140] This much has been made clear in this chapter, and it is strange that some type of rational justification for induction would be ascribed to Hume given how much he has proposed against that view.

Hume describes an experience of all humanity drawing inferences and proposes that the principle accomplishing this feat is called "Custom or Habit."[141]

> For wherever the repetition of any particular act or operation produces a propensity to renew the same act or operation, without being impelled by any reasoning or process of the understanding, we always say, that this propensity is the effect of Custom. By employing that word, we pretend not to have given the ultimate reason of such a propensity. We only point out a principle of human nature, which is universally acknowledged, and which is well known by its effects.[142]

Custom is the ultimate principle Hume finds behind all reasoning concerning matters of fact. Note Hume does not believe he has "given the ultimate reason of such a propensity."[143] Custom alone determines us to expect to find one object with another in future experience because it was found that way in past experience. Hume thinks "This hypothesis seems even the only one which explains the difficulty, why we draw, from a thousand instances, an inference which we are not able to draw from one instance, that is, in no respect, different from them. Reason is incapable of any such variation."[144]

---

140. Hume, *An Enquiry*, 43–44.
141. Hume, *An Enquiry*, 45.
142. Hume, *An Enquiry*, 45.
143. Hume, *An Enquiry*, 45.
144. Hume, *An Enquiry*, 46.

PROBLEM OF INDUCTION 173

This reading of Hume presents a problem for Goodman's view because Hume is clearly differentiating between his skeptical solution and solutions which would pretend to provide some sort of rational basis for induction. Reason is excluded from Hume's solution, while Goodman tries to bring it back in. Hume's concisely stated conclusion reinforces his skeptical view of rationally justified induction.

> What, then, is the conclusion of the whole matter? A simple one; though, it must be confessed, pretty remote from the common theories of philosophy. All belief of matter of fact or real existence is derived merely from some object, present to the memory or senses, and a customary conjunction between that and some other object.[145]

Bertrand Russell agrees, "Experience has shown us that, hitherto, the frequent repetition of some uniform succession or coexistence has been a *cause* of our expecting the same succession or coexistence on the next occasion."[146]

Whether or not induction is reasonable is very much a separate question from whether or not people reason inductively and why it is that they do so. Hume does not at all doubt that people can and must reason inductively. Hume likewise does not doubt that there is some cause for people reasoning in this manner. His skeptical solution is an attempt to formulate an understanding of what this cause is. Russell draws this distinction as well, "We have therefore to distinguish the fact that past uniformities *cause* expectations as to the future, from the question whether there is any reasonable ground for giving weight to such expectations after the question of their validity has been raised."[147]

For Hume, reason has nothing to do with induction, "All these operations are a species of natural instincts, which no reasoning or process of the thought and understanding is able either to produce or to prevent."[148] Hume is merciless in his skeptical conclusion, writing, "Animals, therefore are not guided in these inferences by reasoning: neither are children; neither are the generality of mankind, in their ordinary actions and conclusions: neither are philosophers themselves, who, in all the active parts of life, are, in the main, the same with the vulgar, and

---

145. Hume, *An Enquiry*, 49.
146. Russell, "Problems of Philosophy," 1161.
147. Russell, "Problems of Philosophy," 1161.
148. Hume, *An Enquiry*, 116.

are governed by the same maxims."[149] Russell also writes concerning the appearance of inductive reasoning amongst non-human animals.

> And this kind of association is not confined to men; in animals also it is very strong. A horse which has been often driven along a certain road resists the attempt to drive him in a different direction. Domestic animals expect food when they see the person who feeds them. We know that all these rather crude expectations of uniformity are liable to be misleading. The man who has fed the chicken every day throughout its life at last wrings its neck instead, showing that more refined views as to the uniformity of nature would have been useful to the chicken.[150]

According to Hume and Russell, humans appear to be no different than animals when it comes to the matter of induction. While this is not a conclusion many would be overly zealous to accept, it is a conclusion Hume believes is forced by the premises of his argument. Hume concludes, "It is custom alone, which engages animals, from every object, that strikes their senses, to infer its usual attendant, and carries their imagination, from the appearance of the one, to conceive the other, in that particular manner, which we denominate *belief*. No other explication can be given of this operation, in all the higher, as well as lower classes of sensitive beings, which fall under our notice and observation."[151]

PROBLEM OF INDUCTION AND CHRISTIAN SOLUTIONS

Recall the earlier discussion of the doctrine of divine providence from chapter 1. Not only does God preserve, conserve, or sustain the world in existence, but he also governs, guides, or directs it toward its ends.[152] Further, God does so in virtue of concurrence.[153] Concurrence is a function of the philosophical categories of preservation and government, for God is active in both of the aforementioned categories with respect to the creation itself. God preserves a creation that already exists, and God governs a creation that exhibits secondary causation. Moreover, the doctrine of divine providence establishes that nothing happens according to chance;

---

149. Hume, *An Enquiry*, 116.
150. Russell, "Problems of Philosophy," 1161.
151. Hume, *An Enquiry*, 117.
152. Plantinga, *Where Conflict Really Lies*, 66–67.
153. Plantinga, *Where Conflict Really Lies*, 67.

everything happens in accord with the will of God which preserves and governs the entirety of creation in a *regular* and hence *predictable* way.[154] This regularity and predictability are often noted by the theologians, apologists, and scientists mentioned earlier in chapter 2.

Regularity and predictability are necessary conditions of scientific success.[155] They are also necessary conditions of routine human behavior, or intentional action.[156] However, it is not enough for there to merely be these two prerequisite conditions of scientific endeavor and intentional action. People must also possess warranted belief that the universe exists in the aforementioned way.[157] All of this is available to the Christian theist who has a robust view of the doctrine of divine providence.

It appears to be in the nature of human beings to expect the future to resemble the past in relevant ways, though they do not expect the future to resemble the past in every way.[158] This expectation is what drives the common belief that people are capable of learning from experience. Learning from experience is obviously a significant part of the scientific endeavor. But why should anyone assume that the future will resemble the past? It will not help to claim that since *in the past* the future has resembled the past, it will do so *in the future*, for this response relies upon the very principle which has been called into question, and it is certainly

---

154. Plantinga, *Where Conflict Really Lies*, 67.

155. Plantinga claims, "For science to be successful, the world must display a high degree of regularity and predictability." Plantinga, *Where Conflict Really Lies*, 271. See virtually any book on the philosophy of science.

156. According to Plantinga, "intentional action requires the same thing: we couldn't build a house if hammers unpredictably turned into eels, or nails into caterpillars; we couldn't drive downtown if automobiles unexpectedly turned into tea pots or rosebushes." Plantinga, *Where Conflict Really Lies*, 271. He continues, "Intentional action requires a high degree of stability, predictability, and regularity. And of course the predictability in question has to be predictability *by us*. For intentional action to be possible, it must be the case that we, given our cognitive faculties, can often or usually predict what will happen next. No doubt there could be creatures with wholly different cognitive powers, creatures who could predict the course of events in ways we can't; that might be nice for them, but science as practiced by us humans requires predictability given *our* cognitive faculties." Plantinga, *Where Conflict Really Lies*, 271.

157. Plantinga, *Where Conflict Really Lies*, 271–74.

158. Plantinga, *Where Conflict Really Lies*, 292. Plantinga points out, "Saying precisely how we expect the future to resemble the past is no mean task; we expect the future to resemble the past in relevant respects; but specifying the relevant respects is far from easy. Nevertheless, we do expect the future to resemble the past, and this expectation is crucial to our being able to learn from experience." Plantinga, *Where Conflict Really Lies*, 292.

logically possible that the future will *not* resemble the past in the relevant respects.[159] However, the theist has an answer here insofar as God is that rational will which stands providentially behind every event and object of the universe concurrently preserving and governing his creation. *Nomic necessity* provides the necessary connection between cause and effect that philosophers have sought after in their attempts to account for scientific success. God imposes laws of nature on his creation and thereby enables the scientist to proceed with his tasks. These concepts were discussed earlier in chapter 3. The theist who adheres to a robust doctrine of divine providence is thus *internally justified* in his or her acceptance of inductive reasoning and science.[160]

The theist is also *externally warranted* in holding to induction and science.[161] The Christian theist has every reason to accept inductive reasoning as *rationally warranted*, for human beings who are created in the image of God with "properly functioning cognitive faculties" that match up to a proper cognitive environment take it for granted that inductive reasoning is an acceptable form of reasoning and operate in accordance with it every day.[162]

---

159. Hume pointed this out, but Plantinga clarifies, "There are plenty of possible worlds that match the actual world up to the present time, but then diverge wildly, so that inductive inferences would mostly fail in those other worlds. There are as many of those counter-inductive worlds as there are worlds in which induction will continue to be reliable. It is by no means inevitable that inductive reasoning should be successful; its success is one more example of the fit between our cognitive faculties and the world." Plantinga, *Where Conflict Really Lies*, 295.

160. According to philosophers J. P. Moreland and William Lane Craig, "Roughly, an internalist is one who holds that the sole factors that justify belief are 'internal' or 'cognitively accessible' to the believing agent or subject. These factors are various mental states (experiences, sensations, thoughts, beliefs) to which the agent himself has direct access by simply reflecting on or being aware of his own states of consciousness. Justification is grounded in what is internal to the mind of and directly accessible to the believing subject." Moreland and Craig, *Philosophical Foundation*, 76.

161. Moreland and Craig, *Philosophical Foundation*, 76. According to Moreland and Craig, "An externalist is one who denies internalism, that is, who affirms that among the factors that justify a belief are those to which the believing subject does not have or does not need to have cognitive access." Moreland and Craig, *Philosophical Foundation*, 76.

162. Plantinga believes "Hume is wrong. We human beings, including those among us with properly functioning cognitive faculties, are inveterately addicted to inductive reasoning. And this is another example of fit between our cognitive faculties and the world in which we find ourselves." Plantinga, *Where the Conflict Really Lies*, 295.

The philosopher Thomas Reid believes the skeptical hypotheses of Hume "lead to conclusions which contradict the principles, upon which all men of common sense must act in common life."[163] Reid does praise Hume's attempt to deepen the discussion surrounding induction in virtue of its relationship to science. He writes, "A system of consequences, however absurd, acutely and justly drawn from a few principles, in very abstract matters, is of real utility in science, and may be made subservient to real knowledge."[164] Reid presents Hume as arguing that "there is no ground to believe any one proposition rather than its contrary, and 'all those are certainly fools who reason or believe anything.'"[165] While Reid offers a volley of responses to Hume which call into question many of Hume's assumptions, this principle of common sense is perhaps the most important insight offered by Reid. The reason Reid's observation is so important is that, even conceding Hume's skeptical worry, neither Reid, nor Hume, nor can anyone else circumvent the force of what Reid labels common sense. Before offering a more thorough reply to Hume by way of reasoning concerning probability, Reid runs to the principle of common sense, noting of Hume's skeptical worry, "It is some comfort, that this doctrine can never be seriously adopted by any man in his senses. And after this author had shown that 'all the rules of logic require a total extinction of all belief and evidence,' he himself, and all men that are not insane, must have believed many things, and yielded assent to the evidence which he had extinguished."[166] Again, even Hume must, and does, concede the strength of what Reid calls common sense. Reid writes, "This indeed he is so candid as to acknowledge. 'He finds himself absolutely and necessarily determined, to live and talk and act like other people in the common affairs of life. And since reason is incapable of dispelling these clouds, most fortunately it happens, that Nature herself suffices to that purpose, and cures him of this philosophical melancholy and delirium.'"[167] Reid goes on to reason that nature is the cause of good reasoning with regard to this matter of inductive reasoning, and the philosopher the cause of bad, such that "Whatever was the cause of this delirium, it must be granted, that if it was real and not feigned, it was not

163. Reid, *Essays*, 163.

164. Reid, *Essays*, 163. Reid comments, "This merit Mr HUME's metaphysical writings have in a great degree." Reid, *Essays*, 163.

165. Reid, *Essays*, 562.

166. Reid, *Essays*, 562.

167. Reid, *Essays*, 562.

to be cured by reasoning: For what can be more absurd than to attempt to convince a man by reasoning who disowns the authority of reason. It was therefore very fortunate that Nature found other means of curing it."[168]

Reid's response to Hume fits particularly well within the context of a Christian worldview. God has created people with the potential for knowledge concerning God, the self, and the world around them. People are thus created with the disposition to reason inductively in the cognitive environment of the providentially controlled cosmos which makes such reasoning possible.[169] Inductive reasoning is also an exceedingly practical matter, absurd to deny and useful in the realms of science and everyday life.

It may be a misunderstanding of scientific laws to posit them as stating that the past somehow causes the future, or as holding all things in the universe together in some *causal* sense through time.[170] In this view, scientific laws apply to *objects* and not sequential *events*, though with the assumption that things will tend to go on existing as they have, it is possible to use scientific laws to make predictions about the future.[171] The scientific laws just do not tell us anything regarding that assumption. However, divine preservation may, and might therefore help solve a number of other difficulties in the philosophy of science regarding causality and the laws of nature. One example that was discussed in this chapter is the so-called problem of induction.

Once the laws of nature are established in virtue of the Christian doctrine of divine providence, the short fallings of various attempts to solve the problem of induction are taken care of within the Christian worldview. For example, a Christian might approach science through Popper's hypothetico-deductive method rather than Bacon's inductive method without worrying about the major problem that exists in Popper's

---

168. Reid, *Essays*, 563.

169. Plantinga explains this *deep concord* between theistic belief and science, "Like the others, this fit is to be expected given theism. God has created us in his image; this involves our being able to have significant knowledge about our world. That requires the *adequatio intellectus ad rem* (the fit of intellect with reality) of which the medieval spoke, and the success of inductive reasoning is one more example of this *adequatio*. According to theism, God has created us in such a way that we reason in an inductive fashion; he has created our world in such a way that inductive reasoning is successful. This is one more manifestation of the deep concord between theism and science." Plantinga, *Where Conflict Really Lies*, 295–96.

170. McCann, "Creation and Conservation," 311.

171. McCann, "Creation and Conservation," 311.

solution within the context of a secularist response to the problem of induction. The major problem plaguing science in virtue of the problem of induction is the lack of a cogent account of the laws of nature, which is provided for through recognition of the doctrine of divine providence. Once that problem is resolved, scientists might move forward with any number of different understandings of the scientific method.

Chapter 5

Further Issues

The Introduction claimed that the Christian doctrine of providence and its implications for the laws of nature and problem of induction entail that Christian theism is better equipped to provide a basis for science than are secular and Islamic worldviews. In chapter 1, the Christian doctrine of providence was elaborated upon in great detail before chapter 2 presented a wide variety of thinkers who have noted the implications of the Christian doctrine of divine providence for laws of nature, induction, and science in general. That chapter argued that Islam has failed to produce much by way of science, and one possible explanation for this state of affairs is that Islam lacks a Christian doctrine of divine providence. Chapter 3 provided a closer look at the laws of nature, and chapter 4 dealt with the problem of induction, some secular responses to that problem, why they fail, and how Christianity provides possible solutions to that problem. This chapter, chapter 5, discusses the potential difficulty of miracles for Christian theistic explanations of scientific assumptions, presses a similar difficulty with respect to Islam, then focuses more narrowly on three aspects of Islamic doctrine which appear to create problems for any attempt at constructing scientific thought within the confines of an Islamic worldview. The chapter ends with a brief discussion of apologetic points that might be gleaned from the treatment of the topic at hand in this book.

FURTHER ISSUE OF MIRACLES

One apparent problem with the account of divine providence offered here, especially in its relationship to science, is that of miracles. If God is active in everything that comes about, then what room is left for miracles? Or to put the concern more clearly, what is the difference between God's ordinary providential activity and his miraculous deeds? If miracles are supernatural intervention, then there no longer seems to be any distinction between miracles and the ordinary providential activity of God.

The reply to this concern is not as difficult as it might initially seem. The reason that miracles are distinct from ordinary providence is just that miracles stand out from the normal operations of nature in accordance with the providence of God. Miracles may be said to remain a part of God's providential activity while revealing something special about God and his redemptive purposes through nature behaving in a way that it does not usually behave or the laws of nature even seemingly being defied.[1] Alleged philosophical difficulties pertaining to miracles do not warrant an outright rejection of the positive scriptural, historical, and philosophical case for providence. Miracles are rare, revelatory acts of God. Further, God need not be thought of as bound by the universe in such a way that he is incapable of superseding its natural operations through his divine power.[2]

Theologian John Frame provides a good reminder of what has been understood concerning the doctrine of divine providence, and in particular, concurrence. Frame writes, "Concurrence teaches that God causes events on the micro level as well as on the macro level. He uses second causes, but none of the second causes work without him. He uses second causes, but he is always working in and with those second causes."[3] It follows from what has been stated that God acts in the world in an immediate sense. Immediacy cannot serve to define miracles over against the nonmiraculous.[4] Do miracles as understood in this sense undo the force of the case for laws of nature in the context of divine providence? Plantinga begins to answer this question by describing how the providence of God is responsible for both laws of nature and seeming

---

1. McCann, "Creation and Conservation," 311.

2. McCann, "Creation and Conservation," 311. Those who reject miracles have to explain away any empirical evidence for them.

3. Frame, *Systematic Theology*, 181.

4. Frame, *Systematic Theology*, 181.

exceptions to those laws. The providence of God is not at odds with the providence of God. Plantinga explains, "these laws are not like the laws of the Medes and Persians . . . it is not true that once God has established or instituted them, they limit or constrain his power to act."[5] When God performs miracles, he acts specially. Plantinga thus believes laws of nature take a form, "When God is not acting specially, p."[6] As an example, "When God is not acting specially, no material object accelerates from a speed less than c to a speed greater than c."[7]

The idea that God is somehow in violation of his own laws or providence, or that God is incapable in any other way of acting specially in the context of his law governed universe, is simply false. Plantinga comments on the example of a law provided in the previous paragraph above.

> But of course that doesn't mean that *God* cannot bring it about that some material object accelerate from a speed less than c to one greater than c. Neither we nor any other creature can do this; it doesn't follow that God cannot. If the laws take the above form they are really conditionals: the antecedent of a law specifies that God is not acting specially, and the consequent is a proposition describing how things ordinarily work, how they work when God is not acting specially. For example, when God isn't acting specially, no material object accelerates through the speed of light, any two objects attract each other with a force directly proportional to the product of their masses and inversely proportional to the square of the distance between them, and so on. The thing to see is that while no creatures, no finite beings, can bring about a state of affairs incompatible with the consequent of a law, God has the power to do so.[8]

Laws of nature cannot be violated by creaturely causes. This fact of the natural order is not something easily explained within the context of a naturalistic view of the world. As discussed in chapter 3, the laws of nature are necessary, but not logically necessary. It does not follow that God cannot sometimes act specially in a way that seems to transcend those laws. Thus Plantinga writes, "theism enables us to understand the necessity or inevitableness or inviolability of natural law: this necessity is to be explained and understood in terms of the difference between divine

---

5. Plantinga, *Where Conflict Really Lies*, 281.
6. Plantinga, *Where Conflict Really Lies*, 282.
7. Plantinga, *Where Conflict Really Lies*, 282.
8. Plantinga, *Where Conflict Really Lies*, 282.

power and the power of finite creatures."⁹ Plantinga thus provides an excellent summary of the scenario with God, laws of nature, and miracles. However, pushing the picture a step back into the decree of God may shed even more light on the subject of laws of nature and miracles in their relation to God.

God's prescription of laws of nature is not absolutely unqualified. Recall Plantinga's comment on the providential activity in its relation to laws of nature, "When God is not acting specially, p."[10] The same type of formula is available when focusing on the initial decree of God. According to John Foster, "It might be that what he prescribes, in the case of each mode, is not that things are to conform to it *in all instances*, but that things are to conform to it in all instances *apart from* those where he subsequently decides on a different outcome. If God attaches this qualification to his prescribing, then, even in cases where the prescribed modes assign a definite type of outcome to the course of events on a particular occasion, he leaves himself the freedom to overrule what is thus provisionally determined and get things to turn out differently."[11] Foster appears to think of God as decreeing the laws of nature to be a particular way while allowing openings where he can later on intervene. However, it is just as easy to propose that God already has all such exceptions worked out in terms of his decree without having to make decisions about them *subsequent* to his decree.

Speaking in terms of his decree, when God does not decide on a different outcome in advance, p. Or as Foster puts the matter, "even if the prescribing were thus qualified, it would still succeed in imposing certain regularities on the universe as regularities, in a way that causally obliged certain forms of behaviour in all instances where there was no additional act of divine intervention, and this imposing would still satisfy the requirements for the existence of laws under the causal account that we have embraced."[12] Foster provides the example of gravity, "So, in the case of gravity, we might think of the obtaining of the law as logically excluding the occurrence of counterinstances, but take what is required by the law to be not that bodies behave gravitationally, but that bodies behave gravitationally except in cases where God decides otherwise."[13]

9. Plantinga, *Where Conflict Really Lies*, 283.
10. Plantinga, *Where Conflict Really Lies*, 282.
11. Foster, *Divine Lawmaker*, 176.
12. Foster, *Divine Lawmaker*, 177.
13. Foster, *Divine Lawmaker*, 177.

Miracles are not in "violation" of the laws of nature. Nor does God somehow work against himself in terms of his decree or providential control over creation. Where does this leave us with regard to nomically necessary laws of nature?

> Nomic necessity, as I have constantly stressed, is not a form of *strict* necessity, since it does not exclude altogether the possibility of things being otherwise. The most obvious way in which it falls short of strictness turns on the fact that laws themselves are only contingent and do not even hold constant through all possible worlds which have the sorts of ingredients that are relevant to them. So, for any law, there are compositionally relevant possible worlds in which things fail to conform to the law simply because the law is not present to ensure such conformity.[14]

Foster concedes, "Under the terms of the causal account, the notion of the contravention of a law does not, strictly speaking, make sense, since if a regularity is causally imposed on the universe, there is no logical room for counterinstances: if it is caused to be the case that all Fs are G, then all Fs are G. But once we accept that it is God who is the causal agent, we can see how he can fashion the content of what he imposes in a way that leaves room for cases in which he subsequently intervenes; and, if they occur, such interventions will produce physical outcomes that are out of line with the ways in which the universe normally functions, and which differ from the outcomes that the imposing would have produced if the interventions had not occurred."[15] Foster is right to point out that Judaeo-Christian "theists believe that, on occasions, God intervenes quite dramatically, to bring about outcomes that are *conspicuously* contrary to the normal ways of working of the universe."[16] He explains,

> These dramatic interventions are the ones that carry the title of 'miracles', and cover such putative events as Jesus's turning water into wine and his raising of Lazarus. And they also believe that, as part of his ongoing pastoral care of his human creatures, God sometimes intervenes in less conspicuous ways, doing things that do not, at least to the casual observer, suggest that there is any unusual source of influence at work. Such interventions might occur, for example, in response to petitionary prayer, where the prayer is for some type of outcome (like a good night's

---

14. Foster, *Divine Lawmaker*, 178.
15. Foster, *Divine Lawmaker*, 178–79.
16. Foster, *Divine Lawmaker*, 179.

sleep or calmness before an examination) which could well come about, in circumstances not noticeably relevantly different from the ones that obtain, through the operation of natural factors alone.[17]

Foster writes, "It might be suggested that God could ensure *in advance* that everything conformed to his purposes, simply by fixing the initial state of the universe and the modes of transition in the appropriate ways."[18] Foster objects to this view due to his understanding of creaturely freedom, but if God is omniscient, then God knows even all human actions in advance and could, in theory, adjust his decree accordingly.[19] A much less confused understanding of God's decree in relation to the themes of necessity, contingency, and creaturely freedom comes from the theologian Francis Turretin. Though he does not explicitly address the topic of the laws of nature, it is best to understand their being set forth in terms of what Turretin refers to as hypothetical necessity. The concept of hypothetical necessity, in other words, provides a theological context for understanding the God ordained nomic necessity of laws of nature and the place of miracles. According to Turretin, "a thing is said to be necessary which cannot be otherwise."[20] Beyond that, he sets forth a rather intricate understanding of necessity as it pertains to God and creation in different senses.

> In God, a twofold necessity is commonly remarked: the one absolute, the opposite of which is simply impossible to God (as when God is said to be incorruptible and incapable of denying himself); another hypothetical, arising from the hypothesis of the divine decree which, being made the effect itself willed, must necessarily follow. The former is founded on the immutable nature of God; the latter on his immutable will. This last is again twofold: one of immutability from the immutable decree; another of infallibility from his infallible foreknowledge. In

---

17. Foster, *Divine Lawmaker*, 179.
18. Foster, *Divine Lawmaker*, 180. Foster explains his objection, "But, given that the course of events is partly dependent on how human beings themselves choose to act, and that such choices are made freely (in a way that precludes causal determination by prior events and conditions), there is bound to be a severe limit on what he can ensure by those means alone; and the likelihood is that, whatever initial state and modes of transition he selected, a capacity for subsequent intervention would be of use." Foster, *Divine Lawmaker*, 180.
19. Foster, *Divine Lawmaker*, 180.
20. Turretin, *Institutes of Elenctic Theology*, 320.

things themselves, there also occur various kinds of necessity: (1) physical and internal on the part of second causes which are so determined to one thing that they cannot act otherwise (as in fire the necessity of burning); (2) of coactions, arising from an external principle acting violently; (3) hypothetical of the event or dependence through which a thing, although naturally mutable and contingent, cannot but be (on account of its dependence upon the ordination of God whose will cannot be changed nor his foreknowledge be deceived).[21]

Because of the certainty of the decree of God and Scripture itself, events "must happen necessarily, if not as to the mode of production (which is often contingent), still as to the certainty of the event (which cannot be otherwise)."[22] For Turretin, each event is hypothetical, "ensuring the certainty of the event, but not taking away the nature and properties of second causes."[23] Islamic theology offers a very different account of second causes that has taken away from its theology of miracles and negatively affects its scientific practices.

21. Turretin, *Institutes of Elenctic Theology*, 320. Turretin offers scriptural proofs for his assertions.

22. Turretin, *Institutes of Elenctic Theology*, 320. Turretin writes, "That which maintains a determination to one thing by a physical necessity or a necessity of coactions, takes away liberty and contingency; but not that which maintains it only by a hypothetical necessity. For the certainty does not arise from the nature of second causes, which are free and contingent, but extrinsically from the immutability of the decree (which so determines the futurition of the event as not to change the nature of things, but permits necessary things to act necessarily, free things freely). Hence it is evident that the necessity and immutability of the decree indeed takes away contingency with respect to the first cause. For since all things happen necessarily, nothing can take place contingently. But this does not take it away with respect to second causes because the same decree which predetermined also determined the mode of futurition, so that the things having necessary causes should happen necessarily and those having contingent causes, contingently. Therefore the effect may properly be called both necessary and contingent at the same time, but in different respects (*kat' allo kai allo*): the former on the part of God and relative to the decree; the latter on the part of the thing and relative to second and proximate causes which might be disposed differently." Turretin, *Institutes of Elenctic Theology*, 321.

23. Turretin, *Institutes of Elenctic Theology*, 321. Turretin addresses the concern that leads Foster toward a view more similar to Open Theism, "This necessity (as was just now said) being extrinsic and hypothetical in the highest manner is consistent with the liberty of creatures (who do not cease to act most freely on their part, although the effect is necessary on the part of God). So far therefore from these being mutually opposed to each other, they amicably conspire together because through these means (although free), the events determined by the decree of God are promised and produced." Turretin, *Institutes of Elenctic Theology*, 321.

FURTHER ISSUE OF ISLAM

According to scientist Michael Robert Negus, "Islam justifies natural science by regarding it as a process of studying the acts of the Creator."[24] Of course, these acts will include the miraculous, as above. However, Muslims appear to face great difficulties with presenting a view that even roughly corresponds to the Christian understanding of divine providence and its relationship to the laws of nature. Discussions of laws of nature are almost completely absent from Islam, and hence miracles are believed to occur at random, leading to rather unorthodox "scientific" explanations of events by Muslim scientists.

Astrophysicist Nidhal Guessoum provides a long list of places where Muslims have allowed the concept of the miraculous to destroy their foundations of science. He writes, "Let me start by relating some recent examples to describe and highlight the state of scientific ignorance that prevails in the Arab/Muslim society today."[25]

> In December 2006, the 'Eighth Conference on Scientific I'jaz (Miraculous Aspects) in the Qur'an and the Sunna was organized in Kuwait (at the Sheraton Hotel) by the World Authority on Scientific I'jaz in the Qur'an and the Sunna. Over several days, 'scholars' presented 86 papers (in parallel sessions) on the following topics:
>
> - The scientific I'jaz (miracle) in the destruction by the Mighty shout.
> - The scientific I'jaz in the distinction between the urine of the female maid and that of the suckling boy.
> - The code of human life before birth and after death: scientific signs in the Holy Qur'an.
> - The scientific I'jaz in the prophetic Sunna regarding the stagnant water.
> - Satellites bear witness the truth of Muhammad's prophethood (PBUH).
> - The disease and the remedy in the two wings of the fly.

---

24. Negus, "Islam and Science," 323.
25. Guessoum, *Islam's Quantum Question*, 5.

- The miraculous description of the (re-)creation of human bodies (and not the soul) from the tail bone on the day of resurrection.
- The miracle in the 'descent' of iron (from the sky).
- The scientific *I'jaz* in the Qur'an's description of the movement of shadows (the immobile shadow).
- Study of the effect of bloodletting on the molecular biology of hepatitis-C patients.
- The superiority of the treatment of lower backs by prayers over the treatment by lasers.
- Glimpse into the scientific *I'jaz* in the Prophetic hadith regarding remedying by vinegar.[26]

Commenting on the clearly unscientific nature of this study, he writes, "suffice it here to note the incredible topics that are being 'investigated' nowadays and the implications regarding the understanding (or lack thereof) of science among a large section of the Muslim elite today."[27]

Other conferences on Islamic science follow suit. Guessoum disdainfully explains his experience with another conference. Guessoum writes, "In similar fashion, in April 2007, a conference was organized in Abu Dhabi on 'Qur'anic Healing' at the seven-star Emirates Palace hotel."[28]

> The opening keynote speech was given by Prof. Zaghloul al-Naggar, a former geology university professor who for many years now has specialised in *I'jaz* discourse. In his overview, he decried the 'duality' of the higher education system in the contemporary Muslim world, a result—in his view—of having been culturally influenced and dominated by the Western materialistic civilization. What he meant by that duality is the fact that, on the one hand, medical training does not make room for Qur'anic healing approaches, and, on the other hand, the Islamic theology and jurisprudence curriculum do not include medical subjects. This, then, he says, prevents doctors from appreciating the role and value of Qur'anic healing, while the Qur'anic healers are not knowledgeable enough about scientific methods and facts. He asked for more cooperation between the

---

26. Guessoum, *Islam's Quantum Question*, 5.
27. Guessoum, *Islam's Quantum Question*, 5.
28. Guessoum, *Islam's Quantum Question*, 5. Guessoum states this conference "had a scientific committee and was apparently professionally organized."

two fields and for a greater amount of modern technology in the practice of Qur'anic healing.²⁹

Guessoum continues by explaining some of the bizarre and certainly unscientific explanations of how Qur'anic healing in particular might take place.

> One main theme in the conference was the effect of the recitation of verses of the Qur'an on water, which then heals many ills in patients who drink it. Some speakers, most of whom were university professors, explained the healing on the basis of 'the memory of water' effect (needless to say, a long-discredited idea); others explained it by some electromagnetic waves, which, carried by the 'vibrations' of the Qur'an being read, 'rearrange' the molecular structure of the water, giving it special 'energy' (an overly abused word in that conference as in many others); others invoked the concept of 'information content', which somehow gets passed on from the Qur'an to the water and then to the patient, especially if the Qur'an is read by quasi-saints (*salihun*); others invoked telepathy; and finally some even based their claims on the 'theory' of homeopathy (infinitesimally small concentrations of medicine in water, which, it is claimed, gives it special power). One speaker, a medical instruments technician, even brought with him a device that purported to extract the 'Qur'anic energy' stored in the water (the energy is transferred to the water by just placing one's finger in it and reciting verses aloud or in one's mind); the device then transforms the energy into digital information, records it and even sends it by the Internet to anyone needing it anywhere in the world. I should thus add that the device was hailed as 'a qualitative leap in the development of psychological immunity, and a quantum leap in the concept of 'technological I'jaz' (miraculous Qur'anic technology), the first invention that combines the Holy Qur'an with modern technology.'³⁰

---

29. Guessoum, *Islam's Quantum Question*, 5. Guessoum is clearly disappointed with Muslim science, noting, "But this was just an appetiser. The pièces de resistance were yet to come. Let me present a few highlights." Guessoum, *Islam's Quantum Question*, 5.

30. Guessoum, *Islam's Quantum Question*, 5–6. According to a frustrated Guessoum, "What no one mentioned was the placebo effect or the mind's ability to trigger the release of medicinal chemicals, thereby leading to natural healing that looks quite miraculous sometimes—an important effect." Guessoum, *Islam's Quantum Question*, 6.

The topics of discussion get even worse, as Guessoum continues to describe.

> Another main theme of the conference was the specific methods that should be used for the treatment of cases of exposure to magic, demon possession (*mas bi l-jinn*) and exorcism, and evil eye (*al-'ain*), which was explained as electromagnetic waves radiated by the eye, as the latter is connected to the brain, which can produce evil thoughts.
>
> Reading such reports, I had difficulty reminding myself that all this was being presented in the twenty-first-century conferences and not in dark medieval gatherings.[31]

In case one wonders if these anecdotal stories regarding scientific conferences carry any weight with respect to the greater picture of Islamic science, Guessoum insists, "the fact remains that the above religion–science concoctions are widespread and even prevalent among the public and most of the educated elite."[32] The chaos of modern science in Islam has a long history.

In the late nineteenth and early twentieth centuries, the West had already far surpassed Muslim nations in virtually every way, including, especially science.[33] This state of affairs left Muslim reformers such as Jamal Eddine al-Afghani, Muhammad Abduh, and Mohamed Rashid Rida "fully aware that the Muslim world was in need of modernisation in every sphere of social life, starting from education."[34] The concern, however, is that Islamic theology breeds a culture of scientific retardation. Guessoum's analysis supports this contention. Referencing the aforementioned reformers, he writes, "They were also painfully conscious that even the general understanding of religion was woefully inadequate and dangerous, as full as it was of superstitious beliefs, passive notions of *qadar* (divine destiny), and so on. And, of course, the mechanical

---

31. Guessoum, *Islam's Quantum Question*, 6. Guessoum does note, "To be fair, I should state that other mainstream Islamic scholars decry such hodgepodge approaches to scientific—or at least medical—topics by Muslims." Guessoum, *Islam's Quantum Question*, 7.

32. Guessoum, *Islam's Quantum Question*, 7.

33. Guessoum, *Islam's Quantum Question*, 28. Guessoum explains, "The Renaissance, the scientific revolution, the Enlightenment and the Industrial Revolution had taken place, and these had left Europe not only well ahead of the Muslim world in general development, capability and power but also in colonial control of vast Muslim regions, from India to Morocco." Guessoum, *Islam's Quantum Question*, 28.

34. Guessoum, *Islam's Quantum Question*, 28–29.

and naturalistic model of the world brought in by Newton and Darwin had made the traditional Islamic understanding of phenomena as Allah's 're-creation' of the world at every instant seem totally unphysical if not mystical, and this realisation had forced a re-examination of the very understanding of God and his relation to the world and to humans."[35]

Why is it that Islam, which is so close to Judaism and Christianity in terms of its theistic affirmations, cannot answer questions about science, the laws of nature, and induction in much the same way as proposed above for Christianity? Indeed, Islam is quite similar to the Christian worldview in certain respects, for just as in the classical Christian theology explained in chapter 1, "Classical Muslim theology goes even further than defining Allah as the Creator; He is also considered the Sustainer of the world(s): 'Allah is Creator of all things, and He is Guardian over all things' (Q 39:62); 'It is Allah Who sustains the heavens and the earth, lest they cease (to function): and if they should fail, there is none—not one— can sustain them thereafter: Verily He is Most Forbearing, Oft-Forgiving' (Q 35:41); 'There is no creature on earth but its sustenance is upon Allah' (Q 11:6)."[36]

If a Christian worldview provides the necessary preconditions of science, then it would seem to follow that Islam, insofar as it is similar to Christianity in terms of Allah's relationship to the world, is also in an excellent position to accommodate a scientific worldview, allowing for the progress of science. And yet, as this book has pointed out in numerous ways, Islam is *not* an overly scientific worldview, nor has it provided for much, if any, scientific progress throughout the centuries. In an effort to explain this apparent inconsistency, three characteristics of Islamic theology will be examined and evaluated in regard to the philosophy of science. First, Islam possesses its own strong version of occasionalism which came to dominate the Islamic philosophy of science with negative results. Second, Islam possesses a deity with a questionable moral character which only compounds the problems related to the aforementioned occasionalist view of causation. Third, Islam is not only strictly monotheistic, but focuses on the unity of Allah to the extent that considerations of particulars necessary to the scientific endeavor are forced out of an Islamic understanding of Allah's relationship to the world.

35. Guessoum, *Islam's Quantum Question*, 29.
36. Guessoum, *Islam's Quantum Question*, 43.

The reason Christianity and Islam do not look the same in terms of scientific contributions is that Christianity and Islam are relevantly different in virtue of their respective deities' relations to the world. Though both religions posit a monotheistic creator and sustainer, relevant differences *do* exist between Christianity and Islam. For example, a theological divide within Islam has left Islamic occasionalism the dominant force in Muslim attempts to explain Allah's relation to the world. Commenting on Qur'anic passages that describe Allah as the sustainer of the world, Guessoum writes, "This in fact takes us to a long and unresolved debate among Muslim theologians regarding the way God acts in the world or controls it."[37] He continues, "Some have argued that He sustains the world by way of the laws he built in nature; in Islamic parlance, God uses 'divine habits' (*sunan ilahiyah*)."[38] However, "Others have insisted that God acts directly, that he 'recreates' the world at every instant."[39] Guessoum notes, "Opponents of this position refer to it as 'occasionalism.'"[40] Thus, a historical divide exists within Muslim theological thought that contains potentially major ramifications for scientific reasoning. Rationalist Muslim philosophers took the view that creation is sustained in virtue of laws, whereas traditional Muslims are occasionalists, and this has no doubt affected the way science has been viewed and carried out within Islamic civilizations from the beginning.[41]

Much could be said about various Muslim schools of thought concerning science, but the two most important schools to the discussion of philosophy of science are the Mu'tazilites and the Asharites. According to physicist philosopher Peter E. Hodgson, the Mu'tazilites, seeking to

37. Guessoum, *Islam's Quantum Question*, 43.

38. Guessoum, *Islam's Quantum Question*, 43. This view would appear to be closest to the traditional Reformed Christian view, but it is not the dominant view within Islam and tends to be more rationalistic than Islam is willing to allow.

39. Guessoum, *Islam's Quantum Question*, 43. This view is similar to the non-concurrent theistic understanding of providence described in chap. 1 of this book.

40. Guessoum, *Islam's Quantum Question*, 43.

41. Guessoum, *Islam's Quantum Question*, 43. If Muslims are indeed occasionalists, then the objections of chap. 1 directed toward the non-concurrent theistic view of providence would very likely apply to Islamic theology, in addition to any objections leveled toward occasionalism and pantheism, even if only by way of analogy. Christian occasionalism differs from Islamic occasionalism. For example, the nature of the Christian God and the nature of Allah are relevantly different and affect how occasionalism works. As concerns the topic of this book, Muslim occasionalism has dire consequences for a scientific worldview; hence Islam lends itself to criticism if science is regarded as significant at all.

interpret the Qur'an rationally, "concluded that only God and human beings can cause things to happen, and so causation as a result of natural properties was rejected as unintelligible."[42] The Asharites, who interpreted the Qur'an in strict orthodox manner, "criticized the Mu'tazilites as skeptical rationalists, and restricted causal agency to God alone."[43] These schools are evidence of the difficulty of providing an account of causation that is consistent with the Qur'an. Of the two schools, the Asharite position prides itself as being more faithful to the Qur'an. What did the denial of secondary causation in the Asharite school look like? Hodgson summarizes the thought of the followers of this school:

> Their founder, the mystic al-Ashari, held that the world consists of atomic events in space and time held together by the will of God, so that there is no connection between cause and effect. He was supported by al-Ghazali, who in his book *The Incoherence of the Philosophers* attacked the Mu'tazilites and emphasized that God is the only cause of all events, so that there is no necessary connection between what appears to be the cause and what appears to be the effect. To believe otherwise would be a denial of God's power. Al-Ghazali approved the 'practical' sciences such as arithmetic and medicine, was skeptical about the value of the 'theoretical' sciences and disapproved of metaphysics and some physical sciences.[44]

The Islamic scholar Muzaffar Iqbal echoes Hodgson:

> If God is absolutely free and omnipotent, then the physical world is contingent rather than necessary. This means that there is no necessity that it should be what it is; it is entirely dependent on God's Will in all respects: in its form, function, operation, in fact, in its very existence. The observed physical laws are not necessary, they are imposed by the divine will. The cause and effect relationships, too, are not necessary; they are contingent. Fire burns but not because fire and the act of burning are necessarily connected; rather it is so because God chose to connect them, empowering fire for the function of burning. God is free

---

42. Hodgson, *Theology and Modern Physics*, 45. Hodgson explains, "The Mu'tazilite school sought a rational interpretation of the Qur'an. If, according to the Qur'an, God creates everything, then He also creates evil and our evil actions, so what becomes of divine justice and man's punishment?"

43. Hodgson, *Theology and Modern Physics*, 45.

44. Hodgson, *Theology and Modern Physics*, 45.

and can choose to "disconnect" the relationship between fire and its power to burn....[45]

Physicist Taner Edis likewise observes,

> Indeed, to preserve omnipotence and divine freedom, many Muslim philosophers and orthodox thinkers alike were drawn toward varieties of occasionalism, in which God creates the world anew and decides the motion of its constituent atoms in each moment. Al-Ghazali famously took this to the limit of an almost Humean skepticism about cause and effect. He correctly pointed out that there was no necessary, certain connection between a cause, such as fire, and an effect, such as a piece of cotton burning up. What happened was up to the divine will, which could always go otherwise. Hence philosophical reasoning based on causes and other such alleged necessities of reason could not be trusted.[46]

The implications of these passages must not be missed. Muslims tend to believe that anything resembling laws of nature restricts Allah's freedom. So if Allah is truly omnipotent, as Muslims want to believe he is, then there are no laws of nature. Allah's will alone accounts for all causation, such that secondary causation does not exist.[47] One need not look for a necessary connection between cause and effect, because there is no such connection. Allah is the sole cause of every effect in the world, such that science is rendered unimportant, if not impossible. Science, by its very nature, seeks causal explanations for events that take place in the world. On an Asharite view, science is the mostly useless enterprise of a non-Muslim Western world.

---

45. Iqbal, "Islam and Modern Science: Questions at the Interface," 25.

46. Edis, *An Illusion*, 51–52. Edis writes, "Clearly it was difficult to break out of the mold of the medieval view of reality. Neither the philosophical nor the religious elements in this view had any intrinsic tendency toward modern science. Yes, with hindsight and selective attention again, we can pick out habits of thought that impeded the development of science and we can also see some alternatives that were not taken. But none of this means Muslim thinkers made any mistake, or took a wrong turn. They developed a perfectly sensible, eminently satisfactory philosophical framework for a religious civilization. No one could have anticipated that some of the alternative approaches they failed to emphasize could have led to a new, much more powerful way of understanding nature." Edis, *An Illusion*, 52.

47. What, then, does Allah's will look like in terms of its application to the world? Is Allah good? Is he trustworthy? Is he reliable? Is he harmonious within his nature? Is he rational? Or is he capricious? The answers to these questions affect everything about Islamic science, given the Islamic occasionalist view.

FURTHER ISSUES 195

Al-Ghazali supported the Asharite view. Not only did Al-Ghazali lend support for the aforementioned contention regarding the denial of secondary causation, but he had a reason for thinking this way. According to Hodgson as quoted above, Al-Ghazali thought that to believe Allah created a world involving secondary causation is to deny the power of Allah. Allah's omnipotence, according to the Asharites, precludes the possibility of finding out any cause other than Allah's will, and hence science, which searches for the natural causes of events, is likewise precluded by the very nature of Allah, as well as his relationship to the world.

Like most other philosophical positions, Al-Ghazali's views were not left unchallenged, even within the ranks of Islamic thinkers. As is well known in the study of Islamic philosophy, "Al-Ghazali's views on causation were contested by Ibn Rushd (Averroës), who believed that science and religious beliefs should be kept entirely separate."[48] According to Hodgson, "The world of Averroës is a pantheistic world in which everything behaves according to an intrinsic necessity."[49] Hodgson continues,

> He taught that the world is eternal and is renewed continuously by renewed acts of creation by an external Prime Mover. Thus the world depends on an external cause, but that cause is itself without cause. He also wrote a book called *The Incoherence of the Incoherence of the Philosophers*, which gives detailed answers to the Ashari doctrines. In particular, he maintained that the 'denial of cause implies the denial of knowledge, and the denial of knowledge implies that nothing in the world can really be known.'[50]

---

48. Hodgson, *Theology and Modern Physics*, 45. Of Averroës, Hodgson writes, "He was a thoroughgoing Aristotelian, wrote extensive commentaries on the works of Aristotle and accepted Aristotelian physics as the final truth about the physical world. Aristotle based his philosophy on eternal truths, so no observations could ever disagree with it. There is thus no need ever to make experiments." Hodgson, *Theology and Modern Physics*, 45.

49. Hodgson, *Theology and Modern Physics*, 46.

50. Hodgson, *Theology and Modern Physics*, 46. Hodgson believes the biblical worldview is capable of escaping the scientifically problematic views of both occasionalism and pantheism, as evidenced by Maimonides. He writes, "The Jewish philosopher Maimonides spent most of his life in Cairo writing on medicine, but is best known through his writings on cosmology, which influence Aquinas and hence the medieval discussions on creation. He also wrote the *Guide for the Perplexed*, a very popular treatise on philosophy. His work, guided by the Bible, steered between the occasionalism of the Asharites and the pantheism of the Mu'tazilites." Hodgson, *Theology and Modern Physics*, 46.

Here again it is important to note what is actually being claimed. Averroës is decidedly against the Asharite school and al-Ghazali, arguing that the denial of causation promoted by the former philosophers destroys the very foundation of any and all knowledge of the world. Averroës thus appears to believe that knowledge of the natural world is based upon the necessary law-like character of the world. Averroës rejects the Asharite school of philosophy, but one should not overlook the fact that Averroës attempts to ground his own view of causality in a necessitarian, pantheistic worldview.

By way of review, Mu'tazilites denied natural causation, ascribing causation to God and humans only. Asharites rejected this view, and posited Allah as the sole cause for every event. Al-Ghazali found himself in agreement with the Asharite school of philosophy on this point. Averroës rejected al-Ghazali's view of causation, but in so doing embraced pantheism. Both necessitarian views of nature, as well as pantheistic views of reality, create problems when it comes to the laws of nature, induction, and science. Some of these problems were explained in earlier chapters of this book. These problems affected science within Islamic civilization for the worse, with a marked decline in Arabic science in the thirteenth century.[51] The advance of Western science in Islamic lands corresponded with the general "sidelining of Islamic teaching."[52]

The importance of the Asharite view of causality as it dominated the Muslim world cannot be overemphasized. To summarize, the problem is not merely that such a view is not conducive to scientific enquiry, although that much is certainly true. More importantly, Asharite occasionalism precludes the possibility of doing science at all. The quackery offered as scientific explanation of the miraculous noted at the beginning of this section follows a line of thought where Allah is irrationally free to will whatever he wants without any discernment on humanity's part as to any underlying cause. No underlying physical or scientific causes are found in the Asharite occasionalist scheme, and seeking to find a reason in the will of Allah ends in futility. There is no reason for what Allah does, apart from the affirmation of his omnipotence. The omnipotence of Allah, along with his radical freedom of will, leads one to conclude that Allah is capricious. Indeed, the will of Allah is so free that he is said to be

---

51. Hodgson, *Theology and Modern Physics*, 46.

52. Hodgson, *Theology and Modern Physics*, 46. Hodgson writes, "In spite of much original work in many centres, Arabic philosophy and science declined from the thirteenth century onwards."

responsible for evil itself.⁵³ The importance of this point to the discussion of the laws of nature and induction will be clarified below.

According to Hodgson, "Science can develop only if the world is believed to be contingent, that is, that it is rational but could be otherwise."⁵⁴ Hodgson continues, "This in turn depends on the belief that God is both rational and free so that He freely created the world and gave it an inherent rational nature by which it continues to act unless He decides otherwise."⁵⁵ The difficulty for some Muslims is in balancing the rationality and freedom of Allah. Because of the emphasis on Allah's omnipotent freedom, some Muslim philosophers insist that Allah cannot be "bound" by something like laws of nature. Regarding Asharite theology, Hodgson claims,

> Their theology emphasizes the freedom of Allah more strongly than the inherent rationality of nature; Allah thus decides from instant to instant how everything behaves. Thus, for instance, it is wrong to say that hydrogen and oxygen combine to form water. Instead, we must say that if hydrogen and water [sic] are brought together, by the will of Allah water is created (Hoodbhoy, 1991, p. 54). This is a denial of secondary causality. The theologian al-Ghazali denied causality, saying that any apparent connection is due to the prior decree of God, who creates them side by side (Iqbal, 2002, p. 109). Since science is the search for relations between cause and effect, as they reflect the inherent rationality of things, expressed by exact mathematical formulae, it is inevitably weakened by such beliefs.⁵⁶

Denying secondary causation means all causation is found in Allah alone. Hence everything happens in accordance with his will, divorced from any scientific considerations of the physical realm. Recall that the Asharite view came to dominate Muslim lands. Hodgson tells an anecdotal story that impresses upon the reader the significance of denying secondary causation.

> This is illustrated by a story told me by a traveler in Persia. During a journey the car stopped, and the Muslim driver got out

---

53. But then how can one tell the difference between good and evil on a Muslim view? Appealing to the nature of Allah is of no help, and moral facts do not appear to exist in a Muslim view. See next section.
54. Hodgson, *Theology and Modern Physics*, 53.
55. Hodgson, *Theology and Modern Physics*, 53.
56. Hodgson, *Theology and Modern Physics*, 53. He must mean oxygen, not water.

to find out why. He unscrewed the cap of the petrol tank and peered inside, using a lighted match. My friend tried to dissuade him, but the driver serenely replied: 'If it is the will of Allah that the petrol explodes, it will explode; if it is not, it will not.' It would, I think, be rather difficult to teach physics to that pious man. For science to flourish, belief in the laws of nature must permeate society.[57]

Asharite ideology is generally associated with fundamentalism in Islam. Alternatively, the Mu'tazilites are closer to a more liberal form of Islam.

The Asharite school represents the dominant, fundamentalist interpretation of the Qur'an and Muslim thought regarding science during much of the history of Islam. Hodgson summarizes these truths:

> Following the teachings of the theologians al-Ashari, al-Ghazali and others, the fundamentalist interpretations of the Qur'an gradually dominated Muslim society, to the detriment of the more rational interpretation of the Mu'tazilites al-Kindi, Ibn al-Haytham and Ibn Rushd. This school of theology was strongly supported by some Muslim rulers during the eleventh and twelfth centuries, so that by the end of the fourteenth century Islamic science had been practically destroyed. Mu'tazilism was a revolutionary movement within Islam but it was finally rejected, mainly because it exalted reason over revelation.[58]

The repercussions are far reaching. According to Hodgson, "the Asharite mentality has not been prevalent for the last two hundred years."[59] And yet, science is virtually nonexistent within Islam. Hodgson sets forth the sad reality of science in Islam:

> At the present time Muslim countries constitute one-fifth of the world population, more than the USA, Western Europe and Japan combined. And yet the absolute size of the Islamic scientific community is 'incredibly small', less than 1 per cent per capita compared with Israel. With one or two exceptions, there are no great university departments or world-calibre research institutes. There are fewer physicists in all nineteen universities in Pakistan than in Imperial College of the University of London alone. It is not surprising that most Arabic countries remain poor and underdeveloped. In 1999 the combined GNP

---

57. Hodgson, *Theology and Modern Physics*, 53n3.
58. Hodgson, *Theology and Modern Physics*, 53.
59. Hodgson, *Theology and Modern Physics*, 53.

of all Arab countries amounted to less than that of Spain. The science that now exists in the Muslim world is largely imported from the West.[60]

Muslim scientists do exist, but they were educated in the West, where the necessary presuppositions of science were inherent in their learning.[61] According to Hodgson, "It remains true that there is rather little highly original science in Muslim countries, and the general level of scientific research is disappointingly low; the most famous contemporary Muslim scientist, Abdus Salam (1987; see also Hoodbhoy, 1991, p. 4), described it as 'abysmal.'"[62]

> The fifty-seven nations in the Islamic world, comprising 1.3 billion people, invest less than 0.2 per cent of their combined GNP in research and development (*Physics World*, April 2003, p. 11). The papers written by their scientists and engineers account for just 2 per cent of the world total. Muslims have readily accepted the technology of the West, and have the resources to pay for it, but in the realm of pure science they lag behind, as they have done for centuries (Golshani, 1997, pp. 72-3).[63]

The current state of Islamic science reads like the Golden Age of Islamic science examined in chapter 2, except worse. While probably not wise to attribute the deplorable state of science within Islamic civilization to "this one thing," it seems difficult to conclude that the Asharite view of causality, implying as it does faulty views of the laws of nature and hence induction, had nothing to do with the decline of Islamic science. In fact, Hodgson writes, "This had led many scholars to conclude that the decline of Islamic science from its ancient glories is due to the dominance of the fundamentalist Asharite interpretation of the Qur'an."[64] Not many Muslim scientists adhere to Asharite fundamentalism, but its negative effects endure.[65] Moreover, Islam seems conceptually incapable of restoring itself to its former glory with respect to science. Thus Hodgson writes,

60. Hodgson, *Theology and Modern Physics*, 53.

61. Hodgson, *Theology and Modern Physics*, 53-54. Hodgson, "There are some excellent Muslim scientists, but they have been trained in the West and so have imbibed the necessary presuppositions of science along with the science itself."

62. Hodgson, *Theology and Modern Physics*, 54.

63. Hodgson, *Theology and Modern Physics*, 54.

64. Hodgson, *Theology and Modern Physics*, 54.

65. Hodgson, *Theology and Modern Physics*, 54. Hodgson writes, "Although this interpretation is held by few Muslim scientists today, its legacy remains."

"Unless the Qur'an is interpreted in ways that stress the beliefs that led to the birth of modern science in Western Europe in the High Middle Ages it is not easy to see how it will ever be possible to stimulate a truly indigenous renaissance of science in Islamic countries and thereby remove their scientific and technological dependence on the West."[66]

Such a reinterpretation of the Qur'an is a departure from its true teachings as understood traditionally in Islam. Science operates as a liberalizing force within Islam, or it does not operate at all.

Above, it was demonstrated that Islam possesses its own strong version of occasionalism which came to dominate the Islamic philosophy of science with negative results. Here, it will be argued that Islam possesses a deity with a questionable moral character which only compounds the problems related to the aforementioned occasionalist view of causation. According to Negus, and consistent with the detailed account of Islamic metaphysics presented above, "Allāh acts with an absolute freedom of will, this being the ultimate reason why things are as they are, why things exist and why events happen as they do."[67] The implications of the absolute freedom of Allah, connected with his omnipotence, have already been noted with respect to the laws of nature. In short, there are not any laws of nature, as they are thought to limit the omnipotent freedom of Allah. However, there is another extremely important implication of Allah's absolute omnipotent freedom. Not only is Allah not bound by laws of nature, he is not bound by laws of morality.

Concerning Allah, Negus writes, "He is the Creator of everything, of both good and evil, not just good alone."[68] In case one wonders whether or not this renders Allah responsible for evil in the world, Negus explains, "Allāh punishes those who involve themselves in evil, even though he is responsible for the existence of evil."[69] In Islam, "only God can act."[70]

---

66. Hodgson, *Theology and Modern Physics*, 54.
67. Negus, "Islam and Science," 321.
68. Negus, "Islam and Science," 321.
69. Negus, "Islam and Science," 321. Negus writes, "He punishes those who disobey his command. The correct state of a human is to be a slave (*'abd*) to Allāh, who is his or her Master (*Rabb*). This attitude, of servanthood or more correctly slavery, is manifest in the physical posture of the prayer rite, in which each Muslim touches his or her head on the ground before the majesty of God. Nothing escapes the will or the knowledge of Allāh—yet human beings seem to act with free will and are open to the punishment of hell if they attempt to turn against the will of God." Negus, "Islam and Science," 321–22.
70. Negus, "Islam and Science," 321–22. Negus explains, "The paradox between

Some may object that this is a fundamentalist, Asharite interpretation of the matter of good and evil within the nature and will of Allah. Recall, for example, that "The Mu'tazilite school sought a rational interpretation of the Qur'an."[71] Is the Mu'tazilite school capable of removing the apparent difficulty? No, because, "If, according to the Qur'an, God creates everything, then He also creates evil and our evil actions, so what becomes of divine justice and man's punishment?"[72]

The concern here is not one regarding the question of how humans can be held morally responsible for their actions, as rewarding as the fruits of that discussion may be. Rather, an occasionalist view of Allah's "relation" to creation has been presented. In that view, all causality belongs solely to Allah, such that the causal "reason" for any event following any supposed "cause" has nothing at all to do with that "cause," but everything to do with the will of Allah. And if Allah is not to be confined to behaving in a particular manner, because then he would not be free, and hence not all powerful, then not only is no law-like relation between apparent causes and apparent events discernible, no law-like relation between apparent causes and apparent events is even *possible*. On this view, the very nature of Allah precludes the possibility of such law-like relations. What, then, stands behind every event that happens in the world is the omnipotent will of Allah, which, if anything is to be expected of it, should have the expectation of randomness or capriciousness assigned to it. For otherwise, one might expect some law-like feature of the world is in operation, a feature which has already been seen to be inconsistent with the free omnipotent will of Allah, supposing one takes something like the Asharite view of things. In short, what is being described is a sort of *fatalism* within Islam. Rodney Stark has put the matter as follows,

> Allah is not presented as a lawful creator but is conceived of as an extremely active God who intrudes on the world as he deems

predetermination and free will is a serious problem in most religions, but has an elevated importance in Islam. The main reason for this is the assertion that only God can act, hence the human will can only acquiesce to the act that God makes in the individual's mind. Thus the effective will of God precedes the human will. If God wills something evil in the mind then the mind cannot avoid it even though, as a result of God's command, he or she must not acquiesce to it. By acquiescing the human will takes the responsibility for the evil upon itself, hence the Qur'ān (Koran) says, 'Whatever good happens to you is from Allāh; but whatever evil happens to you, is from your own soul' (Qur'ān 4:79, Sūra, *An-Nisā*, 'Women')." Negus, "Islam and Science," 322.

71. Hodgson, *Theology and Modern Physics*, 45.
72. Hodgson, *Theology and Modern Physics*, 45.

it appropriate. This promoted the formation of a major theological bloc within Islam that condemns all efforts to formulate natural laws as blasphemy in that that they deny Allah's freedom to act. Thus, Islam did not fully embrace the notion that the universe ran along on fundamental principles laid down by God at the creation but assumed that the world was sustained by his will on a continuing basis. This was justified by the statement in the Qur'an that "verily, God will cause to err whom he pleaseth, and will direct whom he pleaseth." Although the line refers to God's determination of the fate of individuals, it was interpreted broadly to apply to all things.[73]

Add to this already extremely fatalistic element of Islam: the theologically affirmed fact that Allah is responsible for evil in the world and one has virtually no basis at all to continue with the scientific endeavor. The Christianized West has traditionally sought wonderful things from scientific inquiry, but Islam is limited to uncertainty regarding the very next event that comes about in the world. Science should be marked by fear, if anything, in Islam. The fruit of a Muslim view of the world is clearly evidenced in historical treatments of science in Islamic society as demonstrated in chapter 2.

The philosopher John Foster believes the goodness of God can be derived from a consideration of what type of divine entity rests behind a nomological explanatory account of the laws of nature.[74]

> On this approach, we are trying to account for the regularities in nature by postulating a supernatural being who deliberately creates the physical universe and the human persons embodied within it. But if this mode of explanation is to be plausible, then we have to be able to envisage a plausible reason why the postulated being should choose to perform this creative work—a reason that both does justice to the character of what has been created and is consonant with the being's own nature, in so far as we can gauge it. Now what makes the claim of moral goodness independently congenial is that it allows us to envisage such a reason. For if the being is morally good, and good to perfection,

---

73. Stark, *Victory of Reason*, 20–21.

74. Foster, *Divine Lawmaker*, 144. Foster claims "the case that has already been made out for accepting the Judaeo-Christian position on the being's knowledge and rationality turns into an equally strong case for accepting its claim with respect to moral goodness. But there is also, I think, an independent reason why we should find this latter claim congenial. For it enables us to fill a crucial lacuna in the explanatory approach we are envisaging." Foster, *Divine Lawmaker*, 144.

then not only is he the sort of being who would want things to go well for other personal beings that exist, but he is also the sort of being who, out of his generosity of spirit, would want there *to be* other personal beings for whom things go well. And so, focusing on the opportunities for significance and fulfillment that human life makes available, we can see his moral goodness as giving him a reason for creating embodied personal beings of our sort, located in our sort of universe.[75]

The same probably cannot be said for Allah, given the statements quoted above. Allah appears to be a capricious entity incapable of providing any reliable basis for the laws of nature, induction, or science.

A case can also be made for the idea that the Christian concept of God enjoys grounding characteristics of goodness (and love) that the Islamic concept of Allah does not. For example, Brian Trapp believes, "accepting a Triune view of God's nature benefits Christian metaethics in a way that is inaccessible to Islamic metaethics."[76] This Trinitarian advantage in ethics will be addressed further below. Trapp discusses a number of metaethical theories within Islam, pointing out a voluntarist strain of thought amongst the Asharites.

> In contrast to the Mu'tazilite position of ethical rationalism, the Ash'arite theologians were determinists and voluntarists. Unlike the Mu'tazilites who believed that humans were free in the sense that their will alone determined their actions, the Ash'arites believed that every event, even human choices, was predetermined by Allah. According to Fakhry, the Ash'arites, "did not devote as much attention to the distinction between right and wrong as

---

75. Foster, *Divine Lawmaker*, 145. Foster writes, "Admittedly, along with its opportunities for significance and fulfillment, human life also leaves ample room for disappointment and suffering; and it may be wondered why a being of perfect goodness and unlimited power should so arrange things. The full answer to this would make a long story—much longer than I could hope to cover here, and, indeed, a story that would take us much more deeply into Christian theology than would be appropriate to my purposes in these lectures. But the basic point is that, unless it left room for disappointment and suffering, human life would not offer the opportunities for the relevant kinds of significance and fulfillment. And it is not implausible to suppose that the intrinsic value of these good things is such that, in order to ensure their availability, it would be rational for a being of perfect goodness to allow for the bad things too." Foster, *Divine Lawmaker*, 145.

76. Trapp, "God and Moral Facts," 180. The metaethical benefits of the Trinity are inaccessible to Islam even though, "The history of ethical thought in Islam is as rich and varied as the history of Christian ethical thought." Trapp, "God and Moral Facts," 180.

their Mu'tazilite rivals had done." However, Fakhry interprets their moral presuppositions such that they, "identified right with what God wills or commands and wrong with what He prohibits." Even before the Ash'arites, early determinists developed sophisticated versions of this view. Muhammad al-Najjar argued that actions were only *performed* by man, but had their ultimate origin in the creative act of Allah.[77]

In this view, good and evil are not found in moral facts or even the nature of Allah, but rather Allah's will alone encompasses all things. Perhaps most significantly for the purposes of the present section, especially in light of Foster's comments on the goodness of God, is Trapp's comment, "Allah himself is not good *necessarily*, but chooses to be merciful to his creations."[78]

Having more than established the arbitrary nature of Allah with the Asharite view in particular, it is helpful to focus on the advantage Trapp ascribes to a Trinitarian position over an Islamic one.

> Moral obligations are not merely abstract entities or philosophical concepts; rather, they are obligations that obtain when two persons have a relationship. Moral obligations do not obtain between a person and a rock, for example. The Christian view of God puts personal relationships at the very heart of reality itself. Since God exists as three divine persons and one divine being, he exhibits a perfect society of personal relationships. His free act of creating others in his image was not some act of desperation or loneliness. Instead, he freely created so that his love might be known and enjoyed by other persons. In other words, his creative act was an overflow of Trinitarian love. Further, God can only act according to his loving nature to these creatures. Since he sees a reflection of himself when he looks upon these creatures, he has the same type of love for them that each member of the Trinity has for each other.[79]

---

77. Trapp, "God and Moral Facts," 182–83. Trapp writes, "The Ash'arites took views like al-Najjar's and built upon them to develop more sophisticated theories. Abu'l Hasan al-Ash'ari, for whom the movement is named, argued directly against the views of the Mu'tazilites on the value of natural reason for knowing moral obligations. According to al-Ash'ari, natural reason delivers a limited understanding of God's will and introduces limited moral notions, but only revelation can introduce actual moral obligations. Even common sense moral notions like gratitude do not become obligatory until necessitated by divine revelation." Trapp, "God and Moral Facts," 183.

78. Trapp, "God and Moral Facts," 183.

79. Trapp, "God and Moral Facts," 184–85.

Muslims have no such recourse.

> The unitary nature of Allah makes for an altogether different scenario. On some Islamic views, Allah created the world so that he would be served and worshipped. Allah is often seen as transcendent in a way that creates a greater discontinuity between his existence and the existence of human beings than the analogous discontinuity offered by Christian theology. Even if an Islamic view proposed that God is good by his nature so that he necessarily loves and commands the good, one might wonder how that goodness is constituted. If Allah existed alone for all eternity before deciding to create, then whatever moral properties he has, they would not be *relational* properties, because there was no other person for him to relate to for that eternal age that passed before his initial creative act. If his moral properties are not grounded in the experience of personal relationship, then how does he view other persons? There is certainly no barrier to having a coherent view of divine goodness on a non-Trinitarian view, even one that can accommodate a coherent metaethics, but the Trinitarian view of orthodox Christianity undoubtedly makes for an easier task.[80]

The unpredictable, causation-denying occasionalism of the Asharites, linked together with the unpredictable, potentially malevolent nature of Allah which stands as cause behind every event in the universe, hardly provides a solid basis upon which to conduct scientific inquiry.

Recall the three main arguments of this section on Islam. First, Islam possesses its own strong version of occasionalism which came to dominate the Islamic philosophy of science with negative results. Second, Islam possesses a deity with a questionable moral character which only compounds the problems related to the aforementioned occasionalist view of causation. The final criticism of Islamic philosophy of science pertains to the non-Trinitarian nature of Allah as well, but not in virtue of love, as above. Rather, the focus is upon potential metaphysical and epistemological difficulties created by the emphasis upon the unity of Allah within Islamic theology. Although Muslim philosophers have clearly thought about the subject to be addressed, discussions are not carried out to the extent that they are here in applying the philosophical difficulty of a non-Trinitarian metaphysic to the Islamic view of science, and in particular, laws of nature.

80. Trapp, "God and Moral Facts," 185.

One such aspect of a non-Trinitarian metaphysic is the concept of emanation. Medieval Muslims, Nasr, and some of his contemporaries emphasized the concept of emanation.[81]

> The cosmos is then viewed as a 'theophany' (*tajalli*), a 'primordial revelation' from Allah, building on the fact that the word *ayat* (signs) is used in the Qur'an to refer both to the revealed scriptural verses and to the phenomena of nature. In earlier writings Nasr had explained that the regularity of natural and cosmic phenomena is a confirmation of all creatures' subservience to God, in fact by no choice of theirs. He also finds in the harmony between religious rites (of Muslims in particular) and natural phenomena (solar-timed prayers, lunar-timed fasting, etc.) further evidence of that divine common origin and connection (between humans, nature and God).[82]

The aforementioned connection is certainly consistent with, if not entailed by, the Islamic emphasis upon the unity of Allah. The absolute unity of Allah appears to lead to an understanding of everything as ultimately unified. For example, "Some Muslim thinkers (e.g. Nasr and Golshani) have stressed the centrality of the Divine Unity in all Muslim intellectual activities, from religious acts to artistic, philosophical or scientific endeavors, all of which aimed at underscoring the Oneness of God."[83] This emphasis on a unity that is derivative of the absolute unity of Allah, when pressed to its logical end, renders science impossible. Thus "Chittick finds it logical and culturally consistent that 'modern science' did not arise in the Islamic civilization."[84] Why? Among other things, according to Chittick, "modern science makes a clear (he calls it 'brute') separation between subject and object and, according to him, refuses to 'admit that consciousness and awareness are more real than material facts.'"[85] The denial of the subject-object distinction is a logical outcome of a monistic metaphysic which is well at home within an Islamic theology of the

---

81. Guessoum, *Islam's Quantum Question*, 44. Guessoum writes, "A different and important perspective on creation is the one proposed by some of the medieval thinkers and espoused by Nasr and a few like-minded contemporaries; it can be summed up in one word, 'emanation', and it represents the 'cosmology' of the old perennial mystical philosophy." Guessoum, *Islam's Quantum Question*, 44.

82. Guessoum, *Islam's Quantum Question*, 44.
83. Guessoum, *Islam's Quantum Question*, 81.
84. Guessoum, *Islam's Quantum Question*, 81.
85. Guessoum, *Islam's Quantum Question*, 81.

absolute oneness or unity of Allah. Some Muslims have even knowingly adopted a view wherein "all is one," though this seems to have been a minority position.[86] However, Muzaffar Iqbal notably takes this position, so that Guessoum writes, "Iqbal, however, adopts a Nasrian view of Islam, nature and science, which considers 'the Qur'anic view of nature [as] characterised by an ontological and morphological continuity with the very concept of God—a linkage that imparts a certain degree of sacredness to the world of nature by making it a Sign (*ayah*, pl. *ayat*) pointing to a transcendental reality.'"[87] Such views, though rare, are an attempt to take the absolute oneness of Allah seriously.

The oneness of Allah is a prime doctrine of Islam, and often cited as the basis for scientific inquiry. Guessoum notes, "the illustrious astronomer al-Battani (Albategnius 850–929) has written: 'By focusing attention, observation, and extensive thought on astronomical phenomena, one is able to prove the unicity of God and to recognize the extent of the Creator's might as well as His wide wisdom and delicate design.'"[88] Guessoum's scholarly study of Islamic science leads him to derive two principles whereby one might begin to grasp an Islamic philosophy of science. He writes, "From the above remarks, two main interrelated principles emerge as a Qur'anic philosophy of science: (1) The exploration of nature, from mere observation to full scrutiny, should clearly point out the order and purpose of the cosmos; and (2) the study of nature should point to a certain unity and thus lead to a (greater) faith in the Creator."[89] A link between the unity of Allah and the unity of the laws of nature is a main premise of Islamic philosophy of science. Thus, "Ghaleb Hasan further extracts some important philosophical principles of science from the Qur'an; he summarises them in the following three points: (1) unity, (2) generalisation and (3) prediction."[90] Note again the emphasis on unity and its link to science (here, generalization and prediction). This view comes directly from the Qur'an:

---

86. Guessoum, *Islam's Quantum Question*, 58. Guessoum writes, "I should stress that this view, although upheld and strongly expounded and publicised by a few prominent thinkers, represents a school of thought that is marginal in the general intellectual landscape of Islamic thought." Guessoum, *Islam's Quantum Question*, 58.

87. Guessoum, *Islam's Quantum Question*, 58.

88. Guessoum, *Islam's Quantum Question*, 59.

89. Guessoum, *Islam's Quantum Question*, 59.

90. Guessoum, *Islam's Quantum Question*, 59.

> He cites various verses in support of his view; for instance: 'For you shall not find any alteration in the ways (laws?) of Allah; and you shall not find any change in His ways' (Q 35:43). He adds that 'science' in the Qur'anic philosophy is meant as the act of interpreting the observed signs (*ayat*) of God, just as—one may add—exegesis is the 'science' of interpreting God's written verses (also *ayat*). Regarding prediction, he notes that the Qur'an points out the regularity in the phenomena of nature and further explains that the computability and predictability of such phenomena is for human benefit: 'It is He Who made the sun a shining brightness and the moon a light, and ordained for it phases that you might know the computation of years and the reckoning (of time)' (Q 10:5). Mujahid finds the concept of cosmic laws in the following Qur'anic verses: 'And the sun runs on to a term/resting-place determined for it; that is the decree of the Exalted in Might, the All-Knowing. And the Moon, We have ordained for it mansions/stages till it becomes again as an old dry palm branch' (36:38–39), where the terms 'determined', 'decree' and 'ordained' are understood to imply a 'natural law.' Mujahid draws the same conclusion from the verse: 'Verily We established Zulqarnain's power on earth, and We gave him the ways and the means to all ends' (Q 18:84), highlighting the words 'ways and means.'[91]

The importance of the doctrine of tawhid (tawheed), both to Islam and Islamic science, cannot be underestimated. The doctrine is not some aberrant or obscure doctrine, but one upon which virtually every Muslim agrees.

Tawhid is crucial to a truly Islamic philosophy of science. Guessoum explains, "Muzaffar Iqbal identifies the three Qur'anic concepts of *tawheed* (unicity), *qadr* (measure) and *mizan* (balance) as 'not only central to the teachings of Islam but . . . also of immense importance for understanding the relationship between Islam and science', a statement and position to which I subscribe wholly."[92]

> Iqbal stresses further that 'God's ways and laws are unchanging', citing the Qur'anic verse 'That was the way of Allah in the case of those who passed away of old, and you will not find for the way of Allah any changes' (Q 33:62), and adds: 'Thus the entire world of nature operates through immutable laws that can be discovered through the investigation of nature.'

91. Guessoum, *Islam's Quantum Question*, 59–60.
92. Guessoum, *Islam's Quantum Question*, 59–60.

Campanini has also pointed out that the Mu'tazilite (rationalistic) theologians 'linked the arranged structure of the universe by God with the exactness of demonstrative proofs'; he refers to 'Abd al-Jabbar (ca. 1024), one of the school's most powerful and influential thinkers, who held that God operates according to rational laws. On this basis, the Mu'tazilites went so far as to severely limit the occurrence of miracles as 'irrational occurrences' that could only be performed by God in order to vouchsafe the claims of his prophets (Moses, Jesus, etc.)[93]

In contrast to theories of Allah's relation to laws of nature from earlier, the theory just explained seems to lock Allah into behaving only in accordance with the laws of nature, which stem from his absolute unity. On this understanding of the laws of nature within Islam, the unity of Allah provides the metaphysical basis for understanding the philosophy of science, because the laws of nature represent the unity of Allah displayed in the world through emanation.[94]

The exceedingly important doctrine of the unity of Allah in Islam creates problems for Islamic science particularly with respect to what the doctrine means for the laws of nature, and this doctrine is central to Islam. The doctrine of the total unity of Allah is central to Islam, first and foremost, because it is given in the Qur'an. The Qur'an is the sacred text of Islam, and fundamental to Islamic belief and practice. One must not miss what this means for science. The Islamic philosopher Ibrahim Kalin explains, "Just as the Islamic revelation determines the social and artistic life of Muslim civilization, it also gives direction to its understanding of the natural environment and its scientific study."[95] The doctrines provided for in the Qur'an thus become basic metaphysical principles whereby the entire realm of nature is to be understood. If the unity of Allah is a core belief for Muslims, then the belief will drastically affect the way Muslims view the world through science. And, as Kalin further explains, it does:

> The doctrine of *tawḥīd*, the most essential tenet of Islamic religion, affirms the unity of the Divine Principle and it is projected into the domain of the natural sciences as the essential unity and interrelatedness of the natural order. A science can

93. Guessoum, *Islam's Quantum Question*, 60.
94. Kalin, "Three Views," 63–64. Kalin explains, "The philosophical underpinnings of Islamic science, as defined by Nasr, Attas, and others are derived from the metaphysical principles of Islam." Kalin, "Three Views," 65.
95. Kalin, "Three Views," 65.

thus be defined as Islamic, Acikgenc states, to the extent that it conforms to and reflects the cardinal principles of the Islamic worldview. In a similar way, Nasr insists that "the aim of all the Islamic sciences—and more generally speaking, of all the medieval and ancient cosmological sciences—is to show the unity and interrelatedness of all that exists, so that, in contemplating the unity of the cosmos, man may be led to the unity of the Divine Principle, of which the unity of Nature is the image." Thus the Islamic sciences of nature function in a two-fold way. First, they look at nature as a single unity with all of its parts interconnected to each other. Second, they are meant to lead both the scientist and the lawman to the contemplation of Nature as the sacred artifact of the Divine.[96]

What is tawhid? According to Edis, tawhid is "the doctrine of the unity and uniqueness of God."[97] More than that, "Tawhid is also often understood to imply the unity of nature under the sovereignty of God."[98] One immediately sees the relevance to science, as do most Muslim philosophers of science.

> Many Muslim thinkers are attracted to the concept of *tawhid*—divine unity—as a way of conceiving of the unity of knowledge under God. According to Ali Shari'ati, "Existence is therefore a living being, possessing a single and harmonious order that is endowed with life, will, sensation and purpose, just like a vast and absolute man."[99]

Ali Shari'ati's view sounds similar to animism or pantheism.

Tawhid serves not just as a basis for science, but as a limiting concept as well. The apparent openness to science "can be very limited where religious matters are concerned, since 'no intellectual enquiry may begin on the premise of denying the fundamental truth of monotheism (*tawhid*) and of the clear guidance which is enunciated in the divine revelation.'"[100] Edis focuses on the numerous difficulties the core doctrine of tawhid causes for Islam with respect to science.

> For example, one reasonably clear and convincing Quranic theme is *tawhid*, the unity and sovereignty of God. Yet this

96. Kalin, "Three Views," 65.
97. Edis, *An Illusion*, 11.
98. Edis, *An Illusion*, 11.
99. Edis, *An Illusion*, 186.
100. Edis, *An Illusion*, 209.

theme of unity has caused no end of headaches for science in the Muslim world. The natural and religiously very understandable inclination of Muslims has been to interpret *tawhid* as demanding the unity of creation under God. So Muslims have been inclined to think that to understand nature properly, one must perceive the signs of divine activity in nature and come to see how the world has been designed by God. In that case, it becomes difficult to maintain a distance between science and the pervasive Muslim sense that revelation holds the key to reality.[101]

Even the greatest of Islamic philosophers cannot seem to escape the difficulties of philosophy, especially philosophy of science, which surround the doctrine of tawhid.

For example, Avicenna's philosophy precludes Allah's ability to know particulars.[102] While some may object that Avicenna affirmed Allah's knowledge of particulars, this affirmation is different from what Avicenna can *logically* claim, and so "the strategy shared by al-Ġazālī and Marmura is to dismiss Avicenna's affirmation of God's knowledge of particulars in light of his explanation of how God knows other things, or specifically that in light of Avicenna's account of divine knowledge it seems impossible that God could know particulars."[103]

Muslims are wholly united on their understanding of Allah as an absolute unity. Amidst the discussion of the unity of Allah is another discussion pertaining to that unity in relation to the knowledge of particulars.

> Unity is another sense Avicenna wants to include within the scope of the term "universal" when he characterizes God's knowledge with universality. God primarily has self-knowledge; however, since he is the origin of everything, his self-knowledge includes his knowledge of other things. Marmura also includes the creative character of divine knowledge and its simplicity in the meaning of universality of God's knowledge. Since God's knowledge is creative, God's relation to his object of knowledge is the opposite of the relation holding between a subject and a

---

101. Edis, *An Illusion*, 226.

102. Acar, "Reconsidering Avicenna's Position," 142. Acar notes, "his frequent confirmations that God knows everything; nothing escapes from God's knowledge, not even the weight of an atom." Acar, "Reconsidering Avicenna's Position," 142. However, it does not follow that Avicenna can *consistently* affirm Allah's knowledge of particulars.

103. Acar, "Reconsidering Avicenna's Position," 143.

known object in human knowledge. Whereas a man acquires his knowledge of things from things themselves, God does not acquire his knowledge from things. To the contrary, things come to exist because of God's knowledge of them. By the simplicity of God's knowledge, Avicenna maintains that God's knowledge does not involve either a temporal or an ontological sequence. God knows everything all at once. There is no transition either from one concept to another or from one event to another.[104]

Unfortunately for Avicenna's theory of knowledge, what follows from this is that Allah cannot know at least some types of particulars. And this lack of knowledge follows immediately from the very nature of Allah's knowing, which is derived from the nature of Allah himself, who is absolute unity.

Philosopher Rahim Acar claims, "If divine universal knowledge includes only the properties of particulars then God does not know particulars individually."[105] Concerning Marmura on Avicenna's epistemology of particulars, Acar writes, "He maintains that (1) Avicenna's conception of universal knowledge of particulars and (2) his criteria for intellectual knowledge imply that for Avicenna God does not know each and every particular entity or event."[106] Regarding an account of Allah's knowledge of particulars, Acar persistently defends Avicenna, claiming, "Avicenna's inability to provide a successful account does not require, or imply, that he denies knowledge of particulars to God."[107] Or again, "The failure of Avicenna's account of how God knows particulars does not require that he believed that God does not know particulars."[108] And again, "Still, al-Ġazālī's and Marmura's arguments, which one might consider representative of the dominant interpretation of Avicenna's position, do not show that for Avicenna God does not know particulars. Granting their arguments, the most one can conclude is that Avicenna does not provide a successful theory for explaining how God knows particulars."[109] But this observation is irrelevant to the current study, since the logical outcome of Islamic metaphysics for laws of nature, induction, and science are in view. The Islamic doctrine of tawhid appears to push Muslims in the direction

---

104. Acar, "Reconsidering Avicenna's Position," 148.
105. Acar, "Reconsidering Avicenna's Position," 149.
106. Acar, "Reconsidering Avicenna's Position," 149.
107. Acar, "Reconsidering Avicenna's Position," 151.
108. Acar, "Reconsidering Avicenna's Position," 152.
109. Acar, "Reconsidering Avicenna's Position," 156.

of some type of monistic worldview. For Allah, upon whom the entire precipice of knowledge rests, can have no knowledge of particulars given his epistemological position derivative of his nature.

That Avicenna, one of Islam's greatest thinkers, could not come up with an account of how Allah knows particulars given the very nature of Allah is telling. Though Acar fights to maintain Avicenna's credibility regarding ascribing knowledge of particulars to Allah, his defense comes up short insofar as Avicenna's position relates to a philosophy of science. With respect to an Islamic philosophy of science, Acar has virtually conceded that Avicenna's theory will move one toward the belief that Allah does not know particulars.

The scholarly consensus on Avicenna is that given the nature of Allah, Avicenna could not come up with a theory to explain how Allah knows particulars. For example, "Gardet thinks that Avicenna, by asserting that God knows particulars, wanted to conceal the real import of his philosophical position on this issue. Hence he finds al-Ġazālī's accusations against Avicenna justified."[110] Beatrice H. Zedler likewise argues that Allah could not know particulars in Avicenna's scheme.

> She considers Avicenna's understanding of God's knowledge of particulars within the context of his theory of cosmogony, i.e., his theory of emanation. She generally agrees with Gardet in arguing why for Avicenna God does not know particulars. She argues that "a direct production of the many is here excluded because a direct knowledge of the many is excluded; and the latter is excluded lest it would thrust multiplicity into the divine essence" (6). She maintains that for Avicenna "God knows singular effects through their universal causes" (10). Since God is not the direct or intentional cause of all things "God can know directly in its singularity only the first effect" (11).[111]

Note that Zedler ties a precluded "many" into the very nature of Allah. If Allah possesses direct knowledge of the "many," or particulars, it would entail that his nature or essence admits of multiplicity, rather than the Qur'anic and traditional Islamic view that Allah is absolute unity, in virtue of the doctrine of tawhid. Acar summarizes, "Gardet's and Zedler's arguments amount to saying that for Avicenna God neither directly nor immediately knows any other thing except for the first intellect, let alone

---

110. Acar, "Reconsidering Avicenna's Position," 142n1.
111. Acar, "Reconsidering Avicenna's Position," 142n1.

particulars in the world of generation and corruption."[112] He adds, "Leaman argues that al-Ġazālī was right in accusing the philosophers of denying God's knowledge of particulars."[113]

Commenting on Allah, philosopher Oliver Leaman asks, "how can a perfect consciousness which is itself immutable include as part of its content the mutable, the changeable?"[114] Elsewhere he writes, "The crucial issue here is whether it is part of the meaning of 'God' that he can know particulars, and can resurrect us physically in the afterlife. According to the *falasifa*, the problem with the idea of his knowing particulars is to explain how a being who is perfect can come to know things which are imperfect."[115] Perhaps what *little* Allah knows would not be a difficulty for the Muslim, except that Muslims take their knowledge to be somehow contingent upon Allah's. For example, "If there is really only God, and the world is just an aspect of his being, then what we count as knowledge is really only an aspect of what is knowledge for God, the perfect and perspicuous grasp of the nature of reality—namely, himself."[116] Given the doctrine of *tawhid*, or *unity* of Allah, an inordinate emphasis is placed upon unity to the exclusion of plurality (or particularity). Allah only knows himself as unity. Creation is supposed to be a reflection of Allah. Thus the *falasifa* go so far as to dismiss knowledge of particulars from the realm of what can be properly labeled knowledge.[117] Not only does Allah not know particulars, humans do not either. Obviously, without this type of knowledge, inductive reasoning is worthless. Contrast this view with Christian theism, which posits a co-ultimate unity and plurality as essential to God.

Lydia Jaeger ties together a number of themes expressed earlier in this book, including the theme of Christ's providential care of creation, laws of nature, the concept of wisdom in the Old Testament, and the Trinity.

> There is one area where the New Testament expresses the Old Testament vision of nature in greater depth: a number of New Testament authors stress Christ's role in the Creation and

---

112. Acar, "Reconsidering Avicenna's Position," 142.
113. Acar, "Reconsidering Avicenna's Position," 143n2.
114. Leaman, *Islamic Philosophy*, 37.
115. Leaman, *Islamic Philosophy*, 37–38.
116. Leaman, *Islamic Philosophy*, 51.
117. Leaman, *Islamic Philosophy*, 59.

maintenance of the world (John 1.3; 1 Cor. 8:6; Col. 1:16–17; Heb. 1:2–3; Rev. 3:14). Here we see an indirect link to the idea of law of nature, insofar as Christ recapitulates, in his person, the role of wisdom in Creation. In the same line of thought, John applies to Jesus the title of *Logos*, which corresponds both to the ḥokmâ of the Old Tetament, with its continuation in the Jewish tradition, and to the unifying principle of the world in Stoic philosophy. These facts allow us to establish a (cautious) link between the natural order and intra-Trinitarian life. In this regard, we must of course recall the fundamental dependence of Creation with respect to God's Trinitarian nature: God can create beings that are radically different from him and yet dependent on him, for he unites in his essence both the One and the Many.[118]

While much could be said about Jaeger's observations, the most obvious point to take away from her comments is how radically distinct the Christian theistic view of divine providence and its implications for laws of nature and the problem of induction are from Islamic views of the same. The mystery of the Trinity promises answers to some of the most fundamental questions in the philosophy of science, such as where to find the source of unity amidst the many seemingly unrelated particulars of human experience. Having earlier explained the role of wisdom in the laws of nature, Jaeger writes, "The essence of God himself reveals a harmonious inner structure, and the Son particularly incarnates, in his person, divine wisdom."[119]

The inductive principle presupposes unity (uniformity, regularity, laws, and the like) while its application presupposes plurality (for example, particular instances of the behavior of objects). While it is not necessary to understand the inductive principle as a universal, if the inductive principle is not understood as exhibiting some form of unity then it is difficult to see how else to understand it. Inductive practice leads to grouping various particulars according to unifying laws. A Christian worldview provides a basis for understanding reality as consisting of both unity and plurality in harmony in virtue of the inner structure of the Trinity, the place of the Son incarnate as creator in union with creation, and the resultant application of the unifying and law-like wisdom of God

---

118. Jaeger, *Einstein*, 141.
119. Jaeger, *Einstein*, 169.

to the particulars of his vast universe. Islam lacks all of these features, making it subject to widespread scientific failure.

FURTHER ISSUE OF APOLOGETICS

Although this book has not focused on offering an apologetic argument *per se*, it has hopefully opened the way for an apologetic argument or arguments premised on contrasting views of philosophy of science relative to religious metaphysics and epistemologies. Chapter 2 described a number of ways apologists have attempted to make an argument based on the type of information provided in this book. Some apologists have offered various forms of what they refer to as transcendental arguments in order to establish Christianity as the only viable worldview. Others have held to a transcendental type argument while weakening the conclusion to include only a generic theism that might later be qualified as specifically Christian in nature. Still others have pointed out the rich historical and cultural argument demonstrating that something is clearly wrong with non-Christian worldviews as they pertain to science, since they are severely lacking in terms of scientific contributions to society. Apologetically speaking, this book attempts to fill out some of the above approaches to the apologetic endeavor, offering what might be thought of as a mere philosophical treatment of divine providence in relation to laws of nature and the problem of induction within Christian theism and its antithetical competitors. If the thesis of the book fits into any particular apologetic approach or argument, then it might be viewed as an abductive case for a Christian theistic philosophy of science. That is, Christian theism is the best candidate of those examined for philosophically sustaining the scientific enterprise. However, there is one other potentially significant line of thought worth pointing out for those interested in developing an apologetic along the lines of the overall argument of this book.

Buried in the depths of pre-Socratic philosophy is an ongoing debate over the make-up of reality.[120] Typically, different groups wanted to explain the universe in terms of a number of different primary elements or as one undifferentiated whole. Philosophers known as the "atomists" might be included in the first group. Atomists held to the metaphysical conviction that reality consists of an infinite number of unperceivable,

---

120. Copleston, *Greece and Rome*, 72–75.

indivisible "atoms" in a void.[121] For them, reality was ultimately made up of an infinite number of particles. Call this view *metaphysical pluralism*. In this view "the world was made up of diverse, separate, discontinuous entities."[122] Epistemologically speaking, atheists, materialists, naturalists, and some empiricists appear to fit the category of metaphysical pluralists. In this view, experience is the only unifying aspect of all of reality. Yet arguments concerning laws of nature and inductive reasoning are not easily made upon the basis of experience, as argued in chapter 3 and chapter 4 of this book.

At least one philosopher has noted "that in terms of a contemporary metaphysical taxonomy, nominalistic materialism provides a paradigmatic case of ultimate plurality."[123] It only makes sense that atheists would have great difficulty explaining how all of the many different objects and events of the world are unified at all. Metaphysical pluralists are trapped with the ways of nature in all of its complex diversity and the only way out is through positing the *uniformity* of nature, the inductive principle, or some other law-like feature of reality. Pluralism is thus not wholly irrelevant to discussions about unifying natural *laws* and a unifying inductive *principle*. A metaphysical pluralist is not able to justify induction in an internalist sense. But, more importantly, a metaphysical pluralist is not rationally warranted in inductive reasoning in an externalist sense. Metaphysical pluralism serves as a defeater for warranted inductive reasoning. Not only does the metaphysical pluralist not have any accessible evidence or reason for believing the inductive principle is true, he or she cannot have an inductive principle. Metaphysical pluralism definitionally precludes any sort of unity, including laws of nature and the inductive principle.

The second group of philosophers noted above who posited that reality exists as one undifferentiated whole.[124] This position may be called *metaphysical monism*. Pantheism is an excellent example of monism.[125] The difficulty with metaphysical monism in the context of laws of nature and induction is that while unity through laws and regularity could, in theory, be affirmed, any application of law (order) to events and

---

121. Copleston, *Greece and Rome*, 72–75.
122. Bahnsen, *Presuppositional Apologetics*, 81.
123. Anderson, "If Knowledge Then God," 64.
124. Coppleston, *Greece and Rome*, 47–53.
125. Anderson, "If Knowledge Then God," 64.

objects in nature is impossible. Not only do the *applications* of law to particular events and objects in nature assume *more than one* application, they assume the existence of many particular *events* and *objects*, not to mention a *differentiation* between the laws, applications, and events or objects. Every instance of plurality involved in inductive inference is inconsistent with a monist metaphysic. Like metaphysical pluralism, metaphysical monism definitionally precludes rationally warranted inductive reasoning.

Muslims quite frequently affirm the absolute *unity* of Allah. Allah exists as a unity, and does not depend in any sense upon his creation. Thus, to affirm the existence of Allah apart from his creation is to affirm metaphysical monism. No plurality exists in Allah. Muslims are not completely ignorant of the difficulties this concept of Allah can create, as demonstrated in the previous section.

Hume's problem of induction, as it is typically posed, emphasizes an internalist scheme of justification. However, sifting through such important issues as the character of the laws of nature and their relationship to the inductive principle is not without merit in the grand scheme of providing a thoroughgoing account of the scientific endeavor as it fits within a particular worldview. The aforementioned sifting reveals that a Christian worldview possesses great strength when it comes to understanding the laws of nature, the justification of the inductive principle, and hence science in a consistent way. Meanwhile, the non-Christian who approaches these same topics will find it difficult, if not impossible, to avoid defeaters which target various inductively held beliefs, even if those beliefs are understood as formed in virtue of an externalist scheme of warrant. Hume's problem of induction, and the metaphysics and epistemologies in terms of which various worldviews can attempt to answer it, cannot be ignored if one is to take seriously the philosophy of science.

Although miracles are rare, revelatory acts of God, they pose no significant difficulty to the doctrine of providence as the basis of the philosophy of science. The same cannot necessarily be said for the idea of the miraculous in Islam. Islam, while seemingly very similar to Christian theism in terms of its metaphysical monotheist creationism and supposedly revelational epistemology, is also dissimilar in relevant ways. Allah is a rather capricious entity, providing little basis for the inferences regarding secondary causation so inherent to the scientific endeavor. Moreover, Allah is not trustworthy in any sense which might bolster confidence in the rational ordering of nature in virtue of good laws. Finally, the concept of the absolute unity of Allah has far reaching metaphysical and hence epistemological consequences which negatively affect the scientific endeavor, if not rendering it, and perhaps Islam as a whole, impossible.

The theological and philosophical observations of this book might be pressed into service in the realm of apologetics as an abductive argument, the conclusion of which is that Christian theism is better equipped to provide a basis for science than are secular and Islamic worldviews. As seen in chapter 2, some apologists have attempted to construct something like a transcendental argument based on the general reasoning discussed in this book. A cultural apologetic also works well with the material examined as also seen in chapter 2. However, much work remains before a sound and convincing argument for Christian theism could be put forth in its entirety based solely upon the line of reasoning selected for the topic of this book.

Chapter 6

Conclusion

This book provides a philosophical account of the Christian doctrine of providence and its implications for the laws of nature and problem of induction before arguing that Christian theism is thus better equipped to provide a basis for science than are secular and Islamic worldviews. Five aspects of defending the aforementioned thesis were divine providence, scientific implications of providence, laws of nature, the problem of induction, and further issues. This chapter provides some concluding remarks regarding each aspect of the thesis stated above.

Three views of divine providence were examined in chapter 1. They were divine providence with non-concurrent theistic preservation and government, divine providence with non-concurrent cosmological preservation and government, and divine providence with concurrent theistic-cosmological preservation and government. After examining each view, concurrent theistic-cosmological preservation and government was chosen as the best understanding of providence for the purposes of this book due to its apparent scriptural and philosophical basis as well as its widespread acceptance throughout history. Various forms of the other two views of divine providence are found within Orthodox Christianity as well, though acceptance of one or the other of those two views over against the one selected in this book might significantly affect the way the thesis of this book is argued. The most important point of the first chapter is that the Christian doctrine of divine providence can be coherently stated in such a way as to remain wholly consistent with science and able to account for the laws of nature and inductive reasoning necessary to scientific inquiry.

In chapter 2, commentary from Christian theologians, apologists, and scientists was offered to show the widespread belief that, far beyond being merely compatible with science, the doctrine of divine providence actually allows for regularity and predictability in the world that is necessary to the scientific endeavor. Some systematic theologians explicitly recognize this regularity and predictability as providing a basis for science. Christian apologists develop arguments surrounding the same theme. Many Christian and even some non-Christian scientists recognize the need for particular tenets of the Christian worldview as a basis for their scientific methodology.

In a Christian theistic worldview, regularity and predictability are most easily described through the concept of laws imposed upon creation by God. What is the *nature* of these laws? This book listed three distinct understandings of the laws of nature. The three distinct ways of understanding the laws of nature are as regularities, logical necessities, or natural necessities. Understanding laws of nature as a type of natural necessity is inherent to the doctrine of divine providence and helps answer the problem of induction. This *nomic necessity* is entailed by the fact that God preserves and governs his creation in accord with his perfect nature and will.

The aforementioned view of laws of nature pertains to the problem of induction, a skeptical worry in philosophy. People typically expect the future to resemble the past in relevant ways, and this expectation drives the belief that people are capable of learning from experience. Learning from experience is a significant part of the scientific endeavor. But why should anyone assume that the future will resemble the past? It will not help to claim that since *in the past* the future has resembled the past, it will do so *in the future*, for this response relies upon the very principle which has been called into question, and it is certainly *logically* possible that the future will *not* resemble the past in the relevant respects. However, the theist has an answer here insofar as God is that rational will which stands providentially behind every event and object of the universe concurrently preserving and governing his creation. *Nomic necessity* provides the necessary connection between cause and effect that philosophers have sought after in their attempts to account for scientific success. God imposes laws of nature on his creation and thereby enables the scientist to proceed with his tasks. The theist who adheres to the doctrine of divine providence is thus justified in his or her acceptance of inductive reasoning and science.

Miracles are rare, revelatory acts of God. Miracles remain a part of God's providential activity while revealing something special about God and his redemptive purposes through nature behaving in a way that they do not usually behave, or the laws of nature even seemingly being defied. God need not be thought of as bound by the universe in such a way that he is incapable of superseding its natural operations through his divine power. Meanwhile, in Islam, everything in nature follows the command of God. General theistic principles initially appear to do for the Muslim what they did for the Christian with respect to establishing the laws of nature and justifying the inductive principle, but this assumption is questionable due to relevant differences. Finally, some apologetic concerns regarding the argument of this book were discussed. The book is best understood as helping fill out a more carefully developed apologetic argument, or as an abductive case that Christian theism provides a better basis for science, at least with respect to laws of nature and inductive reasoning, than do other views such as atheism and Islam.

Bibliography

Abe, Masao. *Zen and Western Thought.* Honolulu: University of Hawaii Press, 1985.
Acar, Rahim. "Reconsidering Avicenna's Position on God's Knowledge of Particulars." In *Interpreting Avicenna: Science and Philosophy in Medieval Islam: Proceedings of the Second Conference of the Avicenna Study Group,* edited by Jon McGinnis, 142–56. Leiden: Brill Academic, 2004.
Al-Ghazali, "The Incoherence of the Philosophers." In *Philosophy in the Middle Ages: the Christian, Islamic, and Jewish Traditions.* 2nd ed. Edited by Arthur Hyman, 283–292. Indianapolis: Hackett, 1983.
Al-Hashimi, Muhammad Ali. *The Ideal Muslim Society: As Defined in the Qur'an and Sunnah.* Translated by Nasiruddin al-Khattab. Riyadh, Saudi Arabia: International Islamic, 2007.
Aland, B., K. Aland, and B. Newman, eds. *Nestle-Aland: Greek New Testament W/ concise Dictionary (Greek Edition).* 27th ed. Stuttgart, Germany: Deutsche Bibelgesellschaft, 2004.
Allison, Gregg R. *Historical Theology: An Introduction to Christian Doctrine: A Companion to Wayne Grudem's Systematic Theology.* Grand Rapids: Zondervan, 2011.
Amstutz, Galen. "Kiyozawa in Concord: A Historian Looks Again at Shin Buddhism in America." *Eastern Buddhist* 41 (2010) 101–50.
Anderson, James. "If Knowledge Then God: The Epistemological Theistic Arguments of Alvin Plantinga and Cornelius Van Til." *Calvin Theological Journal* 40 (2005) 49–75.
———. "No Dilemma for the Proponent of the Transcendental Argument: A Response to David Reiter." *Philosophia Christi* 13 (2011) 189–98.
Armstrong, D. M. *What is a Law of Nature?* New York: Cambridge University Press, 1983.
Arnold, Clinton E. *The Colossian Syncretism: The Interface Between Christianity and Folk Belief at Colossae.* Tübingen, Germany: Coronet Books, 1995.
Arond, David E. "Eye on Religion: Buddhism and Medicine." *Southern Medical Journal* 99 (2006) 1450–51.
Audi, Robert, ed. *The Cambridge Dictionary of Philosophy.* 2nd ed. New York: Cambridge University Press, 1999.
———. *Epistemology: A Contemporary Introduction to the Theory of Knowledge.* Routledge Contemporary Introductions to Philosophy. 3rd ed. New York: Routledge, 2010.

Ayman, Shihadeh. "Al-Ghazali: Faith in Divine Unity and Trust in Divine Providence." *Journal of Islamic Studies* 15 (2004) 78–80.
Bahnsen, Greg L. *The Debate That Never Was*. CD-ROM. Nacogdoches, TX. Covenant Media Foundation, 1994.
———. *The Great Debate: Does God Exist? The Greg L. Bahnsen Vs. Gordon Stein Debate*. Nacogdoches, TX. Covenant Media Foundation, 1985.
———. *Presuppositional Apologetics Stated and Defended*. Power Springs, GA: American Vision, 2010.
———. *Van Til's Apologetic: Readings and Analysis*. Phillipsburg, NJ: P&R, 1998.
Bahnsen, Greg L., and Edward Tabash. "'Does God Exist? A Debate': Dr. Greg L. Bahnsen/Edward Tabash." DVD. Nacogdoches, TX. Covenant Media Foundation, 1993.
Bahnsen, Greg L., and Gordon Stein. *The Great Debate: Does God Exist? Dr. Greg Bahnsen Versus Dr. Gordon Stein at the University of California, Irvine*. 1985. http://andynaselli.com/wp-content/uploads/Bahnsen-Stein_Transcript.pdf
Barclay, William. *The All-Sufficient Christ: Studies in Paul's Letter to the Colossians*. Philadelphia: Westminster, 1963.
———. *The Letter to the Hebrews*. The Daily Study Bible Series. Rev. ed. Philadelphia: Westminster, 1976.
Barr, Stephen M. *Modern Physics and Ancient Faith*. Notre Dame, IN: University of Notre Dame Press, 2006.
Beauchamp. Tom L. *Philosophical Problems of Causation*. Encino, CA: Dickenson, 1974.
Bede. *The Venerable Bede Commentary on the Acts of the Apostles*. Cistercian Studies Series, vol. 117. Kalamazoo, MI: Cistercian, 1989.
Beilby, James K., ed. *For Faith and Clarity: Philosophical Contributions to Christian Theology*. Grand Rapids: Baker Academic, 2006.
Berkhof, Louis. *Systematic Theology*. New ed. Grand Rapids: Eerdmans, 1996.
Beukel, Anthony van den. *The Physicists and God: The New Priests of Religion?* North Andover, MA: Genesis, 1996.
Bloom, Alfred. "The Unfolding of the Lotus: A Survey of Recent Developments in Shin Buddhism in the West." *Buddhist-Christian Studies* 10 (1990) 157–64.
Bonting, Sjoerd L. *Creation and Double Chaos: Science and Theology in Discussion*. Minneapolis: Fortress, 2005.
Born, Max. *Einstein's Theory of Relativity*. New York: Dover, 1962.
Boyce, James P. *Abstract of Systematic Theology*. Cape Coral, FL: Founders, 2006.
Bruce, F. F. *The Epistle to the Hebrews*. Rev. ed. Grand Rapids: Eerdmans, 1990.
Buchanan, George Wesley. *To the Hebrews*. The Anchor Bible, vol. 36. Garden City, NY: Doubleday, 1972.
Calvin, John. *The Epistle of Paul the Apostle to the Hebrews and the First and Second Epistles of St. Peter*. Translated by William B. Johnston, David Wishart Torrance, and Thomas Forsyth Torrance. *Calvin's Commentaries*. Edinburgh: St Andrew, 1963.
———. *Institutes of the Christian Religion*. 2 vols. Phillipsburg, NJ: Westminster John Knox, 1960.
———. *Institutes of the Christian Religion*. Paperback ed. Translated by Ford Lewis Battles. The Library of Christian Classics. Louisville: Westminster John Knox, 2011.
Calvin, John, and John W. Fraser. *The Acts of the Apostles. Calvin's Commentaries*. Edinburgh: St. Andrew, 1966.

Capra, Fritjof. *The Tao of Physics: An Exploration of the Parallels Between Modern Physics and Eastern Mysticism.* 4th ed. Boston: Shambhala, 2000.
Carroll, John W. *Laws of Nature.* Cambridge: Cambridge University Press, 1994.
Cassirer, Ernst. *Determinism and Indeterminism in Modern Physics: Historical and Systematic Studies of the Problem of Causality.* New Haven, CT: Yale University Press, 1956.
Chalmers, A. F. *What Is This Thing Called Science?* 3rd ed. Indianapolis: Hackett, 1999.
Chapple, Christopher Key. "Thomas Berry, Buddhism, and the New Cosmology." *Buddhist-Christian Studies* 18 (1998) 147–54.
Choi, Sean. "The Transcendental Argument." In *Reasons For Faith: Making a Case For the Christian Faith: Essays in Honor of Bob Passantino and Gretchen Passantino Coburn,* edited by Norman L. Geisler and Chad V. Meister, 231–47. Wheaton, IL: Crossway, 2007.
Clark, David L. "Buddhism in America: The Social Organization of an Ethnic Religious Institution by Tetsuden Kashima." *Church History* 48 (1979) 372.
Clark, Kelly James. "A Reformed Epistemologist's Response." In *Five Views On Apologetics,* edited by Steven B. Cowan, 255–63. Grand Rapids: Zondervan, 2000.
Clark, Ronald. *Einstein: The Life and Times.* New York: The World, 1971.
Clarke, J. J. *Oriental Enlightenment: The Encounter Between Asian and Western Thought.* London: Routledge, 1997.
Cockerill, Gareth Lee. *The Epistle to the Hebrews.* The New International Commentary on the New Testament. Grand Rapids: Eerdmans, 2012.
Cohen, L. Jonathan. *An Introduction to the Philosophy of Induction and Probability.* Oxford: Oxford University Press, 1989.
Connell, Richard J. *From Observables to Unobservables in Science and Philosophy.* Lanham, MD: University Press of America, 2000.
Consolmagno, Guy. *God's Mechanics: How Scientists and Engineers Make Sense of Religion.* San Francisco: Jossey-Bass, 2008.
Coogan, Michael D., ed. *The Illustrated Guide to World Religions.* New York: Oxford University Press, 2003.
Cooper, John W. "Pantheism: The Other 'God of the Philosophers': An Overview." *American Theological Inquiry* 1 (2008) 11–24.
Copi, Irving M., and Carl Cohen. *Essentials of Logic.* 2nd ed. Upper Saddle River, NJ: Prentice Hall, 2007.
Copleston, Frederick. *Greece and Rome from the Pre-Socratics to Plotinus.* A History of Philosophy, vol. 1. Reprint, New York: Image, 1993.
Coppenger, Mark T., *Moral Apologetics for Contemporary Christians: Pushing Back Against Cultural and Religious Critics.* Nashville: B&H Academic, 2011.
———. "Therapeutic Nihilism vs. Discursive Judeo-Christianism." *Articles* (blog), ERLC, January 26, 2015, https://erlc.com/resource-library/articles/therapeutic-nihilism-vs-discursive-judeo-christianism.
Corner, David. *The Philosophy of Miracles.* New York: Bloomsbury Academic, 2007.
Crisp, Oliver D. *Retrieving Doctrine: Essays in Reformed Theology.* Downers Grove, IL: InterVarsity Academic, 2011.
Curd, Martin, J. A. Cover, and Chris Pincock. *Philosophy of Science: The Central Issues.* 2nd ed. New York: Norton, 2013.
Danker, Frederick William, ed. *A Greek-English Lexicon of the New Testament and Other Early Christian Literature.* 3rd ed. Chicago: University Of Chicago Press, 2001.

Davenant, John. *Colossians*. Geneva Series of Commentaries. Peoria, IL: Banner of Truth, 2005.

Deleanu, Florin. "Agnostic Meditations on Buddhist Meditation." *Zygon* 45 (2010) 605–26.

Denton, Michael J. *Nature's Destiny: How the Laws of Biology Reveal Purpose in the Universe*. New York: Free Press, 1998.

Draper, James T. *Hebrews: The Life That Pleases God*. Wheaton, IL: Tyndale House, 1976.

Dubs, Homer H. *Rational Induction: An Analysis of the Method of Science and Philosophy*. Chicago: The University of Chicago Press, 1930.

Dunn, James. *Colossians & Philemon*. Grand Rapids: Authentic Media Word, 1996.

Durell, Clement V. *Readable Relativity*. New York: Harper and Brothers, 1960.

Edis, Taner. *An Illusion of Harmony: Science and Religion in Islam*. Amherst, NY: Prometheus, 2007.

Edwards, Jonathan. *Original Sin*. Edited by Clyde A. Holbrook. New Haven, CT: Yale University Press, 1970.

Eigen, Manfred, and Ruthild Winkler. *Laws of the Game: How the Principles of Nature Govern Chance*. New York: Harpercollins, 1983.

Ellis, Brian. *Scientific Essentialism*. Cambridge: Cambridge University Press, 2007.

Elshakry, Marwa. "When Science Became Western: Historiographical Reflections." *Isis* 101 (2010) 98–109.

English, L. Q. "On the 'Emptiness' of Particles in Condensed-Matter Physics." *Foundations of Science* 12 (2007) 155–71.

Erickson, Millard J. *Christian Theology*. 2nd ed. Grand Rapids: Baker, 1998.

Evans, Stephen A. "Epistemology of the Brahmajāla Sutta." *Buddhist Studies Review* 26 (2009) 67–84.

Ewing, Jon D. *Clement of Alexandria's Reinterpretation of Divine Providence: The Christianization of the Hellenistic Idea of Pronoia*. Lewiston, NY: Edwin Mellen, 2008.

Farley, Benjamin Wirt. *The Providence of God*. Grand Rapids: Baker, 1988.

Feinberg, John S. *No One Like Him: The Doctrine of God*. Wheaton, IL: Crossway, 2005.

Fernando, Ajith. *Acts*. The NIV Application Commentary. Grand Rapids: Zondervan, 1998.

Fieser, James, and John Powers. *Scriptures of the World's Religions*. 2nd ed. Boston: McGraw-Hill Humanities/Social Sciences/Languages, 2004.

Flew, Antony and Roy Abraham Varghese. *There Is a God: How the World's Most Notorious Atheist Changed His Mind*. New York: HarperOne, 2007.

Foad, B. Salem. *God's Prophets: Evidence from the Qur'an*. New York: Vantage, 1994.

Foster, John. *The Divine Lawmaker: Lectures on Induction, Laws of Nature, and the Existence of God*. New York: Oxford University Press, USA, 2004.

Frame, John M. *The Doctrine of God*. Phillipsburg, NJ: P&R, 2002.

———. *Systematic Theology: An Introduction to Christian Belief*. Phillipsburg, NJ: P&R, 2013.

Gauch, Hugh G., Jr. *Scientific Method in Brief*. New York: Cambridge University Press, 2012.

Geisler, Norman L., and Chad V. Meister, eds. *Reasons for Faith: Making a Case for the Christian Faith: Essays in Honor of Bob Passantino and Gretchen Passantino Coburn*. Wheaton, IL: Crossway, 2007.

Giberson, Karl W., and Francis S. Collins. *The Language of Science and Faith: Straight Answers to Genuine Questions*. Downers Grove, IL: InterVarsity, 2011.
Gillon, Brendan S. "Dharmakirti and his theory of inference." In *Buddhist Logic and Epistemology*, edited by B. K. Matilal and R. D. Evans, 77-87. Dordrecht, Netherlands: D. Reidel Co., 1986.
Goodman, Nelson. *Fact, Fiction, and Forecast*. Indianapolis: Bobbs-Merrill, 1965.
Grayling, A. C. *The Refutation of Scepticism*. LaSalle, IL: Open Court, 1985.
Greene, Brian. *The Hidden Reality: Parallel Universes and the Deep Laws of the Cosmos*. New York: Knopf, 2011.
Grudem, Wayne. *Systematic Theology: An Introduction to Biblical Doctrine*. Grand Rapids: Zondervan, 1994.
Guessoum, Nidhal. *Islam's Quantum Question: Reconciling Muslim Tradition and Modern Science*. New York: I. B. Tauris, 2011.
Hagner, Donald Alfred. *Hebrews*. A Good News Commentary. San Francisco: Harper & Row, 1983.
Hanzel, Igor. *The Concept of Scientific Law in the Philosophy of Science and Epistemology: A Study of Theoretical Reason*. Boston: Springer, 1999.
Harper, Albert W. J. *Studies in the Interrelationship Between Miracles and the Laws of Nature*. San Francisco: Edwin Mellen Press, 1993.
Harris, Murray J. *Colossians & Philemon*. Grand Rapids: Eerdmans, 1991.
Hasker, William. *God, Time, and Knowledge*. Ithaca, NY: Cornell University Press, 1989.
Heller, Michael. *The New Physics and A New Theology (Vatican Observatory Foundation)*. Vatican City: University of Notre Dame Press, 1997.
Helm, Paul. *Eternal God*. Oxford: Oxford University Press, 1988.
———. *John Calvin's Ideas*. Oxford: Oxford University Press, 2005.
———. *The Providence of God*. Downers Grove, IL: InterVarsity Academic, 1994.
Hodge, Charles. *Systematic Theology*. 3 vols. Peabody, MA: Hendrickson, 1999.
Hodgson, Marshall G. S. *The Venture of Islam, Volume 1: The Classical Age of Islam*. Chicago: University of Chicago Press, 1977.
Hodgson, Peter E. *Theology and Modern Physics*. Aldershot, England: Ashgate, 2006.
Horton, Michael Scott. *Covenant and Eschatology: The Divine Drama*. Louisville: Westminster John Knox, 2002.
Hotchkiss, Brian D. *Buddhism in America: Proceedings of the First Buddhism in America Conference*. Boston: Turtle, 1998.
Howson, Colin. *Hume's Problem: Induction and the Justification of Belief*. New York: Oxford University Press, 2001.
Hughes, Philip Edgcumbe. *A Commentary on the Epistle to the Hebrews*. Grand Rapids: Eerdmans, 1977.
Hume, David. *An Enquiry Concerning Human Understanding and Selections from a Treatise of Human Nature*. Chicago: Paquin, 1963.
———. *A Treatise of Human Nature*. New York: Barnes & Noble, 2005.
Hyman, Arthur. *Philosophy in the Middle Ages: The Christian, Islamic, and Jewish Traditions*. 2nd ed. Indianapolis: Hackett, 1983.
Fair, Frank. "Buddhism, Christianity, and Modern Science: A Response to Masao Abe." *Buddhist-Christian Studies* 25 (2005) 67–74.
Fieser, James, and John Powers. *Scriptures of the World's Religions*. 2nd ed. Boston: McGraw-Hill Humanities/Social Sciences/Languages, 2004.
Fisch, Max. *Classic American Philosophers: Peirce, James, Royce, Santayana, Dewey, Whitehead: Selections from Their Writings*. 2nd ed. New York: Fordham University Press, 1996.

Flint, Thomas P. "Providence and Predestination." In *A Companion to Philosophy of Religion*, edited by P. Quinn and C. Taliaferro, 569–76. Malden, MA: Blackwell, 1997.

Freddoso, Alfred J. "Medieval Aristotelianism and the Case Against Secondary Causation in Nature." In *Divine and Human Action: Essays in the Metaphysics of Theism*, edited by Thomas V. Morris, 74–118. Ithaca, NY: Cornell University Press, 1988.

Ghose, Lynken. "Karma and the Possibility of Purification: An Ethical and Psychological Analysis of the Doctrine of Karma in Buddhism." *Journal of Religious Ethics* 35 (2005) 259–89.

Harrison, Peter. "A Scientific Buddhism?" *Zygon* 45 (2010) 861–69.

Haught, John F. "Is Physics Fundamental? Robert Russell on Divine Action." *Zygon: Journal of Religion and Science* 45 (2010) 213–20.

Helm, Paul. "Calvin (and Zwingli) on Divine Providence." *Calvin Theological Journal* 29 (1994) 388–405.

Hudson, Clarke. "Buddhism in America by Richard Hughes Seager; Luminous Passage: The Practice and Study of Buddhism in America by Charles S. Prebish." *Buddhist-Christian Studies* 22 (2002) 217–21.

Jacobson, Nolan Pliny. "Buddhism, Modernization, and Science." *Philosophy East and West* 20 (1970) 155–67.

Jaeger, Lydia. *Einstein, Polanyi, and the Laws of Nature*. West Conshohocken, PA: Templeton, 2010.

Jammer, Max. *Einstein and Religion: Physics and Theology*. Princeton, NJ: Princeton University Press, 1999.

Jinpa, Thupten. "Buddhism and Science: How Far Can the Dialogue Proceed?" *Zygon* 45 (2010) 871–82.

Jolley, Nicholas. "Occasionalism and Efficacious Laws in Malebranche." *Midwest Studies In Philosophy* 26 (2002) 245–57.

Jowers, Dennis W., ed. *Four Views on Divine Providence*. Grand Rapids: Zondervan, 2011.

Kaiser, Christopher B. *Toward a Theology of Scientific Endeavour: The Descent of Science*. Aldershot, England: Ashgate, 2007.

Kalby, Kais Al. *Prophet Muhammad: The Last Messenger in the Bible*. Logan, UT: American Muslim Cultural Association, 2005.

Kalin, Ibrahim. "Three Views of Science in the Islamic World." In *God, Life, and the Cosmos: Christian and Islamic Perspectives*, edited by Ted Peters, Muzaffar Iqbal, and Syed Nomanul Haq, 43–76. Aldershot, England: Ashgate, 2002.

Kanda, Shigeo H. "Buddhism in America: The Social Organization of an Ethnic Religious Institution by Tetsuden Kashima." *Journal of the American Academy of Religion* 46 (1978) 417–18.

Kant, Immanuel. *Critique of Pure Reason*. Translated by Norman Kemp Smith. New York: St. Martin's, 1965.

———. *Prolegomena to Any Future Metaphysics That Will Be Able to Come Forward as Science, with Kant's Letter to Marcus Herz, February 27, 1772: The Paul Carus Translation Extensively Rev. by James W. Ellington*. 2nd ed. Indianapolis: Hackett, 2001.

Kashima, Tetsuden. *Buddhism in America: The Social Organization of an Ethnic Religious Institution*. Westport, CT: Greenwood, 1977.

Katner, John. *Ishmael Instructs Isaac: An Introduction to the Qur'an for Bible Readers.* Collegeville, MN: Liturgical, 1989.
Katsh, Abraham I. *Judaism in Islam: Biblical and Talmudic Backgrounds of the Koran and Its Commentaries, Surahs II and III.* New York: Bloch, 1954.
Kelly, J. N. D. *Early Christian Doctrines.* Rev. ed. New York: HarperOne, 1978.
Kistemaker, Simon. *Exposition of the Epistle to the Hebrews.* New Testament Commentary. Grand Rapids: Baker, 1984.
Klee, Robert. *Scientific Inquiry: Readings in the Philosophy of Science.* New York: Oxford University Press, 1999.
Knight, Christopher C. *The God of Nature: Incarnation and Contemporary Science.* Minneapolis: Fortress, 2007.
———. "Theistic Naturalism and 'Special' Divine Providence." *Zygon: Journal of Religion and Science* 44 (2009) 533–42.
Kvanvig, Jonathan L., and Hugh J. McCann. "Divine Conservation and the Persistence of the World." In *Divine and Human Action: Essays in the Metaphysics of Theism,* edited by Thomas V. Morris, 13–49. Ithaca, NY: Cornell University Press, 1988.
Lange, Marc. *Laws and Lawmakers: Science, Metaphysics, and the Laws of Nature.* New York: Oxford University Press, 2009.
Larmer, Robert. "Divine Agency and the Principle of the Conservation of Energy." *Zygon: Journal of Religion and Science* 44 (2009) 543–57.
Layman, Emma McCloy. *Buddhism in America.* Chicago: Nelson-Hall, 1976.
Leaman, Oliver. *Islamic Philosophy.* 2nd ed. Cambridge: Polity, 2009.
Lee, Sukjae. "Necessary Connections and Continuous Creation: Malebranche's Two Arguments for Occasionalism." *Journal of the History of Philosophy* 46 (2008) 539–56.
Lennox, John C. *God's Undertaker: Has Science Buried God?* Updated ed. Chicago: Kregel, 2009.
Lewis, Bernard. *What Went Wrong? The Clash Between Islam and Modernity in the Middle East.* New York: Harper Perennial, 2003.
Lindberg, David C., and Ronald L. Numbers, eds. *When Science and Christianity Meet.* Chicago: University Of Chicago Press, 2003.
Lohse, Eduard. *Colossians and Philemon.* Hermeneia. New York: Fortress, 1972.
Lopez, Donald S., Jr. "The Future of the Buddhist Past: A Response to the Readers." *Zygon: Journal of Religion and Science* 45 (2010) 883–96.
Lumpkin, William. *Baptist Confessions of Faith.* Rev. ed. Valley Forge: Judson, 1969.
MacDonald, Margaret Y. *Colossians and Ephesians.* Collegeville, MN: Liturgical, 2000.
Martin, Michael. *Reply to Butler, Ventrella, and Fields.* The Secular Web, 1996. https://infidels.org/library/modern/michael_martin/reply.html.
Matilal, Bimal K., and Robert D. Evans, eds. *Buddhist Logic and Epistemology: Studies in the Buddhist Analysis of Inference and Language.* Hingham, MA: Springer, 1986.
Matthews, Bruce. "Luminous Passage: The Practice and Study of Buddhism in America by Charles S. Prebish." *The Journal of Religion* 81 (2001) 510–12.
McCance, Dawne. "Physics, Buddhism, and Postmodern Interpretation." *Zygon* 21 (1986) 287–96.
McCann, Hugh J. "Creation and Conservation." In *A Companion to Philosophy of Religion,* edited by P. Quinn and C. Taliaferro, 306–12. Malden, MA: Blackwell, 1997.
McDonough, Jeffrey K. "Berkeley, Human Agency and Divine Concurrentism." *Journal of the History of Philosophy* 46 (2008) 567–90.

———. "Leibniz: Creation *and* Conservation *and* Concurrence." *The Leibniz Review* 17 (2007) 31–60.
McGhee, Michael. "The Turn Towards Buddhism." *Religious Studies* 31 (1995) 69–87.
Miller, Timothy. "Continuous Creation and Secondary Causation: The Threat of Occasionalism." *Religious Studies* 47 (2011) 3–22.
Mizuno, Kogen. *Essentials of Buddhism: Basic Terminology and Concepts of Buddhist Philosophy and Practice.* 1st Eng. ed. Tokyo: Kosei, 1997.
Moad, Omar. "Al-Ghazali's Occasionalism and the Natures of Creatures." *International Journal for Philosophy of Religion* 58 (2005) 95–101.
———. "Al-Ghazali on Power, Causation, and 'Acquisition.'" *Philosophy East and West* 57 (2007) 1–13.
Mohler, R. Albert. *Atheism Remix: A Christian Confronts the New Atheists.* Wheaton, IL: Crossway, 2008.
More, Louis Trenchard. *The Life and Works of the Honourable Robert Boyle.* New York: Oxford University Press, 1944.
Moreland, J. P., and William Lane Craig. *Philosophical Foundations for a Christian Worldview.* Downers Grove, IL: InterVarsity Academic, 2003.
Morris, Thomas, ed. *Divine and Human Action: Essays in the Metaphysics of Theism.* Ithaca, NY: Cornell University Press, 1988.
———. *Our Idea of God.* Notre Dame, IN: University of Notre Dame Press, 1991.
Morris, Tim, and Don Petcher. *Science and Grace: God's Reign in the Natural Sciences.* Wheaton, IL: Crossway, 2006.
Musgrave, Alan. *Common Sense, Science, and Scepticism: A Historical Introduction to the Theory of Knowledge.* New York: Cambridge University Press, 1993.
Nadler, Steven. "Occasionalism." In *The Cambridge Dictionary of Philosophy.* 2nd ed. Edited by Robert Audi, 626–27. New York: Cambridge University Press, 1999.
Nash, Ronald H. *Life's Ultimate Questions: An Introduction to Philosophy.* Grand Rapids: Zondervan, 1999.
Negus, Michael Robert. "Islam and Science." In *God, Humanity, and the Cosmos,* 2nd ed., edited by Christopher Southgate, 321–39. New York: T. & T. Clark, 2005.
Numbers, Ronald L. *Science and Christianity in Pulpit and Pew.* New York: Oxford University Press, 2007.
Okasha, Samir. *Philosophy of Science: A Very Short Introduction.* New York: Oxford University Press, 2002.
Oliphint, K. Scott. *Covenantal Apologetics: Principles and Practice in Defense of Our Faith.* Wheaton, IL: Crossway, 2013.
———. *God with Us: Divine Condescension and the Attributes of God.* Wheaton, IL: Crossway, 2012.
Olson, Roger E. *Arminian Theology: Myths and Realities.* Downers Grove, IL: InterVarsity Academic, 2006.
Omnès, Roland. *Quantum Philosophy: Understanding and Interpreting Contemporary Science.* Princeton, NJ: Princeton University Press, 1999.
O'Murchu, Diarmuid. *Quantum Theology.* New York: Crossroad Classic, 1997.
Owen, John. *Hebrews: The Epistle of Warning.* Grand Rapids: Kregel, 1985.
Pannenberg, Wolfhart. *Toward a Theology of Nature: Essays on Science and Faith.* Edited by Ted Peters. Louisville: Westminster John Knox, 1993.
Parrish, Stephen E. *God and Necessity: A Defense of Classical Theism.* Lanham, MD: University Press of America, 1997.

Pearcey, Nancy R., and Charles B. Thaxton. *The Soul of Science: Christian Faith and Natural Philosophy*. Wheaton, IL: Crossway, 1994.

Peirce, Charles S. *Philosophical Writings of Peirce*. New York: Dover, 2011.

Pessin, Andrew. "Does Continuous Creation Entail Occasionalism? Malebranche (and Descartes)." *Canadian Journal of Philosophy* 30 (2000) 413–39.

Peters, Ted, Muzaffar Iqbal, and Syed Nomanul Haq, eds. *God, Life, and the Cosmos: Christian and Islamic Perspectives*. Burlington, VT: Ashgate, 2003.

Peterson, David. *The Acts of the Apostles*. The Pillar New Testament Commentary. Grand Rapids: Eerdmans, 2009.

Piper, John, Justin Taylor, and Paul Kjoss Helseth. *Beyond the Bounds: Open Theism and the Undermining of Biblical Christianity*. Wheaton, IL: Crossway, 2003.

Plantinga, Alvin. "Precis of Warrant: The Current Debate and Warrant and Proper Function." *Philosophy and Phenomenological Research* 50 (1995) 393–96.

———. "Appendix: Two Dozen (or so) Theistic Arguments." In *Alvin Plantinga*, edited by Deane-Peter Baker, 203–27. Cambridge: Cambridge University Press, 2007.

———. *Where the Conflict Really Lies: Science, Religion, and Naturalism*. New York: Oxford University Press, 2011.

Platt, Andrew R. "Divine Activity and Motive Power in Descartes's Physics." *British Journal for the History of Philosophy* 19 (2011) 849–71.

Polhill, John B. *Acts*. The New American Commentary, vol. 26, Nashville: Broadman, 1992.

Polkinghorne, John. *Quantum Physics and Theology: An Unexpected Kinship*. New Haven, CT: Yale University Press, 2007.

Pollard, William G. *Physicist and Christian: A Dialogue Between the Communities*. Greenwich, CT: Seabury, 1961.

Popper, Karl R. *Objective Knowledge: An Evolutionary Approach*. Oxford: Clarendon, 1972.

Poythress, Vern S. *Redeeming Science: A God-Centered Approach*. Wheaton, IL: Crossway, 2006.

Pratt, James Bissett. "Buddhism and Scientific Thinking." *The Journal of Religion* 14 (1934) 13–24.

Prebish, Charles S. *American Buddhism*. North Scituate, MA: Duxbury, 1979.

Prebish, Charles S., and Kenneth K. Tanaka, eds. *The Faces of Buddhism in America*. Berkeley: University of California Press, 1998.

Queen, Christopher S., and Duncan Ryuken Williams. *American Buddhism: Methods and Findings in Recent Scholarship*. Edited by Duncan Ryūken Williams. Richmond, England: Routledge, 1999.

Quinn, Philip L. "Divine Conservation, Secondary Causes, and Occasionalism." In *Divine and Human Action: Essays in the Metaphysics of Theism*, edited by Thomas V. Morris, 50–73. Ithaca, NY: Cornell University Press, 1988.

Quinn, Philip L., and Charles Taliaferro, eds. *A Companion to the Philosophy of Religion*. Cambridge, MA: Wiley-Blackwell, 1999.

Radford, Lewis B. *The Epistle to the Colossians and The Epistle to Philemon: With Introduction and Notes*. London: Methuen and Company, 1931.

Rahman, Fazlur. *Major Themes of the Qur'an*. 2nd ed. Chicago: University Of Chicago Press, 2009.

Reid, Thomas. *Essays on the Intellectual Powers of Man: A Critical Edition*. Edited by Derek R. Brookes and Knud Haakonssen. Edinburgh: Edinburgh University Press, 2002.

Reiter, David. "Rejoinder to James Anderson." *Philosophia Christi* 13 (2011) 199–202.
Reymond, Robert L. *A New Systematic Theology of the Christian Faith*. Nashville: Thomas Nelson, 1998.
Ridderbos, Herman. *Paul: An Outline of His Theology*. Grand Rapids: Eerdmans, 1975.
Roberts, John Russell. "'Strange Impotence of Men': Immaterialism, Anaemic Agents, and Immanent Causation." *British Journal for the History of Philosophy* 18 (2010) 411–31.
Roberts, John T. *The Law Governed Universe*. Oxford: Oxford University Press, 2012.
Rockwell, Teed. "Minds, Intrinsic Properties, and Madhyamaka Buddhism." *Zygon* 44 (2009) 659–74.
Rosner, Brian S., T. Desmond Alexander, Graeme Goldsworthy, and D. A. Carson, eds. *New Dictionary of Biblical Theology*. Downers Grove, IL: InterVarsity Academic, 2000.
Rowe, William. "Does Panentheism Reduce to Pantheism? A Response to Craig." *International Journal for Philosophy of Religion* 61 (2007) 65–67.
Russell, Bertrand. "Problems of Philosophy." In *Classics of Western Philosophy*. 6th ed. Edited by Steven Cahn, 1143–66. Indianapolis: Hackett, 2002.
Sanders, John. *The God Who Risks: A Theology of Providence*. Downers Grove, IL: InterVarsity, 1998.
Schmidt, Alvin J. *How Christianity Changed the World*. Grand Rapids: Zondervan, 2004.
Schmidt, Roger et al. *Patterns of Religion*. 2nd ed. Belmont, CA: Wadsworth, 2005.
Schwöbel, Christoph. "Divine Agency and Providence." *Modern Theology* 3 (1987) 225–44.
Seager, Richard Hughes. *Buddhism in America*. New York: Columbia University Press, 2000.
Sharma, Aparna. "Buddhism and Science: Breaking New Ground by B. Alan Wallace." *Leonardo* 37 (2004) 78–79.
Smith, Buster G. "Buddhism in America: An Analysis of Social Receptivity." *Contemporary Buddhism* 7 (2006) 149–64.
Smith, Huston; Philip Novak. *Buddhism: A Concise Introduction*. New York: Harper One, 2003.
Smith, Robert H. *Hebrews*. Augsburg Commentary on the New Testament. Minneapolis: Augsburg, 1984.
Spielberg, Nathan, and Bryon D. Anderson. *Seven Ideas That Shook the Universe*. 2nd ed. New York: John Wiley & Sons, 1995.
Stark, Rodney. *The Victory of Reason: How Christianity Led to Freedom, Capitalism, and Western Success*. New York: Random House, 2005.
Stern, Robert, ed. *Transcendental Arguments: Problems and Prospects*. New York: Oxford University Press, 2000.
―――. *Transcendental Arguments and Scepticism: Answering the Question of Justification*. New York: Oxford University Press, 2000.
Storhoff, Gary, and John Whalen-Bridge, eds. *American Buddhism as a Way of Life*. Albany: State University of New York Press, 2010.
Stott, John R W. *The Message of Acts: The Spirit, the Church and the World*. The Bible Speaks Today. Leicester, England: InterVarsity Press, 1994.
Sudduth, Michael. *The Reformed Objection to Natural Theology*. Farnham, England: Ashgate, 2009.

Suzuki, Daisetz Teitaro; Wayne S. Yokoyama. "The Prospects for Buddhism in Europe and America." *Eastern Buddhist* 39 (2008) 69–77.
Swinburne, Richard, ed. *The Christian God*. New York: Oxford University Press, 1994.
———. *Justification of Induction: Readings in Philosophy*. New York: Oxford University Press, 1974.
Talisse, Robert B., and Scott F. Aikin. *Pragmatism: A Guide for the Perplexed*. London: Continuum, 2008.
Thurman, Robert A.F. "Toward an American Buddhism." In *Buddhism in America: Proceedings of the First Buddhism in America Conference*, edited by Brian D. Hotchkiss, 450–68. Boston: Turtle, 1998.
Tiessen, Terrance L. "Why Calvinists Should Believe in Divine Middle Knowledge, Although They Reject Molinism." *Westminster Theological Journal* 69 (2007) 345–66.
Tipler, Frank J. *The Physics of Christianity*. New York: Doubleday Religion, 2007.
Towne, Edgar A. "The Plausibility of Panentheism." *Encounter* 67 (2006) 273–95.
———. "The Variety of Panentheisms." *Zygon: Journal of Religion and Science* 40 (2005) 779–86.
Tracy, Thomas F. "Divine Action." In *A Companion to Philosophy of Religion*. Edited by P. Quinn and C. Taliaferro, 299–305. Malden, MA: Blackwell, 1997.
Tracy, Thomas F., ed. *The God Who Acts: Philosophical and Theological Explorations*. University Park, PA: Pennsylvania State University Press, 1994.
Trapp, Michael Brian. "God and Moral Facts: A Trinitarian Realist Model of Christian Metaethics." PhD diss., The Southern Baptist Theological Seminary, 2010.
Trefil, James. *The Nature of Science: An A-Z Guide to the Laws and Principles Governing Our Universe*. New York: Houghton Mifflin, 2003.
Turretin, Francis. *Institutes of Elenctic Theology*. Edited by James T. Dennison, Jr. Phillipsburg, NJ: P&R, 1993.
Tweed, Thomas A. *The American Encounter with Buddhism, 1844–1912: Victorian Culture and the Limits of Dissent*. Bloomington, IN: University Press, 1992.
Vailati, Ezio. "Leibniz on Divine Concurrence with Secondary Causes." *British Journal for the History of Philosophy* 10 (2002) 209–30.
Vallicella, William F. "God, Causation and Occasionalism." *Religious Studies* 35 (1999) 3–18.
Van Til, Cornelius. *The Defense of the Faith*. 4th ed. Edited by K Scott Oliphint. Phillipsburg, NJ: P & R Pub., 2008.
Von Wright, Georg Henrik. *A Treatise on Induction and Probability*. London: Routledge and Kegan Paul, 1951.
Wahl, Russell. "Occasionalism, Laws and General Will." *British Journal for the History of Philosophy* 19 (2011) 219–40.
Wallace, Daniel B. *Greek Grammar Beyond the Basics 5.0*. Grand Rapids: Zondervan, 2006.
Wallis, Glenn. "The Faces of Buddhism in America by Charles S. Prebish; Kenneth K. Tanaka." *International Journal of Hindu Studies* 4 (2000) 89–91.
Walls, Jerry L. "Why No Classical Theist, Let Alone Orthodox Christian, Should Ever Be a Compatibilist." *Philosophia Christi* 13 (2011) 75–104.
Ware, Bruce A. *God's Greater Glory: The Exalted God of Scripture and the Christian Faith*. Wheaton, IL: Crossway, 2004.
———. *God's Lesser Glory: the Diminished God of Open Theism*. Wheaton, IL: Crossway, 2000.

Ware, Bruce A., ed. *Perspectives on the Doctrine of God: 4 Views*. Nashville: B&H Academic, 2008.

Wettimuny, R. G. de S. *Buddhism and its Relation to Religion and Science*. Colombo, Sri Lanka: M.D. Gunasena and Company, 1962.

White, Edward A. *Science and Religion in American Thought: The Impact of Naturalism*. Stanford: Stanford University Press, 1952.

White, James R. *What Every Christian Needs to Know about the Qur'an*. Grand Rapids: Bethany House, 2013.

Worthing, Mark William. *God, Creation, and Contemporary Physics*. Minneapolis: Fortress, 2000.

Yong, Amos. "Buddhism and Science: Breaking New Ground by B. Alan Wallace." *Buddhist-Christian Studies* 25 (2005) 176–80.

———. "Mind and Life, Religion and Science: His Holiness the Dalai Lama and the Buddhism-Christianity-Science Trialogue." *Buddhist-Christian Studies* 28 (2008) 43–63.

www.ingramcontent.com/pod-product-compliance
Lightning Source LLC
Chambersburg PA
CBHW050850230426
43667CB00012B/2230